The French Revolution

The French Revolution

LINDA S. FREY AND MARSHA L. FREY

Greenwood Guides to Historic Events 1500–1900

GREENWOOD PRESS
Westport, Connecticut • London

3 1257 01516 2299

Library of Congress Cataloging-in-Publication Data

Frey, Linda.
  The French Revolution / Linda S. Frey and Marsha L. Frey.
      p. cm. — (Greenwood guides to historic events, 1500–1900, ISSN 1538–442X)
    Includes bibliographical references and index.
    ISBN 0–313–32193–0 (alk. paper)
    1. France—History—Revolution, 1789–1799. I. Frey, Marsha. II. Title. III. Series.
    DC148.F728 2004
    944.04—dc21   2003048543

British Library Cataloguing in Publication Data is available.

Library of Congress Catalog Card Number: 2003048543
ISBN: 0–313–32193–0
ISSN: 1538–442X

First published in 2004

Greenwood Press, 88 Post Road West, Westport, CT 06881
An imprint of Greenwood Publishing Group, Inc.
www.greenwood.com

Printed in the United States of America

The paper used in this book complies with the
Permanent Paper Standard issued by the National
Information Standards Organization (Z39.48–1984).

10 9 8 7 6 5 4 3 2 1

This book is dedicated to our family and friends, particularly Dolores Frey, Debbie Bellisari, and H. W. Palen, and to our canine companions, who refused to suffer in silence.

CONTENTS

SERIES FOREWORD

American statesman Adlai Stevenson stated, "We can chart our future clearly and wisely only when we know the path which has led to the present." This series, Greenwood Guides to Historic Events, 1500–1900, is designed to illuminate that path by focusing on events from 1500 to 1900 that have shaped the world. The years 1500 to 1900 include what historians call the early modern period (1500 to 1789, the onset of the French Revolution) and part of the modern period (1789 to 1900).

In 1500, an acceleration of key trends marked the beginnings of an interdependent world and the posing of seminal questions that changed the nature and terms of intellectual debate. The series closes with 1900, the inauguration of the twentieth century. This period witnessed profound economic, social, political, cultural, religious, and military changes. An industrial and technological revolution transformed the modes of production, marked the transition from a rural to an urban economy, and ultimately raised the standard of living. Social classes and distinctions shifted. The emergence of the territorial and later the national state altered man's relations with and view of political authority. The shattering of the religious unity of the Roman Catholic world in Europe marked the rise of a new pluralism. Military revolutions changed the nature of warfare. The books in this series emphasize the complexity and diversity of the human tapestry and include political, economic, social, intellectual, military, and cultural topics. Some of the authors focus on events in U.S. history such as the Salem witchcraft trials, the American Revolution, the abolitionist movement, and the Civil War. Others analyze European topics, such as the Reformation and Counter-Reformation and the French Revolution. Still others bridge cultures and continents by examining the voyages of discovery, the Atlantic slave trade, and the Age of Imperialism. Some focus on intellectual questions that have shaped the modern world, such as Charles Darwin's *Origin of Species,* or on turning points such as the Age of Romanticism. Others examine defining economic, religious, or legal events or issues such as the building of the railroads, the Second Great Awakening, and abolitionism. Heroes (e.g., Meriwether Lewis and William Clark), scientists (e.g., Darwin), military leaders (e.g., Napoleon Bonaparte), poets (e.g., Lord Byron) stride across the pages. Many of these events were seminal in that they marked profound changes or turning points. The Scientific Revolution, for example, changed the way individuals viewed themselves and their world.

The authors, acknowledged experts in their fields, synthesize key events, set developments within the larger historical context, and, most important, present well-balanced, well-written accounts that integrate the most recent scholarship in the field.

The topics were chosen by an advisory board composed of historians, high school history teachers, and school librarians to support the curriculum and meet student research needs. The volumes are designed to serve as resources for student research and to provide clearly written interpretations of topics central to the secondary school and lower-level undergraduate history curriculum. Each author outlines a basic chronology to guide the reader through often-confusing events and presents a historical overview to set those events within a narrative framework. Three to five topical chapters underscore critical aspects of the event. In the final chapter the author examines the impact and consequences of the event. Biographical sketches furnish background on the lives and contributions of the players who strut across the stage. Ten to 15 primary documents, ranging from letters to diary entries, song lyrics, proclamations, and posters, cast light on the event, provide material for student essays, and stimulate critical engagement with the sources. Introductions identify the authors of the documents and the main issues. In some cases a glossary of selected terms is provided as a guide to the reader. Each work contains an annotated bibliography of recommended books, articles, CD-ROMs, Internet sites, videos, and films that set the materials within the historical debate.

Reading these works can lead to a more sophisticated understanding of the events and debates that have shaped the modern world and can stimulate a more active engagement with the issues that still affect us. It has been a particularly enriching experience to work closely with such dedicated professionals. We have come to know and value even more highly the authors in this series and our editors at Greenwood, particularly Kevin Ohe and Michael Hermann. In many cases they have become more than colleagues; they have become friends. To them and to future historians we dedicate this series.

Linda S. Frey
University of Montana

Marsha L. Frey
Kansas State University

PREFACE

There is moreover in this disease of the French Revolution something very strange that I can sense, though I cannot describe it
properly or analyse its causes.
Alexis de Tocqueville, in *Interpreting the French Revolution*
by François Furet

The French Revolution often has been perceived as the dawn of the
modern era, the divide between the ancien régime and the contemporary world. The revolutionaries shared that perception because they
saw the Revolution as a decisive break with the past or as "a kind of
crucible in which the past was abolished, the present was constituted
and the future was shaped."[1] Undergirding this view are two assump-
tions: the inevitability of the Revolution and the Revolution as a radical
break. Both have been questioned. Some historians emphasize the
importance of contingency and the influence of individuals, such as
Louis XVI, on the Revolution. The nineteenth-century aristocrat Alexis
de Tocqueville argued that the Revolution should be seen not as the
dawn of a new era, but as an acceleration of certain trends already present in the ancien régime, such as the growth of the centralizing state.
This view underscores the divergence between intentions and out-
comes. The revolutionaries intended to create a new world but ended
up using "the debris of the old order."[2] Others argue that "much that
was attributed to it would in all probability have come about in any
case":[3] free trade, religious toleration, codification and reform of the
law, the independence of the Latin American colonies, and so forth.
Some emphasize the continuity in areas such as agriculture that were
not changed. Still others downplay the contributions of the Revolu-

tion. Many of the ideals, including the Western idea of universality of rights, touted by the French revolutionaries had been articulated in the American Revolution. Historian Jacques Godechot emphasizes that the Revolution was not limited to France but was part of an "Atlantic revolution" and the American historian R. R. Palmer argues that the eighteenth century was "the age of the democratic revolution" that transcended France. It was an era of universal agitation in western, central, and eastern Europe, in North and South America, and in the Caribbean. Still it can be argued that the revolution in France posed and continues to pose a new challenge to the established order. In 1858, Alexis de Tocqueville noted, "There is moreover in this disease of the French Revolution something very strange that I can sense, though I cannot describe it properly or analyse its causes. It is a *virus* of a new and unknown kind. There have been violent Revolutions in the worlds before; but the immoderate, violent, radical, desperate, bold, almost crazed and yet powerful and effective character of these Revolutionaries has no precedents, it seems to me, in the great social agitations of past centuries. Where did this new race come from? . . . For the same men are still with us, even though the circumstances are different now; and they have a progeny everywhere in the civilized world."[4] It is to an examination of that "*virus*" and these questions that we now turn.

Notes

1. François Furet, *Interpreting the French Revolution,* translated by Elborg Forster (Cambridge: Cambridge University Press, 1977), 19.

2. Alexis de Tocqueville, *The Old Régime and the French Revolution,* translated by Stuart Gilbert (Garden City, N.Y.: Doubleday, 1955), vii.

3. William Doyle, *The Oxford History of the French Revolution* (Oxford: Clarendon Press, 1989), 423.

4. Furet, *Interpreting the French Revolution,*163.

ACKNOWLEDGMENTS

This book would not have been possible without the tolerance and good humor of our family and friends, especially our canine companions, who, despite limited patience, gave unconditional support as did our friends and colleagues at the United States Military Academy West Point, particularly Colonel Robert Doughty, the University of Montana, and Kansas State University. A particular note of thanks must go to Richard Drake, Ken Lockridge, Michael Mayer, Pamela Voekel, and Jeff Wiltse, who each read part of the manuscript; to Diane Rapp, who helped at critical junctures with such good will; to Todd Allen, our local computer genius; and to Margaret Robertson, who lugged many an unwieldy tome and who checked many an obscure reference. We also would like to thank the Earhart Foundation, the International Center for Jefferson Studies, Kansas State University, and the University of Montana for funding this research. The directors and staff of the Library of Congress, the London Public Record Office, the Archives Nationales, the New York Public Library, the Newberry Library, Hale Library at Kansas State University, the library at the United States Military Academy, the Maureen and Mike Mansfield Library at the University of Montana, and the William O. Thompson Library at The Ohio State University graciously assisted us. Last, a word of thanks must go to our editors at Greenwood Press: Barbara Rader for her unfailing encouragement and Kevin Ohe and Michael Hermann for their unstinting support and unquenchable humor.

CHRONOLOGY

1715–1774		**Reign of Louis XV, king of France**
1740–1748		War of Austrian Succession
1748–1762		Great period of Enlightenment publications, including the following:
1748		Montesquieu's *Spirit of the Laws*
1751		Voltaire's *Century of Louis XIV*
1751		Diderot and others, *Encyclopédie*
1759		Voltaire's *Candide*
1762		Rousseau's *Emile; Social Contract*
1756		Diplomatic Revolution; France allies with Austria
1763		Treaty of Paris ends Seven Years' War
1771–1774		Maupeou Parlements
1774–1792		**Reign of Louis XVI, king of France**
1778		France allies with United States
1781		Necker publishes *Compte Rendu*
1786		Eden Treaty (Anglo-French commercial treaty)
1787	February 22	Meeting of Assembly of Notables
1788	May	Suspension of *parlements*
	August 8	Decision to convoke the Estates General
	August 25	Appointment of Necker
	September	Recall of *parlements*

	September 25	The Paris *parlement* recommends the Estates General be held as in 1614
	December 27	Doubling of the Third Estate
1789	May 5	Estates General assembles at Versailles
	June 17	Adoption of title of "National Assembly" by the Third Estate
	June 1789–September 30, 1791	**National Assembly (Constituent Assembly)**
	June 19	Majority of clergy votes to join the Third Estate
	June 20	Excluded from their meeting place, the members of the Third Estate assemble in a tennis court and swear not to disband until a constitution is established
	June 23	The royal session
	June 27	The clergy and nobility are ordered by the king to join the Third Estate
	July 11	Dismissal of Necker
	July 14	Fall of Bastille
	July–August	Great Fear
	July 16	Recall of Necker
	August 5–11	Decrees of National Assembly abolishing feudalism and privileges
	August 26	National Assembly approves the text of a Declaration of the Rights of Man and the Citizen
	September	Publication of Sieyès's *What Is the Third Estate?*
	September 10	Assembly rejects bicameral legislature
	September 11	Assembly approves suspensive veto for the king
	October 5–6	The October Days followed by removal of the royal family and National Assembly to Paris
	October 29	Decree distinguishing electoral rights of active and passive citizens
	November 2	Nationalization of the property of the church
	December 19	First issue of assignats

1790	February 13	Suppression of religious orders (unless engaged in teaching or charitable work) and of monastic vows
	May 22	Renunciation of wars of conquest
	June 19	Decree abolishing titles and status of hereditary nobility
	July 12	The Civil Constitution of the Clergy
	September 4	Necker resigns from ministry
	November 27	First decree imposing civic oath on clergy
1791	April 13	Papal Bull *Caritas* condemns the Civil Constitution
	May 16	Self-denying ordinance
	June 20	Abortive flight of royal family to Varennes
	July 10	Padua Circular
	August 27	The Declaration of Pilnitz by the king of Prussia and emperor of Austria
	September 14	The king formally accepts the constitution Avignon annexed
	September 30	Dissolution of the Constituent Assembly
	October 1, 1791–September 20, 1792	**Legislative Assembly**
	November 9	Decree against émigrés (king vetoes November 12)
	November 29	Decree against nonjuring priests (king vetoes December19)
1792	February 9	Sequestration of property of émigrés
	April 20	Declaration of war against Francis II, ruler of Austria, Hungary, and Bohemia
	June 20	A mob invades the royal palace of the Tuileries, and the king and royal family are insulted and menaced
	July 25	Manifesto by the Duke of Brunswick threatens Paris with dire consequences if the city does not submit to the king
	August 3	Petition from 47 out of 48 Paris sections demanding deposition of the king

	August 10	Insurrection: the storming of the Tuileries is followed by the suspension of the king from his functions and the reinstatement of ministers dismissed in June (ministry of Roland)
	August 19	Defection of Lafayette to the Austrians
	September 2	Prussian army takes Verdun
	September 2–6	The September Massacres
	September 20	French victory at Valmy
	September 20, 1792–October 26, 1795	**National Convention**
	September 21	The monarchy abolished by unanimous vote
	September 22	Convention orders all acts to be dated from year I of the *republic*, the first time the word is officially used
	September 29	French occupation of Nice (Sardinian territory)
	November 6	Battle of Jemappes; French invasion of Belgium under way
	November 19	Decree offering aid to subject people wishing to be free
1793	January 21	Execution of King Louis XVI
	February 1	Declaration of war against Great Britain and the Dutch republic
	March 7	Declaration of war against Spain
	March 9	First authorization of missions by members of the Convention (*représentants en mission*) to the provinces and armies
	March 10	Decree setting up the Revolutionary Tribunal
	March	Rising in the Vendée
	March 21	*Comités de surveillance* set up in each commune
	April 5	General Dumouriez defects to Austrians
	May 4	The first Maximum, on grain prices
	June 2	Arrest of 31 members of the Convention (the fall of the Gironde)
	June 3, 1793– July 28, 1794	**Reign of Terror**

	July 10–July 23, 1794	Great Committee of Public Safety
	August 1	Adoption of the metric system
	August 23	Decree of *levée en masse* (universal obligation to service)
	August 27	Toulon surrendered to the British
	September 5	Terror is henceforth the order of the day
	September 17	Law of Suspects
	September 29	New law of the general Maximum on prices and wages
	October 5	Adoption of revolutionary calendar
	October 9	Reconquest of Lyons, in federalist hands since May
	October 10	Decree declaring that the government is "revolutionary until the peace"
	October 16	Execution of Marie Antoinette
	October 31	Execution of the Girondin leaders
	December 4	Law of 14 Frimaire on revolutionary government
1794	March 14–24	Arrest, trial, and execution of *Hébertistes*
	March 30–April 5	Arrest, trial, and execution of *Dantonistes*
	June 8	Festival of the Supreme Being (20 Prairial)
	June 10	Law of 22 Prairial speeds up work of the Revolutionary Tribunal
	July 26	Robespierre's last speech in the Convention calls for a new purge
	July 27 (9 Thermidor)	Arrest of Robespierre
	July 28	Execution of Robespierre
1794–1795		**Thermidoreans**
	July 30–31	Reorganization of Committee of Public Safety
	November 12	Jacobin club closed
	December 8	Deputies who protested Girondin purge readmitted to Convention
	December 24	Repeal of the Maximum
1795	April 1 (12 Germinal)	Popular demonstrations in Paris. Attack on Convention

	May 20 (1 Prairial)	Attack on Convention
	June 8	Death of Louis XVII
	August 22	Constitution of year III
	August 30	Two-thirds decree
	October 5 (13 Vendémiaire)	Uprising. Napoleon's troops protect the Convention. Army brought into politics
	October 26	Dissolution of the Convention
1795–1799		**The Directory**
1796	May 10	Arrest of Babeuf
1797	April	Elections. Reform and peace coalition wins
	September 4 (18 Fructidor)	Coup d'état; 177 deputies removed; elections annulled in 49 departments
1798	March	Election, three-fifths of legislature chosen, democrats' victory
	May 11 (22 Floréal)	Coup d'état; 105 elections quashed
	August 1	Battle of the Nile; Nelson destroys French fleet at Aboukir Bay
1799	November 9–10	Coup d'état of Brumaire
1799–1804		**Consulate**
1799	December 13	Constitution of year VIII, appearance of republic but in reality, dictatorship
1804–1814		**First Empire**
1814	April 11	Napoleon abdicates; exiled to Elba
1814–1824		**Reign of Louis XVIII, king of France**
1814	September–June 1815	Congress of Vienna
1815	March 1	Napoleon lands in France
1815	**March 20–June 18**	**Hundred Days**
	June 18	Battle of Waterloo
	June 22	Second abdication of Napoleon
	July 7	Return of Louis XVIII
	October	Napoleon arrives at St. Helena
1821	May 5	Napoleon dies in captivity

Note on the Revolutionary Calendar: On October 5, 1793, the revolutionaries adopted a new calendar in an attempt to underline the importance of the revolution, to open another front in the anticlerical campaign, and to put in place a more rational system. The new calendar underscored that the Revolution, not Christ's birth, was the defining event in man's history. September 22, 1729, the proclamation of the republic, became day 1, year I. Several revolutionaries noted that September 22 also marked the autumnal equinox and that the equality of day and night coincided with civil equality. The system was expressly designed to displace the old calendar and all its associations with Christianity by ridding the year not only of Sundays but of saint days, Advent, and so forth. There were still 12 months, but these were divided not into 7 days but into 3 *décades*, or 10-day units. The revolutionaries also suggested, although it was never really implemented, that each day be divided into 10 "hours," each revolutionary "hour" into 100 decimal "minutes," and each "minute" into 100 decimal seconds. The decimalization of time was the counterpart to the decimalization of weights and measures. Because this unnamed system, for example, day 1, of second *décade* of third month of year I, hardly promoted amity or facilitated its use, the dramatist Philippe François Nazaire Fabre d'Eglantine divided the new republican year into units that corresponded to the seasons. Fall consisted of Vendémiaire (wine harvest), Brumaire (fog), and Frimaire (frost); winter, of Nivôse (snow), Pluviôse (rain), and Ventôse (wind); spring, of Germinal (germination), Floréal (flowering), and Prairial (meadows); summer, of Messidor (harvest), Thermidor (heat), and Fructidor (fruition). The five (or six) days in leap year were named *sans-culottides*. The emphasis on nature and agriculture also was reflected in the decision to name each *quintidi* (fifth day of the *decade*) after a bird, fish, or animal; each *décadi* after an agricultural implement; and most of the other days after flowers, fruits, trees, or grains. The revolutionary calendar was never adopted outside of France. Neither was it particularly popular inside France except with the zealous few for whom it meant a day of rest every tenth instead of every seventh day. It offended the religious sentiments of many and perhaps the traditional attachments of even more. When the official newspaper began using both Christian and republican dates in 1802, it was a harbinger of its end. Napoleon orchestrated its official suppression on January 1, 1806. The calendar reveals not only the importance of symbols for the revolutionaries, but also their belief that restructuring time could help mold man in a new image.

CHAPTER 1

HISTORICAL OVERVIEW

Experience teaches us that, generally speaking, the most perilous
moment for a bad government is when it seeks to mend its ways.
Alexis de Tocqueville, in *France in Modern Times*
by Gordon Wright

The French Revolution was triggered not by one cause or event but by
several. Ironically, many, such as Alexis de Tocqueville, argue that the
various attempts to reform the ancien régime by Louis XV and Louis
XVI led to its demise. When they failed, revolution swept France. Many
blame Louis XIV, Louis XV, or Louis XVI, or all three for the outbreak of
revolution. Louis XIV (reigned 1643–1715) weakened the nobility, but
left them strong enough to thwart a weak king, and neither Louis XV
(reigned 1715–74) nor Louis XVI (reigned 1774–92) were strong leaders. In the early eighteenth century, the nobility insisted on retaining or
recovering their old rights and privileges, and they blocked the social
advancement of those, for example, who wanted to become officers in
the navy or army or to hold certain positions in the government. This
resurgence of the nobility created more tensions in society and made it
more difficult for the king to enact meaningful reform. In addition,
Louis XIV bequeathed to his successors a nation mired in debt because
of his ruinous engagement in several wars, the last of which, the War of
the Spanish Succession (1702–14), impoverished France.

Neither Louis XV nor Louis XVI strengthened the institution of
kingship. During their reigns, France suffered numerous diplomatic
and military defeats, which created disaffection at home and eroded the
morale of both the army and navy, the support of which the monarch
needed to retain his throne. Although Louis XV was greeted at the
beginning of his reign as "the well beloved," by the end of his reign he
was mocked as "the pleasure of ladies" because of his flamboyant mis-

tresses, notably Madame de Pompadour and Madame Du Barry, who intervened in politics to advance the interests of their favorites. Only toward the end of his reign did Louis XV take a more active role in governance and become convinced of the need for reform. Frederick the Great's verdict of Louis XV, "his only defect was that of being king,"[1] was both damning and true.

His grandson and successor, Louis XVI, a well-intentioned and conscientious ruler, became conscious of the necessity of reform and brought in a variety of ministers, such as Anne-Robert-Jacques Turgot (see document 1, "Letter of Turgot to Louis XVI"), to enact such measures. But a phalanx of powerful enemies moved against Turgot, who was "just, but inflexible in his principles" and a man "whom no credit could bend or favour corrupt."[2] His expedients and those of others failed in part because of the strength of the opposition and the weakness of the king, who articulated at the outset of his reign that he wished "nothing so much as to be beloved."[3] As one contemporary observed, "A well meaning man at Court is a foreign plant that a thousand insects set out to devour."[4] The populace also unfairly derided Louis XVI as impotent and his wife, the Austrian-born Marie Antoinette, as extravagant and promiscuous. Although the queen was unfairly libeled, for she was a devoted wife and mother, it is true that she had done nothing to enhance the reputation of the king. Undoubtedly, Louis XVI faced a daunting task at a time when the institution of kingship was being challenged by intellectuals known as *philosophes.*

The *philosophes,* men such as François-Marie Arouet de Voltaire, Jean-Jacques Rousseau, Charles-Louis de Secondat, baron de Montesquieu, and Denis Diderot, challenged the basic institutions of the state, most notably the monarchy and the church, the pillars of the old regime. They used reason and criticism to attack existing inequities, such as unfair taxation, unjust laws, slavery, the evils of war, religious intolerance, bigotry, superstition. But in leveling such charges they eroded the prestige and power of the king and weakened his ability to bring about the very changes they advocated.

Economic conditions also played an important role in bringing about revolution. The government primarily relied on direct taxation, and neither the clergy nor the nobility paid this tax. Those who had the least paid the most, and those who had the most paid the least. This situation could not last for long—and it did not. France was on the verge of bankruptcy when Louis XVI came to the throne, and the situation only deteriorated during his reign. Because expenditure exceeded revenue, especially in wartime, the government had to use more and more of the revenue to service the debt. Because Louis XVI became convinced that only in peacetime could fundamental reform be enacted, he avoided commitment abroad, further eroding his prestige and ironically making it more difficult to enact reform. The increase in population, the European-wide recession, the growing unemployment, and the imbalance between the food supply and the population coalesced in 1788–89 when a drought in the spring, a hailstorm in the summer, and a bitterly cold winter devastated the crops and drove up the price of grain, the basic subsistence item, and caused rioting and then revolution.

It was in such an atmosphere that the king agreed to call the Estates General, a representative body that had not met since 1614, to deal with the endemic problems that France confronted. The Paris *parlement* (1 of 13 law courts throughout France), which was staffed by members of the nobility, decided that the estates should meet and vote as they had in the past—by estate: the first, the clergy; the second, the nobility; and the third, everyone else in France—and that each estate would have one vote. The members of the Third Estate, lawyers, merchants, artisans, and peasants, were furious with the *parlement,* which before this decision championed their rights against a despotic king—or so they thought. Individuals, such as Emmanuel-Joseph Sieyès, denounced the *parlement's* decision and championed the rights of the Third Estate in pamphlets such as *What Is the Third Estate?* In this tract, Sieyès argued that the Third Estate represented the nation and that "if the privileged order were removed, the nation would not be something less, but something more."[5] Many urged the king to agree to the doubling of the Third Estate; that is, the Third Estate would have twice as many members as each of the other estates. At the insistence of his financial adviser Jacques Necker, the king agreed.

In the spring of 1789, elections were held to vote for the representatives to the Estates General. These elections varied throughout France, depending on local customs. The process was indirect in the case of the Third Estate and placed a premium on speaking ability. At this same time, *cahiers des doléances* (lists of grievances such as inequitable taxation) were also being drawn up. They provide a glimpse into the public opinion of various constituencies on the eve of the Revolution; they listed area concerns, complaints about abuses, and sometimes recommendations for change. But the king throughout the Revolution was led by events; he did not lead. When the Estates General convened on May 5, 1789, the king presented no reform program, and the members grew restive. The Third Estate wanted all the estates to meet as one and refused to act until the king agreed. The representatives of the Third Estate called on the other estates to meet with them as the National Assembly and refused to disband until they established a constitution for France. The king initially did nothing, perhaps paralyzed by grief over the death of his son. In the beginning, the king sided with the first two estates, but on June 27, 1789, the king wavered and finally ordered the members of the other estates to meet with the Third. Troops began to converge on Versailles, and on July 11 the king dismissed Necker, the symbol of reform.

The mustering of troops, the dismissal of Necker, the escalating price of wheat, fear of vagrants and the unemployed washed over the capital, and crowds started to arm themselves. On July 14, they went, seeking weapons, to the Bastille, a symbol of royal despotism because it was at one time both a prison and a fortress. The governor of the fortress finally agreed to let the mob in and ordered his troops not to fire. The mob, however, practicing no such restraint, murdered six soldiers, the governor, and the mayor of Paris and later paraded their heads on pikes. This was not the first time nor would it be the last that the mob played a decisive role. One contemporary, horrified by the bloodshed, condemned the murders and observed that "a cold-blooded cruelty was accounted virtue, and humanity was accounted weakness."[6] The seizure of the Bastille, today marked by a national holiday in France, triggered the first of the great emigrations from France as the king's brothers, failing to convince the king to punish the rioters and suppress the Assembly, fled. It also marked the beginning of violence that would become endemic in the Revolution.

The king made yet another concession; he ordered all of the clergy and nobles who had not yet done so to meet with the Third Estate and dismissed the troops. Meanwhile, violence escalated both in Paris and in the countryside. Attempting to restore order, some nobles in the National Assembly on August 4–5 moved to abolish seigneurial rights, such as *corvée,* which is forced manual labor, gaming rights, and other dues. The call for reform intensified. The Assembly also abolished tithes, the taxes collected by the church, and all exemptions from taxation and stipulated that all offices were open to anyone, to name but a few of the more important acts. These reforms dismayed the king, who, writing candidly to an archbishop, contended, "I will never consent to the spoilation of my clergy and my nobility."[7] Faced with decrees that he could not condone, the king did nothing. But the passage of these decrees virtually ended disorder in the countryside. A few days later, on August 26, the Assembly issued the Declaration of the Rights of Man and the Citizen. This fundamental document, influenced by the American Declaration of Independence, the cahiers, and the ideas of the *philosophes,* stressed man's natural rights, the rule of law, and freedom of thought and religion. (See document 4, "Declaration of the Rights of Man and the Citizen.")

The economic situation, however, had not improved. The Flanders regiments were called into Versailles, and a banquet was held to celebrate their arrival. Rumors circulated that the white of the Bourbons and the black of the house of Austria were flaunted and the tricolor trampled. Agitators, such as Jean-Paul Marat and Camille Desmoulins, also spread stories that the king intended to disavow the work of the Assembly. As the tocsin rang out, crowds gathered in Paris. On October 5, a large crowd of women gathered around the Hôtel de Ville (city hall) demanding cheap bread and marched the 12 miles to Versailles. Both the king and the Assembly graciously received the women. The king, later that evening, accepted the Assembly's decree, yet another sign that the mob had dictated the resolution. Early the next morning, the mob stormed the palace, killed some of the bodyguards, paraded the bloody trophies on pikes, and surged up the steps toward the queen's apartments. Half dressed, the queen fled to the king. A contemporary observer, André-François, Comte Miot de Mélito, recoiled from the scene and recalled that at the time he was "dumb with horror."[8] The regiments, in the meantime, had turned over their cartridges to the National Guard. Marie Joseph Paul Yves Roch Gilbert du Motier, Marquis de Lafayette, the commander of the National Guard, attempted to restore order and convinced the king to come to Paris. The Assembly followed shortly thereafter. Thus, the mobs had again captured the Revolution. In the succeeding days, disgusted by the violence and disquieted by the idea of meeting in Paris, some members of the Assembly resigned and returned home; still more emigrated. The king had become a prisoner of Paris and increasingly was to realize it.

The most important legislation of the Revolution was passed in the period after the autumn of 1789. It was at this time that political clubs, such as the Jacobins, started to form. The Jacobins were members of a group who called themselves the Society of Friends of the Constitution. They were dubbed Jacobins because they usually met in the buildings formerly occupied by the Jacobin order. In the fall of 1791, there were over 1,000 such clubs scattered throughout France, but their number mushroomed to approximately 2,000 during the radical phase of the Revolution. This large network of affiliated societies and its active membership enabled the Jacobins to wield enormous power. As the membership, initially limited to the upper middle class, was opened to the poorer elements, the society became more radical. By 1793, the Jacobins fell under the influence of the Mountain. This group of left-wing deputies, so called because they sat high up on the left of the Convention, was estimated to include between 258 and 302 members. It most famously included Maximilien Marie Isidore Robespierre, George Jacques Danton, and Jean Paul Marat.

Those who wanted a stronger role for the king lost on pivotal issues: the king received a suspensive, not an absolute, veto; the Assembly voted for a unicameral, not a bicameral, legislature. Even more distressing from the king's point of view was the confiscation of church land. This church land was to be sold and the bonds, the assignats, were to be used to pay down the debt. Shortly thereafter, the Assembly passed the Civil Constitution of the Clergy (July 12, 1790), which reorganized the church. The new diocesan boundaries corresponded to the departments, with one bishop for each department, a reduction from 130 to 83 bishoprics. In addition, the civil constitution treated all officials of the church as officials of the state and paid them on a graduated scale, provided that all officials be chosen by local election, and demanded that all clergy take an oath of loyalty to the state. This legislation, probably one of the most ill-conceived of the Revolution because it fueled Catholic resistance, further disenchanted the king with the Revolution and created a schism in French society. As one observer notes about this legislation, it "cut all the bridges."[9] Only 7 of the 138 bishops agreed to take the oath (see document 7, "Memoirs of the

Duchess of Tourzel on the Oath to the Civil Constitution of the Clergy,"
and document 8, "Letter of the Archbishop of Embrun"). Of the parish
priests throughout France, about half took the oath. Of those who took
the oath, many retracted it (see document 9, "Declaration of Guillaume
Tollet") when the pope denounced the Civil Constitution of the Clergy
in the spring of 1791 and threatened all those who did not retract the
oath within 40 days with excommunication. The regions with the highest percentage of refractory clergy—also called nonjuring clergy, that is,
those who had not taken the oath—tended to be rural and to have
native-born priests.

The Revolution had created two churches, one official and one
clandestine. In so doing, it had alienated many irrevocably. In setting
state against church, Paris against Rome, the Assembly unwittingly
forged the leaders and troops of the counterrevolution. The schism in
the clergy lasted until 1801, when Napoleon Bonaparte signed the Concordat with the papacy. That agreement bound church and state even
more tightly together. Even then some on both sides refused to accept
it. Many Catholics, including the king, took the sacraments from the
refractory clergy. The National Assembly at this time also tried to eliminate many of the institutions of the old regime—the provinces, the
parlements, local laws—and to replace them with departments, uniform
municipal organizations, and uniform laws.

As the king's disenchantment with the Revolution grew, so did his
sense of being a prisoner. In the spring of 1791, when the royal family
attempted to go to the countryside to celebrate Easter as they did tra-
ditionally, the National Guard refused to let them leave Paris. The realization that they were in fact prisoners combined with the growing and
hostile demonstrations of the crowd outside the Tuileries persuaded
the king and his family to flee the capital. They did so on June 20,
1791. Unfortunately, the king left behind a note condemning the Revolution (see document 10, "Letter of Louis XVI"), and the escape was
bungled. The royal family was brought ignominiously back to the capital. The flight forced the Constituent Assembly to recognize an
inescapable fact: the king had not accepted the Revolution. Nonetheless, when the constitution was presented to the king, he signed it, and
the Constituent Assembly ended and the new Legislative Assembly
convened. A constitutional monarchy had been established that would
last less than a year.

War proved to be the crisis that helped to end the constitutional monarchy. Other European powers had refused up to this time to intervene in the Revolution because many hoped that the Revolution would weaken France internally and prevent the French from becoming the aggressors they had been in the seventeenth century. Still other powers were more concerned with other international issues, such as the partition of Poland. But the émigrés kept clamoring for intervention, and those who feared the spread of the Revolution abroad, such as Edmund Burke, became more vocal. On July 6, 1791, the emperor Leopold II issued the Padua Circular in which he urged other European sovereigns to act in concert and "limit the dangerous extremes of the French revolution."[10] The French only gave credence to their enemies' fears: they annexed papal territory inside France, Avignon and Venaissin, and violated international treaties. The dominant political group in the Assembly, the Girondins, or the Brissotins, so called because many came from an area called the Gironde or were followers of Jacques Pierre Brissot, became the war party. These left-wing deputies, numbering approximately 130, relied on the considerable oratorical talents of their members, which included Marie-Jean-Antoine-Nicholas de Caritat, Marquis de Condorcet. The king favored war because he expected that disaster would ensue; that is, the army would fall apart and the nation would rally around him. The Girondins favored war because they thought victory would be assured, foreigners would flock to the Revolution, and only then would the Revolution be secured. In the Declaration of Pillnitz of August 1791, Leopold II of Austria threatened to invade France to reestablish order if the other European powers would join him. Although the infamous "if" clause in effect made this an empty gesture, the declaration only added to the war hysteria. Some, such as Robespierre, argued—but futilely—that no one loves "armed missionaries."[11] In April 1792, the French declared war on Austria. Shortly thereafter, Prussia joined with Austria. Disaster soon followed for France. By the summer, both Austria and Prussia were on the verge of invading France. This advantage prompted them to issue the Brunswick Manifesto (July 25), which threatened Paris with retribution if anything happened to the king or queen. Instead of ameliorating the situation of the royal family this declaration exacerbated it and confirmed the suspicions many harbored of the king's betrayal of the Revolution.

As many had predicted, the French suffered serious losses in initial clashes with the enemy. Many of the officers had either emigrated or resigned and the troops lacked discipline—sometimes murdering their own commanders. Because of these disasters the reputations of those, such as Robespierre who had opposed the declaration of war, increased and the suspicions of the court—particularly of the king and the Austrian-born queen—increased. In France, meanwhile, conditions had deteriorated: the paper money, the assignat, steadily lost value; prices climbed; and scarcities of vital items escalated. Recruits streamed into Paris; those from Marseilles chanted a new, bellicose song that would later become the national anthem, the *Marseillaise.* Demagogues such as Marat, Robespierre, and Danton whipped up revolutionary hysteria and submitted petitions to the Assembly urging the dethronement of the king.

It was in such an atmosphere that the "second revolution" took place: a mob invaded the Tuileries, massacring 600 of the Swiss Guard, who protected an empty palace because the royal family had fled to the Assembly for protection. Mobs again determined the path of the Revolution. The Assembly voted to suspend the king and establish a new republican constitution. But mob violence was not yet over. After Lafayette defected to the Austrians and as the Prussian troops advanced, capturing Verdun, the last fortress defending the road to Paris, mobs, acting on ill-founded rumors that counterrevolutionaries were cooperating with the enemy, massacred over 1,300 defenseless men, women, and children imprisoned mainly in Paris in what has come to be called the September Massacres. (See document 12, "Journal of Jourgniac de Saint-Meard.")

Shortly thereafter, the French took the offensive. French troops repulsed the allies at Valmy (September 30), stopping the Prussian advance on Paris, and invaded the Austrian Netherlands, the Left Bank of the Rhine, and Savoy. It was in celebration of such victories and the certitude of more to come that the French issued the "propaganda decrees" (see document 26, "The First Propaganda Decree, November 20, 1792," and document 27, "The Second Propaganda Decree, December 15, 1792"), which offered fraternity and aid to all people who wished to recover their liberty, and which confirmed the fears of many, such as Edmund Burke (see document 32, "Edmund Burke's Condemnation"), that the French intended to export their revolution. Burke and others also worried about the fate of the king.

Those who wanted the establishment of a republic, such as Louis-Antoine de Saint-Just, argued that the king should not be tried, that he should be executed because kingship itself was a crime. "One cannot reign innocently," Saint-Just contended.[12] The discovery of a hidden cache of the king's letters denouncing the Revolution and requesting foreign aid decided the king's fate. Although the well-respected lawyer Chrétien Guillaume de Lamoignon de Malesherbes and two others came forward courageously to defend the king, the issue was never in doubt. By a wide margin, the king was found guilty of treason and condemned to death. Louis XVI was executed in January 1793. His wife's execution followed within less than a year. Of the regicides, those who voted for the death of the king, 34 died under the "national razor" (the guillotine), 21 died by violence, 28 expired naturally, and 127 later served under Napoleon.[13] The execution of the king combined with the issuance of the propaganda decrees and the increased violations of international law provoked Britain, the United Provinces, and Spain to join Austria, Prussia, and Sardinia in the War of the First Coalition (1792–95) against France.

As the allies drove the French from the Austrian Netherlands and the Rhineland and prepared to invade France, and yet another celebrated French general, Charles-François du Périer Dumouriez, defected to the allies (April 1793), the French government responded to the crisis by conscripting men into the army, provoking resistance and shortly thereafter counterrevolution in an area called the Vendée. France found herself at war within and without her borders. The assignat plunged in value and scarcities of critical items increased. In the Convention, the Girondins, the group who had argued for a national referendum on the fate of the king, opposed giving in to the demands of the Parisian crowds invaded the Tuileries and threatened the Assembly. They advocated a diminution of the role of the capital and pushed for an extension of the war, but found their fate at issue.

On May 31, 1793, approximately 80,000 Parisian *sans-culottes*, so called because they did not wear the culottes of the aristocracy, invaded the Convention. With cannon primed and pointed at the chamber, they demanded the expulsion and arrest of the Girondins. Mobs again determined the fate of the Revolution. As historian Simon Schama has pointed out, what was abandoned was "the last scrap of pretense that the revolution was founded on legality and indeed on representation."[14] Some Girondins escaped and fled to the provinces; these "federalist" rebels would later demand a more decentralized revolution. Revolts broke out in Marseilles, Bordeaux, and Lyons, and the great port of Toulon was handed over to the British. The champion of the *sans-culottes,* the journalist Jean-Paul Marat, was murdered in his bath. The Mountain concurred with the demands of the *sans-culottes* and assumed more power. Their opposition to the group led by Brissot and their support for the Terror defined them. During the king's trial, they voted against the referendum and for the king's death. Moreover, they shared the dangerous conviction that "liberty must conquer at all costs,"[15] or, in the words of Robespierre, "to despair is equivalent to treason."[16] Inherent in that view was an absolutism far more terrifying than that of the monarchy.

Once the Mountain dominated the Convention, they assumed control of the pivotal Committee of Public Safety, which itself assumed more power during the Terror. The Terror began in the summer of 1793 and lasted through the summer of 1794. During that period, more than 40,000 were executed. More than 400,000 died in the civil war that wracked France. Many in the Convention thought that the republic was beleaguered from within as well as without. To combat the invasion of the allies, the Convention decreed the *levée en masse* (August 23, 1793), calling on the entire population to aid in the war effort (see document 25, "Decree of August 23, 1793, the *Levée en masse*"). In the words of one revolutionary, "Every citizen should be a soldier and every soldier should be a citizen."[17] On September 5, 1793 "terror" was proclaimed the "order of the day."[18] Shortly thereafter, the Convention passed the Law of Suspects (September 17, 1793) which stipulated in very vague terms that anyone even suspected of disloyalty could be arrested (see document #15, "The Law of Suspects"). On October 10 the constitution was suspended and France was declared to be "revolutionary until the peace."[19] The Convention also passed three decrees called the Maximum (May 4, 1793, September 29, 1793, and February 24, 1794) that set prices on necessities, such as grain, flour, butter, oil, brandy, coal, candles, salt, and tobacco, and regulated wages. They also requisitioned goods for the war effort, executed many generals for failing to act aggressively enough, and resorted to mass executions in the provinces to suppress federalist revolts or counterrevolutionary uprisings. Many agreed with the assessment of Saint-Just that "prosperity can not be hoped for while the last enemy of liberty still breathes."[20]

The spirit of that sentiment was incarnated in the Law of 22 Prairial (June 10, 1794), which marked the beginning of the Great Terror, or "the Republic of Virtue." This law accelerated the judicial processes of the Terror by, in effect, depriving the accused of any defense and requiring little evidence to convict. During that period of 7 weeks more people were condemned to death than in the preceding 14 months, although ironically both the internal and external threats were no longer significant.

Opposition developed on both the left and the right. On the left, the followers of Jacques Hébert, a spokesman for the *sans-culottes* who advocated more radical economic reforms and espoused atheism, threatened the Mountain because of their support in Paris. On the right, the *Dantonistes*, or Indulgents, challenged the continuance of the Terror by pointing out that both the external danger from France's enemies abroad and the internal threat from counterrevolutionaries and federalists had been checked. Both the *Hébertistes* and the Indulgents ultimately met the same fate: death on the guillotine.

When the Committee of Public Safety failed to answer all of its critics, when many became convinced that the Terror was no longer necessary, and when many feared that they too would be targeted, the fate of Robespierre and his colleagues was decided. Ironically, the very success of the Terror ensured its demise. In the revolutionary month of Thermidor, Robespierre and his colleagues, notably Saint-Just and Georges Couthon, were arrested. Although Robespierre's followers secured their release, they were soon rearrested and promptly executed. Of the 12 members of the Committee of Public Safety, 3 were executed and 3 sentenced to deportation. William Wordsworth, an early, but subsequently disenchanted, admirer of the Revolution, would condemn the "heinous appetites"[21] of the terrorists and write evocatively of the Terror and the "domestic carnage [that] now fill'd all the year":

> The Old Man from the chimney nook,
> The Maiden from the bosom of her Love,
> The Mother from the Cradle of her Babe,
> The Warrior from the Field, all perish'd, all
> Friends, enemies, of all parties, ages, ranks,

Head after head, and never heads enough
For those who bade them fall.[22]

The Thermidoreans, who governed from 9 Thermidor (July 27, 1794) until the installation of the Directory in October 1795, dismantled the machinery of the Terror. They repealed the Law of 22 Prairial, suppressed the Revolutionary Tribunal, freed thousands of prisoners, closed the Jacobin clubs, and weakened the power of the Parisian commune (which had supported Robespierre), the Committee of Public Safety, and the representatives on mission (those dispatched to the army or to the departments to enforce the will of the Convention). During this time, those who had indulged in some of the worst atrocities, such as Jean-Baptiste Carrier (see document 19, "Letter of Carrier"), who had conducted "republican baptisms" (mass executions by drowning), and over 70 others died under the national razor. The government offered an amnesty to those in the Vendée, which temporarily brought peace to that region (see document 20, "Proclamation of the Royalists in the West," and document 21, "Charette's Declaration, February 17, 1795"). But revolt broke out again in 1796, 1813, and 1815.

After the government dismantled the economic controls in December 1794, thus sparking and fueling inflation, the assignat plunged in value, forcing many to pay their taxes in kind rather than in currency. Although in 1795 the Directory stipulated that no more assignats would be issued, by 1796 the assignat was worth 0.025 percent of its original value. In 1797, the assignats were formally demonetized. The inflation of this currency ruined creditors, devastated wage earners and those on fixed incomes, and undermined confidence in the economy.

Twice in the spring of 1795, 12 Germinal (April 1) and 2 Prairial (May 21), the crowd again tried to play a role in the Revolution. In Prairial, they invaded the Convention, beheading a deputy who tried to stop them, and surrounded the hall with cannons. On this occasion, however, the Convention called in the National Guard and arrested the militants. In both instances military force was used against the crowd. Never again did the *sans-culottes* rise and change the path of this Revolution. A general revulsion toward Robespierre and the Terror and all that that implied swept over France. As one historian notes, "The pursuit of pleasure replaced the republic of virtue."[23] Contemporaries often commented on the immorality that seemed endemic in France after Thermidor. For a British traveler, "the depravity of all ranks . . . " was "past belief."[24]

The Thermidoreans also perceived the necessity of drawing up yet another constitution for France with elaborate checks and balances, including annual elections and a five-man directorate. Each year one of the five would be replaced. To avoid threats from both the left and the right, the two elected bodies, the Council of Ancients and the Council of Five Hundred, were to include at least two-thirds of the members of the existing government. At this time, too, peace was concluded with Prussia (April 1795), the United Provinces (May 1795), and Spain (July 1795). Only Austria, Sardinia, and Great Britain remained at war with France under the Directory.

The Directory was a government obsessed with war and with staying in power. The French, under able generals such as Jean Victor Moreau, Jean Baptiste Jourdan, and Napoleon Bonaparte, took the offensive in the German and Italian lands, forcing Sardinia (1796) and Austria (1797) out of the war. The British continued fighting. They retained naval superiority because of the able leadership of such officers as Samuel Hood, Richard Howe, John Jervis, and Horatio Nelson, and they won strategic victories, such as Aboukir Bay (1798), which marked British naval supremacy and which incidentally stranded Napoleon and his troops in Egypt. Back in Europe, the French invasion of Italy and Switzerland and the creation of the satellite republics meant war yet again and the formation of the Second Coalition with Russia, Austria, Great Britain, Turkey, Portugal, and Naples (1799).

Both those on the left and those on the right, dissatisfied with the Directory, assailed it for being corrupt and self-seeking. The royalists, hoping for free elections, staged a mass protest in the capital in Vendémiaire (October 5, 1795), but they were quelled by the army under the orders of an aggressive commander, Napoleon Bonaparte. It was only then, as historian T. C .W. Blanning points out, that the deputies were able to escape "from the thrall of the revolutionary crowd."[25] The next threat came from the left under François-Noël Babeuf, a journalist who frequently had been imprisoned for advocating more radical reforms. He called himself Gracchus Babeuf after the famous brothers of ancient Rome who advocated, among other things, distribution of land to the landless. In 1796, he, together with disenchanted Jacobins, planned an uprising called the Conspiracy of Equals. The government, apprised of the plot, arrested them and executed two, including Babeuf. In the 1797 (Fructidor) elections, those on the right won, but three of the directors, faced with a royalist majority and the possibility of peace, nullified 49 elections and purged 177 of those legally elected with the assistance of the military. The elections of 1798 (Floréal) and 1799 (Germinal) also were "adjusted."

The Directory, increasingly under attack and ridiculed for its greed, corruption, and tenacious insistence on staying in power, came to rely more on the army. Yet, at the same time, it came to fear a young general whose reputation had been earned during the revolutionary wars: Napoleon, whom one contemporary referred to as "that wild-haired little runt." It was Napoleon to whom Sieyès turned when he realized that the government under the Directory was neither workable nor supportable. As Sieyès put it, what France most needed was "authority from above and confidence from below."[26]

On 18 Brumaire (November 1799) in another coup, Napoleon became first consul and then later emperor (1804). In 1799, Napoleon called on all Frenchmen to recognize a new reality: "Citizens, the Revolution is established on the principles on which it began. It is over."[27] And so it was. After numerous years of warfare and privation and the loss of many fellow citizens, the French found themselves under a government more despotic than the monarchy they had overthrown. This is but one of many ironies of the French Revolution.

Notes

1. T.C.W. Blanning, *The French Revolutionary Wars, 1787–1802* (New York: St. Martin's, 1996), 21.

2. Jean François Marmontel, *Memoirs of Marmontel* (London: H. S. Nichols, 1895), 2:148–50.

3. Ibid., 2:288.

4. George Armstrong Kelly, *Victims, Authority, and Terror: The Parallel Deaths of d'Orleans, Custine, Bailly, and Malesherbes* (Chapel Hill: University of North Carolina Press, 1982), 214.

5. Sieyès, quoted in Keith Michael Baker, ed., *The Old Regime and the French Revolution* (Chicago: University of Chicago Press, 1987), 156.

6. Marmontel, *Memoirs*, 2:294.

7. Quoted in M. J. Sydenham, *The French Revolution* (New York: Capricorn Books, 1966), 57.

8. André-François, Comte Miot de Mélito, *Memoirs of Count Miot de Mélito,* edited by General Wilhelm August Fleischmann (New York: Scribner, 1881), 15.

9. Nigel Aston, *The End of an Elite* (Oxford: Clarendon Press, 1992), 46.

10. Quoted in Albert Goodwin, *The French Revolution* (New York: Harper, 1953), 104.

11. Quoted in Blanning, *The French Revolutionary Wars,* 65.

12. Quoted in Simon Schama, *Citizens: A Chronicle of the French Revolution* (New York: Knopf, 1989), 651.

13. John Hall Stewart, ed., *A Documentary Survey of the French Revolution* (New York: Macmillan, 1951), 385.

14. Schama, *Citizens,* 724.

15. Sydenham, *The French Revolution,* 189.

16. *Speeches of Maximilien Robespierre with a Biographical Sketch* (New York: International Publishers, 1927), 14.

17. Blanning, *The French Revolutionary Wars,* 83.

18. Sydenham, *The French Revolution,* 176.

19. Ibid., 187.

20. Ibid.

21. William Wordsworth, *The Prelude or Growth of a Poet's Mind, 1805* (London: Oxford University Press, 1970), line 339.

22. Ibid., lines 329–36.

23. Sydenham, *The French Revolution,* 231.

24. Ibid.

25. Blanning, *The French Revolutionary Wars,* 181.

26. William Doyle, *The French Revolution: A Very Short Introduction* (Oxford: Oxford University Press, 2001), 63.

27. Ibid.

CHAPTER 2

CRISES OF THE ANCIEN RÉGIME

Man was born free and everywhere is in chains.
Jean-Jacques Rousseau, *The Social Contract
and Discourse on the Origin of Inequality*

Many events triggered the outbreak of that complex event, the French Revolution. Some historians, such as Hippolyte Adolphe Taine, blame the *philosophes* (intellectuals who in the late seventeenth and eighteenth centuries were concerned with the basic problems of the day) because they used criticism and reason to undermine the very foundations of the ancien régime and to advocate freedom, whether from arbitrary power or unjust laws. These *philosophes,* who stressed individuals' rights rather than their duties, came from different social classes: Montesquieu was a member of the nobility; Voltaire, the middle class; and Rousseau, the lower class. Although the Enlightenment was centered in France, it was not exclusively a French phenomenon. *Philosophes* could be found in many countries: John Locke was English; Adam Smith and David Hume, Scottish; Cesare Beccaria, Italian; Montesquieu, Diderot, and Voltaire, French; Rousseau, Swiss; and Immanuel Kant, German. They critiqued existing injustices but often differed on the solution and fought among themselves, prompting historian Peter Gay to compare them to a stormy family.[1] Carl Becker also compared the *philosophes*— but to medieval theologians. Just as theologians in the Middle Ages were trying to construct a heavenly city in the hereafter using faith, in the eighteenth century *philosophes* were using reason to construct a heavenly city on earth. The *philosophes* attacked the authority of the church and the Bible, but they believed in the authority of reason.[2]

They also believed in the importance of education. The project advanced by Diderot and Jean le Rond d'Alembert to assemble an *encyclopédie* symbolized the Enlightenment spirit: to spread knowledge and to encourage a critical evaluation of society and its institutions.

The *philosophes* attacked a variety of abuses. John Locke, Pierre Bayle, and Voltaire, for example, undermined the position of the church by advocating religious toleration. Locke also propagated the idea that man had natural rights and that government was formed to protect those rights, the contractual theory of government. Should the government fail to do so, man had the right to rebel. This philosophy proved a potent rationale for revolution. Other *philosophes,* notably Rousseau and Montesquieu, attacked corrupt governments but did not agree on the remedy. Montesquieu argued that climate, the size of the country, customs, and so forth influenced the type of government. A large tropical country needed a despotic government. A small country in a northern climate was best suited to a republic. In a medium-sized country, such as France, with a moderate climate, the best government was a mixed government, a monarchy whose power was restricted by various corporate bodies. In particular, the nobility were important because they could prevent a monarchy from becoming a despotism. Rousseau argued that man's defects were given him by society; institutions had corrupted man. "Man was born free and everywhere is in chains."[3] The general will, which incarnated the will of the community, a hazy concept at best, should govern society. Other *philosophes* attacked superstition, slavery, unfair laws, and taxes. Some, such as Voltaire, attacked optimism because such a philosophy implied acceptance of the status quo and precluded any change. Over time the *philosophes* became more radical. For example, at the end of the seventeenth century, Locke and Bayle argued for limited toleration of others' religions; but by the late eighteenth century, Paul-Henri Thiry, Baron d'Holbach, was contending that there was no God. These ideas helped to undermine the legitimacy of the old regime. To philosophize, as one contemporary noted, was "to shake off the yoke of authority."[4]

Some historians, however, stress the importance of economic issues. They point, for example, to the great increase in population in the eighteenth century and the ensuing dislocation, especially in France. In 1700, there were approximately 19 million French people, and by 1789, there were 24 million. The population increased in part because more scientific farming and animal-breeding methods were employed and new crops, such as the potato and the turnip, were introduced, which provided people in the eighteenth century with a better diet than their predecessors. The death rate declined for many reasons: the recession of various diseases, such as the plague; medical advances; and the growing philanthropic spirit, which translated into better care of the ill and the poor.

The growth of the population also meant that there was an imbalance between the population and the food supply. More people survived but on a marginal level. Approximately 30 percent of the population lived in poverty. The gap between the rich and the poor was not lessening but growing. Some historians emphasize the direct link between the high price of bread and the outbreak of revolts. For example, in 1774, when the harvest was poor, bread prices rose more than 50 percent and ignited what has been called the "Flour War"; that is, riots in Paris and northeastern France. In the late 1780s, bread prices increased because of a series of natural disasters. In 1788, a drought in the spring, a hailstorm in the summer, and a bitterly cold winter devastated crops. All these natural disasters drove up the price of grain, which peaked on July 14, 1789, the day the Bastille fell. In a century, the price of goods rose 62 percent, but wages did not.[5] In addition unemployment also spiked upward because of the European-wide recession from 1785 to 1788.

The fundamental fiscal problem in France was structural. The government primarily relied on direct taxation, the *taille,* for financing. But neither the clergy, who owned about 10 percent of the land, nor the nobility, who owned between 25 and 30 percent, paid this tax. The clergy, who ran the hospitals, schools, and orphanages and kept the local records of births, marriages, and deaths, collected the tithe, in theory one-tenth of an individual's income. They did present the king with a "free gift," but they determined the amount. To compound the problem, in many areas tax farmers collected the taxes and forwarded only part of that money to the government. What precipitated the Revolution more than anything else was the fiscal crisis. Expenditure exceeded revenue, especially in wartime. Throughout the eighteenth century, France was involved in many wars, most notably the War of the Austrian Succession (1740–48) and the Seven Years' War (1756–63), which helped to bankrupt the state. The French devoted about 25 percent of the budget to the army and navy and about 50 percent to pay off the debt.[6] The various finance ministers, who had no central bank to turn to, relied on a variety of expedients to stave off disaster, such as loans, but to no avail. The creaky edifice known as the ancien régime finally collapsed.

Socially, the most fundamental paradox in the ancien régime was the king, who claimed a monopoly on all legitimate power. The king was thus both the defender of privilege and at the same time the fountainhead of justice; that is, the source of reform. This role would have challenged the most talented and resourceful of kings, and neither Louis XV nor his grandson Louis XVI were either. The Second Estate, the nobility, most directly contested the king's power. Although Louis XIV had undermined the power of the nobility, they nonetheless remained strong enough to challenge his successors. After the death of Louis XIV (1715), the nobles increasingly assumed more power, a phenomenon called the resurgence of the nobility. The nobles claimed a variety of privileges, such as trial in special courts and execution by decapitation rather than by hanging. They could not be conscripted into the army nor could troops be billeted in their households. Only nobles could hold the most prestigious offices in the realm, whether it be bishop or minister or ambassador or general officer in the army or navy. In effect, the old order made it impossible for talented men who were not members of the nobility to achieve high office. Even more dangerous, the nobles of the sword, the older, more prestigious nobility, and the nobles of the robe, the officeholders, started to intermarry and join forces against the king. It was the nobility who acted as judges of the 13 *parlements* (law courts) that registered the edicts of the king. Thus, the nobles were able to block the king's reforms. Some historians allege that the Revolution started long before the seizure of the Bastille in July 1789. They argue that the first stage of the Revolution was the struggle between the king and the nobility.

Both Louis XV (reigned 1715–74) and Louis XVI (reigned 1774–92) realized that reform was essential. Unfortunately, both kings damaged the image of monarchy at a time when the old rationalization for the king's rule, divine right (the belief that the king was appointed by and answerable only to God), was being contested. Louis XV was both lazy and pleasure loving. In particular, he loved women and supported a number of mistresses, the most famous of which was Jeanne

Antoinette Poisson Le Normant d'Etioles, Marquise de Pompadour. During his reign, a number of favorites dominated the court and a number of ruinous wars drained the treasury. But Louis XV became increasingly committed to reform as France tottered on the edge of bankruptcy. When Madame de Pompadour's funeral cortege passed by, he allegedly said: she picked a good time to take a journey. He also is attributed incorrectly with the remark, *"Après moi, le déluge"* (After me, the deluge). In 1745, he appointed Jean Baptiste de Machault d'Arnouville controller general of finances. Machault persuaded the king that France could be saved only by the imposition of a new tax, the *vingtième* (the twentieth), which would replace the old taxes. This tax that would be levied on all Frenchman directly attacked the exemption of the nobles and the church. Because of stiff resistance, this plan was eventually abandoned, but the king increasingly reasserted his right to govern, arguing that he alone held power in the state. Eventually, Louis XV realized that the only way to enact reform was to abolish the old *parlements,* establish new ones, and eliminate the sale of judicial offices. This reform, the "Maupeou *parlements,*" however, lasted less than three years (1771–74).

When Louis XVI came to the throne in 1774, he wanted to be loved by his people and immediately dismissed the Maupeou *parlements* and recalled the old ones. Some historians contend that from this time onward revolution was inevitable. Louis XVI, too, attempted numerous reforms; he appointed a number of controllers generals of finance dedicated to eliminating abuses. In 1774, he appointed Anne Robert Jacques Turgot, a former intendant (agent of the king) in Limoges who was noted for his many reforms, notably the introduction of new crops, the development of industry, and the abolition of compulsory labor (*corvée*) for public projects. In the Six Edicts, Turgot attacked many of the privileged groups in France (see document 1, "Letter of Turgot to Louis XVI"). He advocated the abolition, for example, of most guilds, *corvée,* and the tariffs levied on grain and proposed the establishment of a new tax on landowners. The *parlements* defended the privileged and opposed Turgot. Turgot, however, was both tactless and politically inept. He was determined to push his reforms through no matter what the cost, and he imprisoned many of his opponents in the Bastille. On being advised to be patient and put through his reforms slowly he replied, "In our family we die at fifty."[7] He paid for his haste.

He soon lost the support of other ministers and the queen and was dismissed by the king. However, his assessment that only significant reform could avert revolution proved accurate. His other prediction of his own demise was fairly accurate as well: he died at age 54. Turgot's dismissal, in the words of an eminent historian, showed the "impossibility of overcoming entrenched privilege."[8]

The king then turned to a number of other ministers to resolve the fiscal crisis: Jacques Necker, Charles Alexandre de Calonne, and Etienne Charles Loménie de Brienne. Necker served as director of the treasury in 1776 and then director general of finances starting in 1777. His opposition to free trade in grain had made him enormously popular. The king, however, refused to name him controller general because he was a Protestant and a commoner. Necker, who was an international financier, hoped to restore financial confidence by reducing expenses and borrowing at high interest rates. He also conducted a survey of all venal offices (offices that were bought and sold and regarded as property) with the hope of abolishing them. His publication of the *Compte Rendu* in 1781 revealed a modest surplus in the king's accounts but did not detail the loss in the extraordinary accounts that funded the military debt. His image as financial savior survived intact, but his attempt to increase his power and gain admittance to the council backfired. When the king refused his demand for even more stringent reforms, he resigned in 1781.

The next significant reform effort came with the appointment of Calonne, who served as controller general from 1783 to 1787. In his words, "All the funds were empty . . . [the] alarm was general and confidence destroyed."[9] Like Turgot, he too had been an intendant, but, unlike both Turgot and Necker, he realized that economizing would not solve the fundamental economic problem. Instead, he adopted a spending policy to restore confidence in the government. The recession that gripped Europe at the end of the eighteenth century doomed that effort. Calonne rejected the idea of printing more money, fueling inflation and thus lowering the costs of the loans, and refused to repudiate the kingdom's debts. The only solution was to institute a new tax on land to be levied on all, even the privileged. To garner support for this fundamental reform, Calonne urged the king to call an Assembly of Notables, the most eminent men in the nation. Unfortunately, many of Calonne's enemies and Necker's supporters were in the Assembly, and they refused to authorize any fundamental reform. The king accordingly dismissed Calonne, who fled to Great Britain not to return to France until 1802. He was the first of many who sought safety abroad.

The king turned next to Brienne, Calonne's main adversary in the Assembly. Brienne fared little better with the Assembly, and the king had to resort to various expedients to raise money, including forcing laws through the reluctant *parlements*. Brienne's attempts to save France from bankruptcy also failed. The ancien régime simply collapsed. The king had no choice but to call the Estates General, the representative body of France that had not met since 1614.

Louis XVI was neither capable enough nor imaginative enough to deal with this new situation. He was both conscientious and well intentioned but also "hopelessly irresolute"[10] as well as politically inept. He did not direct events; events drove him. He was an extremely private man whose great passions were eating and hunting. His failure to sire a child after almost eight years of marriage was ridiculed widely. His wife, Marie Antoinette, also gravely impaired the reputation of the monarchy. She was tactless, frivolous, extravagant, and poorly advised. She also was unpopular because she was from Austria, France's traditional enemy, and seemed to many to advance the interests of her homeland rather than those of France. The Diamond Necklace Affair, in which a credulous churchman thought that he was buying an expensive bauble for the queen, unjustly implicated the queen, who was notorious for her extravagance, even though she knew nothing of the swindle. Both Louis XVI and Marie Antoinette did little to narrow the widening gulf between the court and the people. It was not hatred that the people felt for the monarchy but contempt, and as Goethe once astutely remarked, it was not hatred but contempt that destroys a regime.[11]

Because the king's primary duty and exclusive prerogative was to defend the kingdom, the disasters that befell France militarily and diplomatically were blamed on him. In the eighteenth century, the French army oftentimes was humiliatingly defeated just as they were at Rossbach in 1757 by the greatly outnumbered Prussians. The diplomatic picture was no better. France's participation in the War of the Polish Succession (1733–35), the War of the Austrian Succession (1740–48), and the Seven Years' War (1756–63) garnered France little.

Rather, France lost most of its colonies abroad. The Diplomatic Revolution of 1756 in which France allied with her age-old enemy, Austria, was not popular. One observer echoed the opinion of many when he described this ill-fated alliance as "monstrous in principle and disastrous . . . in practice."[12] France was also ashamedly unable to help its traditional allies. She stood by helplessly while Poland was partitioned among Austria, Prussia, and Russia and while Russia seized Turkish territory, such as the Crimea. When the Prussians invaded the United Provinces in 1787, the French were also unable to come to their aid. These series of defeats eroded the respect France had formerly enjoyed in Europe. In the words of Joseph II of Austria, "France has collapsed and I doubt whether it will rise again."[13] In addition many blamed the recession and unemployment in France on the Eden Treaty of 1786 in which the British and the French agreed to reduce the tariffs on certain goods. The reaction in France to these military disasters and diplomatic setbacks was "humiliation, anger, and disaffection."[14]

The disaffection of the army also played a role in the coming of the Revolution. The army, demoralized over recent losses, particularly in the War of the Austrian Succession and the Seven Years' War, was furious with the king for his refusal to send French troops to aid their Dutch ally. The poor morale was so critical by 1789 that the king believed he could not rely on his own troops. He was told that the army would mutiny if ordered to fire on the Parisians.[15] The army's loyalty was never tested on the field, but the large number of soldiers who were willing to sit in the Estates General (of the 278 deputies of the noble estate, 221 were officers, active or retired) and to speak out against abuses reflects their discontent.[16]

The only notable diplomatic and military success of the French in the eighteenth century was their assistance to the colonials in the war for American independence—support for which was not universal. Turgot, for example, had advised the king to remain neutral because of the precarious state of French finances. The financial aid to the Americans constituted more than twice the ordinary yearly revenue.[17] The American Revolution also played another role in causing the French Revolution: the French saw that protest against arbitrary actions and unjust laws could succeed, that new societies could be established, that despotism could be resisted. The American example would prove a potent one (see document 2, "*Mémoires* of Weber").

Notes

1. Peter Gay, *The Enlightenment: An Interpretation; the Rise of Modern Paganism* (New York: Vintage Books, 1968), 4.

2. Carl L. Becker, *The Heavenly City of the Eighteenth-Century Philosophers* (New Haven, Conn.: Yale University Press, 1932).

3. Jean-Jacques Rousseau, *The Social Contract and Discourse on the Origin of Inequality* (New York: Washington Square Press, 1967), 7.

4. Quoted in Sydenham, *The French Revolution*, 24.

5. William Doyle, *Origins of the French Revolution* (New York: Oxford University Press, 1990), 195.

6. Ibid., 43.

7. Schama, *Citizens*, 87.

8. Daniel Roche quoted in T. C. W. Blanning, *The Culture of Power and the Power of Culture: Old Regime Europe 1660–1789* (New York: Oxford University Press, 2002), 409.

9. Quoted in Doyle, *Origins of the French Revolution*, 49.

10. Blanning, *The Culture of Power*, 416.

11. Goethe quoted in ibid., 141.

12. Quoted in Blanning, *The French Revolutionary Wars*, 23.

13. Blanning, *The Culture of Power*, 423.

14. Orville Murphy, *The Diplomatic Retreat of France and Public Opinion on the Eve of the French Revolution, 1783–1789* (Washington, D.C.: Catholic University of America Press, 1998), 4.

15. Samuel Scott, *The Response of the Royal Army to the French Revolution: The Role and Development of the Line Army, 1787–1793* (Oxford: Clarendon Press, 1978), 60.

16. Blanning, *The Culture of Power*, 427.

17. Peter McPhee, *The French Revolution, 1789–1799* (New York: Oxford University Press, 2002), 35.

CHAPTER 3

THE TERROR

Pity is not revolutionary.

François Joseph Westermann, in
The French Revolution, 1789–1799 by McPhee

Although historians disagree about when exactly the Terror began, 1793 witnessed the suspension of many laws and rights and the establishment of the basic institutions that would support the Terror. The Terror, which took place between the summer of 1793 (June 2, the fall of Jacques Pierre Brissot and his colleagues—the Girondins) and the summer of 1794 (July 27, the fall of Robespierre and his colleagues), was marked by an acceleration of arrests and the execution of many. More than 17,000 were brought before the Revolutionary Tribunal and condemned to death, approximately 12,000 were killed by representatives on mission or after surrendering on the battlefield, and another 11,000 died in the prisons awaiting trial; a total of approximately 40,000 fell victim to the Terror.[1] These victims included the queen, Marie Antoinette; the great poet, André Chénier; the founder of modern chemistry, Antoine Lavoisier; the philosopher and mathematician, Marie-Jean-Antoine-Nicolas de Caritat, Marquis de Condorcet; many members of the Academy of Science; the mayor of Paris, Jean Sylvain Bailly; the Girondins; the *Dantonistes*; and the *Hébertistes*. Of those executed, more than 70 percent were from the lower classes, and 84 percent were from the Third Estate.[2] The scale and inhumanity of such executions prompted the great historian Taine to describe the Terror as "a political philosophy written in blood."[3] The Terror more than any other event disillusioned many with the Revolution.

Historians disagree over what caused the Terror. Some contend that the Terror was the inevitable offspring of ideology or that it was an intrinsic part of the revolutionary ethos. Others argue that events drove the Terror: war, civil conflict, and the deteriorating economy. For them, the Terror was necessary to save France from its enemies and the Revolution from failure. By the spring of 1793, France found herself at war with Austria, Prussia, Spain, Great Britain, the United Provinces, and Sardinia. Revolutionary armies were being defeated on many fronts. Some French officers, such as General Dumouriez, were defecting to the allies, and French land was being occupied by foreign troops. Discipline had broken down in the armies, and soldiers often lynched their officers. In addition France faced civil war. Parts of France, notably the area called the Vendée in the western part of the country, rejected the authority of the Convention. The effort to conscript men into the army triggered the revolt, but many there already opposed some of the policies of the Convention, such as the execution of the king and the Civil Constitution of the Clergy. In the Vendée more than 50,000 men fought the revolutionary government, taking as their symbol the Sacred Heart of Jesus with a superimposed cross. These individuals included counterrevolutionaries who supported the king and wanted a restoration of the royalist government, federalists who opposed the centralization of power in Paris, and others. The great provincial cities such as Lyons, Marseilles, and Bordeaux defied the Convention. At Toulon the royalists handed the city over to the British and surrendered the fleet. In addition, the assignat, the revolutionary paper currency, plummeted in value. By the summer of 1793, it had lost about 77 percent of its value. France also faced a shortage of basic necessities, such as food and fuel. Such was the situation that the government faced in the spring of 1793.

In response to these threats, the revolutionaries urged that control be centralized in Paris. The more moderate individuals on the committee, such as Danton, were replaced by the more radical, such as Robespierre and Saint-Just and, later in September, Jean-Marie Collot d'Herbois and Jean Nicholas Billaud-Varenne. The Montagnards (the Mountain) dominated the key committees in the National Convention, especially the Committee of Public Safety, which arrogated to itself more power. To ensure that its policies were carried out, the committee sent out representatives on mission. Increasingly, the Committee of Public Safety assumed the responsibility of running the government. By the winter of 1793, this committee, for example, named individuals to the other committees. It also worked closely with the Committee of General Security, which supervised the police.

The Committee of Public Safety, comprising 12 members, governed France during the Terror. Its most prominent member was Robespierre, a provincial lawyer dubbed the "Incorruptible" because of his chastity and self-righteousness. Robespierre and his allies wanted to establish a "republic of virtue." For Robespierre, those who did not share this vision were "vile and base beings who eternally conspire against the rights of man and the happiness of all peoples."[4] Seven of the 12 who governed with Robespierre were also lawyers: Saint-Just, Billaud-Varenne, Couthon, Robert Lindet, Pierre-Louis Prieur, Bertrand Barère, Marie-Jean Hérault de Séchelles. Two, Lazare Carnot and Claude-Antoine Prieur-Duvernois, were engineers; one, Jeanbon Saint-André, was a minister; and one, Collot d'Herbois, an actor. Of the 12, only 1 was a member of the nobility and 1 a member of the lower classes; the rest were professionals. The group was also young: 4 had not reached age 30 and only 1 was over 40.[5] Within the committee, some members handled specific problems: Carnot, for example, directed the armies. But they all shared a commitment to the Revolution.

Robespierre echoed the opinion of many when he argued that the Revolution owed "its enemies nothing but death."[6] Those who opposed such policies he labeled "foolish or perverse sophists who seek to reconcile black with white and white with black: They prescribe the same system for peace and war."[7] According to Robespierre, "If the mainspring of popular government in time of peace is virtue, the mainspring of popular government in time of revolution is both virtue and terror: virtue, without which terror is evil; terror, without which virtue is helpless. Terror is nothing but justice, prompt, severe and inflexible; it is therefore an emanation of virtue."[8] The Convention decreed on September 5 that "terror was the order of the day," and on October 10 that France would remain "revolutionary until the peace."[9]

To deal with the threat of foreign invasion the Convention decreed the *levée en masse* on August 23, 1793. It called on the entire population to aid in the war effort: unmarried men between the ages of 18 and 24 were conscripted, married men were to make munitions and transport munitions and provisions, women were to make uniforms and tents, the children bandages. Even the very old and the very young were to join in the effort. The goal was to mobilize the entire population and its resources for the war effort (see document 25, "Decree of August 23,

1793, the *Levée en masse*"). The Committee of Public Safety also put the economy on a wartime basis; it requisitioned goods and imposed a maximum price on essential items. A Maximum, passed on September 29, 1793, set prices on necessities such as butter, oil, brandy, coal, candles, wheat, and flour and regulated wages. In practice many flouted the regulations. In addition the French did not hesitate to execute their own; more generals (84) were executed by the Convention for either failure or timidity than were killed in the war.[10] Such efforts were so successful that by the end of 1793 the French had repulsed the foreign armies and gained control of all of France except for a small piece of territory in the north. By the spring of 1794, over 800,000 men were in arms and on the offensive, seizing the Austrian Netherlands and the Left Bank of the Rhine.

By the spring of 1794, the revolutionaries also had defeated the counterrevolutionary movement known as the Vendée and suppressed the federalist rebellions. They had not spared their enemies; they often resorted to mass executions. For example, at Lyons they slaughtered over 1,665 people by forcing them to stand in front of predug graves (the *mitraillades*) where the army fired cannons at them, leaving them to fall in. The revolutionaries even eliminated the old name of the city and called it instead "liberated city" (Ville Affranchie). Mass executions took place at other places as well. At Toulon, *fusillades,* mass executions by firing squad, killed at least 1,109 people. At Gonnord, 32 women and children were buried alive. At Nantes, the representative on mission, Carrier, ordered "vertical deportations," or "republican baptisms": those accused were forced on boats with hacked-out bottoms and left to drown in the Loire. Other revolutionaries proposed but did not implement even more horrific schemes such as poisoning the wells with arsenic and gassing their enemies in mines. The "infernal columns"[11] of the republican army were ordered to destroy or kill anything in their path; they burned crops, slaughtered animals, and razed buildings. They made the Vendée a desert and killed approximately one-third of the population—and this after the main royalist army had been defeated. The Vendée was aptly renamed *Vengé* (Avenged). The republican General François Joseph Westermann reported: "The Vendée is no more. . . . We did not take any prisoners: it would have been necessary to give them the bread of liberty, and pity is not revolutionary."[12] Carnot epitomized the philosophy of many when he wrote: "We need expect no peace from our enemies, and those at home are worse than those abroad. We must smash them, or they will crush us."[13] And smash them they did. Another revolutionary argued, "We can be humane when we are assured of being victorious,"[14] or in the words of a member of the Committee of Public Safety, "that which constitutes a Republic is the total destruction of that which opposes it."[15] The members of the Committee of Public Safety and the representatives on mission were accused of many things, but humanity was not one of them.

In Paris the Convention passed a number of laws to govern France and to weed out the traitors in the body politic. The Law of Suspects, passed on September 17, 1793, stipulated that anyone suspected of disloyalty could be arrested. The criteria were so vague that virtually anyone could be arrested: those who were partisans of tyranny or federalism or enemies of liberty, those who could not prove their means of existence, those who did not perform their civic duties, those who did not have a certificate of civism, public officials who were dismissed from their offices and not reinstated, former nobles and their relatives, and those who had emigrated and who had not proved their loyalty to the Revolution. Because of this legislation about 300,000 people were arrested.[16] The revolutionaries determined that anyone who opposed the Revolution would die.

Yet another critical piece of legislation was the Law of 14 Frimaire (December 4, 1793), which served as the "constitution of the Reign of Terror."[17] It centralized and consolidated power in Paris by providing for the publication and distribution of laws. It placed all governmental agencies, except for the police who were under the direction of the Committee of General Security, under the control of the Committee of Public Safety. Even the representatives on mission had to report to the Committee of Public Safety.

The last significant piece of revolutionary legislation, the Law of 22 Prairial (June 10, 1794), was co-authored by Robespierre and Couthon, both members of the Committee of Public Safety. This law often is termed the "high tide of revolutionary legislation"[18] because it speeded up the processes of the Terror and reformed the Revolutionary Tribunal. It stipulated that everyone must be tried in Paris. In addition the law deprived the accused of any legal defense, defined enemies of the people in vague terms, provided that the only verdict possible was acquittal or death, and required little evidence to convict. In effect, this legislation identified legal justice with morality and reduced trials to mere appearances. In Paris alone, 1,376 were executed in six and a half weeks. As the prisoners flowed in from the provinces, the jails in Paris were soon overflowing, as were the courtrooms. Mass trials, or *journées,* took place in which individuals were tried as a group. In one such trial, more than 60 people were condemned at once. This legislation marked the beginning of the 7-week period called the Great Terror because more people were condemned to death in those 7 weeks than in the preceding 14 months, even though both internal and external threats had subsided. If the thesis of "circumstance," the theory that the Terror was a reflexive and self-defensive response to certain crises, does not offer a satisfactory explanation, what does? For many the answer lies in ideology grounded in the revolutionary mentality. Perhaps violence was an intrinsic part of the Revolution, or perhaps it was a result of the religious fervor of the revolutionaries whose "arrogant self-confidence," whose "fanatical faith" in their ability to transform mankind blinded them to the monstrosity of their actions.[19]

In addition to relying on the guillotine to establish this new republican order the Convention tried to establish a new revolutionary culture in which everything that reminded the people of the old regime was eliminated. For example, the revolutionaries abolished the old Christian calendar and replaced it with a republican one divided into 12 months, each with 3 periods of ten days, the *décades.* The Committee of Public Safety also established a far more rigorous system of censorship than existed under the ancien régime because they regarded criticism as tantamount to disloyalty. Many abandoned their Christian names, others urged the abolition of the constitutional clergy and the closure of all churches, the destruction of all religious icons, and the substitution of revolutionary ceremonies for religious ones. But some on the Committee of Public Safety disapproved of the more radical ideas such as dechristianization, which Robespierre labeled a "philosophical masquerade."[20] Robespierre accused the dechristianizers "under pretense of destroying superstition . . . [of making] a kind of religion of atheism itself."[21] For Robespierre, who believed in a Supreme Being, such a movement was blasphemous and would alienate moderates from the Revolution. Atheism Robespierre equated with the aristocracy, immorality with despotism, and virtue with republicanism. For him, the answer lay in the cult of the Supreme Being.

Opposition to these policies arose from both the left and the right. On the left, the *Hébertistes*, an ill-defined group, challenged the Committee of Public Safety. Hébert acted as a radical spokesman for the *sans-culottes*, the group of mainly artisans and shopkeepers who wore long trousers instead of the knee breeches or culottes of the upper classes. A radical journalist, Hébert threatened Robespierre because of his support in the Commune of Paris. Hébert had not only advocated the tightening of the Maximum and the Law of Suspects but also, as an atheist, had supported the Cult of Reason. He and his followers were arrested and executed in March 1794. On the right, the *Dantonistes*, or the Indulgents who advocated a lessening of the Terror, also challenged the policies of the committee. The defeat of France's internal and external enemies prompted many to urge a lessening of the Terror. The deputy Jacques-Alexis Thuriot, for one, contended, "We must check this torrent which is sweeping us back to barbarism."[22] Desmoulins, one of Robespierre's friends, attacked the increasing repression and wrote, "I shall die in the belief that to make France free, republican, and prosperous, a little ink would have sufficed, and only one guillotine."[23] In a brilliant article, allegedly a translation of the Roman historian Tacitus, Desmoulins depicted a society riven by fear (see document 17, "Camille Desmoulins's Plea for Clemency"). The comparison with France was unmistakable. Danton, noted for his zest for life and popularity with the Parisians, also opposed the creation of a state based on terror. Danton and Desmoulins were executed in April 1794. Subsequently, the widows of Hébert and Desmoulins were executed—a clear signal that no dissidence would be tolerated. Shortly thereafter, Malesherbes, the courageous lawyer who had left his retirement to defend the king, was executed along with his daughter, son-in-law, and grandchildren.

After these executions the Committee of Public Safety went on to abolish the various ministries in the government, such as war and foreign affairs, and replaced them with commissions, each of which had to report to the committee. It also consolidated its hold over the Commune of Paris, executing its archbishop and mayor. The committee also started to relax price controls, and, predictably, inflation recurred, with the assignat plummeting to 36 percent of its original value.

But the Committee of Public Safety had not been able to silence all of its critics. Fear of a new purge or of Robespierre, discontent with Robespierre's policies, and personal enmity towards the so called Incorruptible, prompted these men to act. Many also may have been convinced that the Terror was no longer necessary since French armies were increasingly victorious over their enemies at home and abroad. Others lamented that the Terror did not go far enough. The divisions within the Committee of Public Safety, which in the past had been kept within the committee, became public. For example, some disliked the Cult of the Supreme Being; others opposed the execution of Hébert or Danton. The Committee of General Security resented the growing dominance of the Committee of Public Safety. Robespierre, angry with his colleagues, began to isolate himself. His absence gave his enemies the opportunity they sought. The Terror ended on 9 Thermidor (July 27, 1794) when a number of revolutionaries denounced Robespierre and some of his colleagues. Robespierre, Couthon, and Saint-Just were arrested but then released by Robespierre's followers and taken to the Hôtel de Ville (city hall). On the following day, the Convention mobilized enough troops to re-arrest them. They were guillotined that evening. Three other members of the committee were put on trial and condemned in the spring of 1795 to the "dry guillotine"; that is, deportation to Guiana. Only Barère managed to evade the sentence.

The subsequent dismantling of the revolutionary government is often dubbed the Thermidorean reaction. The Thermidoreans governed from 9 Thermidor until the installation of the Directory in October 1795. The Thermidoreans repealed the Law of 22 Prairial, suppressed the Revolutionary Tribunal, and freed thousands of prisoners. In addition they punished those who had supported Robespierre by closing the Jacobin clubs and reducing the powers of the Commune of Paris. They also repealed the Maximum and reduced the power of the Committee of Public Safety and the representatives on mission. Many in Paris disavowed the radical terrorists; in the provinces the "white terror" (so called because white was the color of the Bourbons) of reaction ensued and militant Jacobins were killed. The Convention also guillotined the most zealous advocates and executors of the Terror, including Carrier, who had overseen mass executions, and Antoine-Quentin Fouquier-Tinville, the prosecutor of the Revolutionary Tribunal. Eventually, 108 Robespierrists died on the guillotine. Those who had killed in the name of the Revolution met the same fate as those they earlier had mercilessly condemned.

Notes

1. R. Bienvenu, "The Terror," in *Historical Dictionary of the French Revolution, 1789–1799,* edited by Samuel F. Scott and Barry Rothaus (Westport, Conn.: Greenwood Press, 1985), 942–46.

2. Donald Greer, *The Incidence of the Terror during the French Revolution: A Statistical Interpretation* (Gloucester, Mass.: Peter Smith, 1935), 97.

3. Quoted in ibid., 5.

4. Ibid., 126.

5. For an extensive analysis of these men, see R. R. Palmer, *Twelve Who Ruled: The Year of the Terror in the French Revolution* (Princeton, N.J.: Princeton University Press, 1973).

6. Sydenham, *The French Revolution,* 207.

7. Jeremy D. Popkin, *A Short History of the French Revolution* (Englewood Cliffs, N.J.: Prentice Hall, 1995), 84.

8. R. R. Palmer, *The Age of the Democratic Revolution* (Princeton, N.J.: Princeton University Press, 1964), 2:126.

9. Popkin, *A Short History of the French Revolution,* 82.

10. Blanning, *The French Revolutionary Wars,* 181.

11. Sydenham, *The French Revolution,* 197.

12. Quoted in McPhee, *The French Revolution,* 112.

13. Quoted in ibid., 151.

14. Quoted in Greer, *The Incidence of the Terror,* 15.

15. Quoted in ibid., 19.

16. Sydenham, *The French Revolution,* 177.

17. Palmer, *Twelve Who Ruled,* 127.

18. Ibid., 365.

19. Alexis de Tocqueville, *The Old Regime and the French Revolution,* translated by Stuart Gilbert (Garden City, N.Y.: Doubleday, 1955), 156.

20. Palmer, *Age of the Democratic Revolution,* 2:115.

21. Palmer, *Twelve Who Ruled,* 121.

22. Sydenham, *The French Revolution,* 181.

23. Ibid., 198.

CHAPTER 4

A NEW POLITICAL CULTURE

Nothing in the Revolution, no, not to a phrase or a gesture, not to
the fashion of a hat or a shoe, was left to accident.
Edmund Burke, "Letters on a Regicide Peace,"
in *The Works of Edmund Burke*

The revolutionaries strove to transform France, to create a new political
culture, to reshape mankind in the revolutionary mold and in the process to destroy any remnant of the ancien régime. They aimed at nothing less than the regeneration of man. Revolutionaries were filled with
what has been called "possibilism": "the sense of boundless possibility."[1] The nineteenth-century historian Tocqueville talked of the revolutionaries' "fanatical faith" in "transforming the social system, root and
branch and regenerating the whole human race." In so doing they were
prepared to act with "unprecedented ruthlessness."[2] They possessed a
utopian energy that convinced them that it was possible to change not
only the public sphere but also the private one. As one revolutionary
explained: "A revolution is never made by halves; it must either be total
or it will abort. All the revolutions which history has conserved for
memory as well as those that have been attempted in our time have
failed because people wanted to square new laws with old customs and
rule new institutions with old men . . . REVOLUTIONARY means outside of all forms and all rules."[3]

The revolutionaries realized that, in the words of historian Robert
Darnton, the ancien régime's "system of power was embedded in the
language, the social codes, and the behavior patterns of everyday life"
and that "political systems are held together, are made to stick, by the
force of culture."[4] They acknowledged that although the state was

invisible, "it must be personified before it can be seen, symbolized before it can be loved, imagined before it can be conceived."[5] The revolutionaries strove to transform man's entire world, to invest everything with political significance: dress, speech, manners, education, religion. All must bear the revolutionary imprint. As Edmund Burke noted at the time: "Nothing in the Revolution, no, not to a phrase or a gesture, not to the fashion of a hat or a shoe, was left to accident."[6] The republicans stressed how to speak, dress, and act just as the aristocrats had done. Unconsciously, the revolutionaries, who were never aware of the irony, adopted a system as structured as the one they strove to overturn. They wanted to eliminate all symbols of the ancien régime, to delegitimate and desacralize those symbols and to legitimate and sacralize the symbols of the Revolution. Instead of exalting divine-right absolutism as symbolized by the king and the king's color—white—they exalted popular sovereignty and the national cockade—red, white, and blue. The king symbolized the old paternal, despotic order, and Marianne, the new symbol of France, the new revolutionary world and a rejection of the old patriarchal regime. Just as the crown symbolized the monarchy, so the red liberty cap, initially worn by freed slaves in ancient Rome, symbolized the republic. The slogans of the new republican order, *Liberté, Egalité, Fraternité,* were all feminine nouns. Virtuous republicans wore liberty caps, painted or sculpted female figures of liberty or the Revolution, and planted liberty trees at home and abroad as a sign of their republican ardor.

Under the ancien régime, dress was a political sign and differentiated the various groups in society. Professions, such as judges and masons, had their own unique apparel. When the Estates General met, the members dressed in traditional garb: the Third Estate in all black and the First and Second Estates in colors with lace and plumes. (See document 3, "Memoirs of Miot de Melito.") Since aristocrats had worn culottes (breeches) and powdered their hair, revolutionaries adopted the fashion of the *sans-culottes;* they wore trousers, a liberty cap, natural hair, and a *carmagnole* (a short jacket). For women, the elaborate hairstyles of the ancien régime, which sometimes towered three feet high, were abandoned. Instead, their hair was worn flat, their necklines were higher, and their heels lower. The revolutionaries wanted to eliminate what they termed "odious distinctions of dress."[7] The authoritarian dress of the ancien régime was replaced—but with an equally authoritarian republican one. Men who dressed in the old noble garb were assaulted and often lynched because the revolutionaries were convinced that dress reflected political convictions. Because of such views the republic required all men to wear the national cockade after July 5, 1792.

Language also was to be regenerated. Revolutionaries were urged to adopt an energetic and frank tone because only that was suitable to a great nation. Those who encountered foreigners were given some latitude and cautioned not to give offense if foreigners did not adopt "our revolutionary style"; that is, using *tu,* the familiar form, instead of *vous,* the more formal term of address. Nor were ambassadors, envoys, consuls, or others outside France to be greeted as anything other than *citoyen.* As late as 1796, a revolutionary discovered what he termed a "real scandal." Some were substituting the word *monsieur* for that of *citoyen.* Those who wished to "*monsieuriser* can return to coteries who accept this language but these messieurs ought to resign as employees of the republic," he warned. "We know the influence of words on things."[8] Revolutionaries even went so far as to purge from the vocabulary certain words that intimated any sort of privileged status, such as *privilège exclusif,* which means 'patent.' *Avocats* of the ancien régime became *hommes de loi* (men of the law). Letters were to be signed with "*Salut et fraternité*" or "*Vive la République une et indivisible.*" Furthermore, all Frenchman were expected to speak French, not the various languages and dialects tolerated under the ancien régime, which included Breton, Provençal, Basque, Italian, German, and Flemish.

The revolutionaries also wanted to tear aside what Rousseau had damned as that "perfidious veil of politeness,"[9] which they equated with the monarchy and the aristocracy. They repudiated the etiquette and ceremonial of court society because it validated the ancien régime and reinforced the aristocratic code. One revolutionary articulated this mentality bluntly: "Politeness is not a republican virtue."[10] Manuals were written to inculcate the new codes. Such things as manners were not insignificant; according to Burke, they were more important than laws: "Manners are what vex or soothe, corrupt or purify, exalt or debase, barbarize or refine us, by a constant steady, uniform, insensible operation, like that of the air we breathe in. They give their whole form and colour to our lives."[11]

Diplomats who represented the new republican France abroad were particularly careful to project republican mores in style, language, dress, and etiquette. The old aristocratic dress was replaced by a simple republican costume; the deferential and circuitous language, with a frank and direct speech; and the elaborate court etiquette, with a simple, egalitarian style. Envoys had to avoid "diplomatic" habits. French envoys were to live "with simplicity, with friendship, and with fraternity."[12] They were expected to act like true republicans and forego, for example, the custom of genuflecting when they presented their credentials, which revolutionaries regarded as one of the "obsequious forms of the despotic regime."[13] As one revolutionary explained in 1793: "To be truly Republican, each citizen must experience and bring about in himself a revolution equal to the one which has changed France. There is nothing, absolutely nothing in common between the slave of a tyrant and the inhabitant of a free state; the customs of the latter, his principles, his sentiment, his action, all must be new."[14] The attire of French diplomats prevented them from being confused with others who were "still branded by the shackles of servitude."[15] On June 22, 1796, a decree stipulated that French representatives must wear a blue coat, vest, and pants, a red and white sash with tricolor fringes, and a hat with a tricolored plume.[16] One of the most accomplished, Jean-Baptiste Treilhard, who represented France at the congress of Rastatt, deliberately ignored the restraint so characteristic of the old school. He stupefied his fellow delegates when he pounded violently on the table. Treilhard avoided acting like a diplomat of the ancien régime because he did not want to be accused of behaving like an envoy of the king as one of his colleagues had been. This colleague had traveled very slowly with a numerous entourage and with a great deal of pomp and ostentation.

In this vast program of indoctrination the revolutionaries purged the administration of old civil servants and often hired inept or corrupt political cronies. Having held a position in the ancien régime was often grounds for dismissal (see document 13, "Memoirs of Miot de Mélito"). The revolutionaries were often preempted, however, by the nobility, who resigned the important positions they held in the diplomatic corps, the army, and the navy. By March 1792, in the navy, for example, 7 of 9 vice admirals, 15 of 18 rear admirals, and 128 of 170 captains had resigned.[17] These massive resignations, however, cleared the way for the talented to move quickly up in rank, as Napoleon did.

In order to inculcate loyalty, the revolutionaries staged carefully orchestrated festivals to commemorate key events or to incite anger against their enemies. These festivals took the place of the ancien régime celebrations. For example, the French staged a *fête sanglante* (bloody fete) to commemorate the killing of two French envoys as they left the congress of Rastatt (1799). The Festival of Federation of July 14, 1790, was a celebration of national reconciliation and unity. In this festival the National Guard, the army, and groups of children took an oath to be faithful to the nation, the law, and the king. As the Revolution became more radical, revolutionaries not only beheaded the king but also purged him or any symbol of him from future celebrations. The festival held on August 10, 1793, not only reminded observers of the overthrow of the king exactly one year earlier but also underscored revolutionary messages, such as the defeat of federalism. Delegates from various departments set fire to the symbols of monarchy. Festivals also were staged to celebrate liberty, reason, the supreme being, victory, and so on. Artists, such as Jacques Louis David, used symbols, such as liberty caps, liberty trees, and the national cockade, to reinforce their message. At festivals liberty trees often played a pivotal role. Generally, young people would dig up a tree in the woods and then replant it. These young people had to be patriots, and the tree watered and often sprinkled with wine by a mother, a symbol of fertility. The locals would then festoon the tree with tricolor garlands and bedeck it with a liberty cap. If other trees were planted, they were designated fraternity trees, or equality trees, or unity trees. Those who planted the tree would then sing appropriately revolutionary songs and dance around it.

The revolutionaries also tried to destroy the old system of education. Many revolutionaries had a pronounced anti-intellectual attitude. One outspoken revolutionary argued that "the republic has no need of savants," and David, the artist, argued that academies could not "exist under a free government."[18] Because academic privileges were inconsistent with republican ideals, academies were abolished as well as universities in 1793. The Bouquier law (December 19, 1793) established universal primary education—but it was an education carefully regulated by the state. Because revolutionaries feared that teachers might harbor royalist or counterrevolutionary ideas, all instructors were queried on their adherence to republican ideals and had to produce certificates of civism proving they were good republicans. The teaching of history was particularly doctrinaire and slanted to show the corruption and decadence of the monarchy. Books were examined as well. One revolutionary urged his colleagues, "Burn all the books . . . they are useless and harmful."[19] Yet another wanted to establish an "index of reason" to replace the old index of forbidden books established by the church. A commission was established to collect all the books confiscated from royal, noble, and church libraries. One revolutionary wanted to purge or deport all unacceptable books. Intentional acts of book burning did take place, but, fortunately, many nobles and clergy either hid or sold their books and the sheer volume of printed material overwhelmed the authorities. Unfortunately, a number of documents in royal, noble, and church archives were destroyed. The revolutionaries also wrote new manuals to replace the religious ones. Instead of a religious catechism there was a republican one. For example, in a manual for *sans-culottes,* the following questions were asked: What is the form of government? Republican. What does this word mean? Concern for everyone. On what is the government founded? On justice. What is baptism? Regeneration of the French begun on July 14, 1789, and soon supported by the entire nation. Republicans used newspapers, pamphlets, even tricolored candy wrappers to convey the republican message. Even games did not escape revolutionary scrutiny. Neither the deck of cards nor chess pieces could include queens or kings; Liberty, Equality, Fraternity, or Genius took their place. Revolutionaries could buy miniature guillotines that even included a little basket to collect heads. Block models of the Bastille could be built and then demolished with toy cannons. Patriotic songs such as *Ça ira* and *La Carmagnole* were chanted in the schools and included lyrics such as "What does a republican demand? What does a republican demand? Liberty of the entire human race, Liberty of the entire human race."

The revolutionaries also relied on the arts to convey the republican message. Theaters, "schools of the Revolution," reenacted pivotal events of the Revolution, such as the taking of Toulon, or staged republican tragedies such as Gaius Gracchus, the celebrated Roman reformer, with its implicit comparison of revolutionary France and republican Rome. Painters and artists, such as Jacques Louis David, also played a role; they portrayed republican heroes, such as Marat, slumped dead in his bathtub, or commemorated revolutionary events, such as the Oath of the Tennis Court when the men of the National Assembly refused to disband until a constitution was in place. The neoclassicism of artists such as David with its stress on austerity, simplicity, order, proportion, and balance contrasted with the rococo of the ancien régime and artists such as François Boucher whose art was frivolous, elegant, artificial, and often cluttered. Furniture and everyday objects such as snuffboxes, playing cards, furniture, ladies' fans, bedposts, to cite but a few, did not escape the revolutionary imprint either. Bedposts, for example, were carved in the shape of pikes adorned with liberty bonnets. Ladies' fans often were decorated with key events of the revolution.

Little architecture of the Revolution has survived. As in other areas, the revolutionaries strove to destroy anything reminiscent of "royalty, feudalism and superstition."[20] Revolutionaries pulled statues from churches, tore down or defaced pillars and columns. They decapitated the statues of the kings of Juda on the portal of Notre Dame Cathedral, engaging in a type of ritual regicide. At the Basilica of Saint Denis, the burial place of the French kings, they melted down the bronze and copper statues of their former rulers and their wives and demolished the tombs and mausoleums. They destroyed all except the shells of the papal palace at Avignon and the monastery of Mont-Saint-Michel. At Avignon they stabled their horses in the palace and the horse urine ruined the frescoes. They destroyed statues, paintings, tapestries, frescoes. Except for vandalism, Paris changed little during the Revolution. The only exception was the razing of the Bastille. Throughout France, as in Paris, the Revolution had little positive impact architecturally. Some columns of liberty were erected, as in Montpellier, but these were leveled during the Bourbon restoration. The Louvre, transformed by the revolutionaries into a national museum on August 10, 1793, reflected the revolutionaries' desire to maintain the cultural hegemony France enjoyed under the ancien régime. The revolutionaries filled the museum with objects expropriated from the king, the nobles, and the church, and war booty looted from areas occupied by the French. It has survived and remains one of the great museums of the world. Streets and buildings throughout France were renamed to efface the old names of saints and kings and queens. For example, Notre Dame Cathedral became the Temple of Reason. The Place Louis XV became the Place de la Révolution and later the Place de la Concorde. The revolutionaries even renamed themselves: if they were named Louis, for example, they changed their names to those of ancient

Romans, such as Spartacus, or of fruits or vegetables, such as Green Bean. They also eliminated the old provinces and transformed them into departments, which were given names based on geography. Some of these changes have survived, and the observant traveler can find streets such as rue de l'égalité, and rue de la fraternité.

The revolutionaries also sought to reorganize both the measurement system and time on a rational basis. To do the latter they had to combat both ingrained habit and religion, which supported the old Gregorian calendar. The new revolutionary calendar was rational and commemorative. The *décade* included 10 days and replaced the old 7-day week. The days were rationally named: *primidi* (first day), *duodi* (second day), and so forth; and the months were named for the seasons, for example, Nivôse (snow), Frimaire (cold). The new republican year started on September 22 to commemorate the first day of the republic's existence on that date in 1792 and was called 1 Vendémiaire, year I. Although the Convention adopted the new calendar on October 5, 1793, the French never accepted it and Napoleon abolished it on January 1, 1806.

The revolutionaries adopted a more rational and simpler system of measurement as well: the metric system. It has been estimated that before the Revolution, over 60,000 different measures of weight were used in France. The *cahiers des doléances* (lists of grievances) often included demands for "one king, one law, one weight, one measure."[21] Many revolutionaries thought that the adoption of the meter, one of the few enduring legacies of the Revolution, would be a "benefit to humanity."[22] And so it was.

One of the more radical policies of the Revolution was dechristianization. This desire to eradicate Christianity and its alleged corollary, superstition, began in September 1793. Monasteries and religious houses were dissolved and priests were urged to abdicate and abjure their faith. The cathedral of Notre Dame was transformed into the Temple of Reason. Hymns of liberty replaced religious hymns; festivals of reason replaced Christian holy days. But this movement never gained widespread support and was denounced by Robespierre and many of his followers. The Jacobins, however, did use religious metaphors; they had republican hymns, civic altars, republican martyrs. Moreover, they constantly used expressions, such as "the holy fatherland," "holy liberty," or "the holy constitution." They and other revolutionaries aimed at nothing less than the regeneration of mankind and the establishment of a civic religion. But, other than the destruction of irreplaceable art and architectural and literary treasures, the legacy of the Revolution remains the acceptance of the metric system, the establishment of the Louvre as a great national museum, and the adoption of a national anthem and flag. The attempted transformation of mankind did not come without costs.

Notes

1. Robert Darnton, *The Kiss of Lamourette: Reflections in Cultural History* (New York: W. W. Norton, 1990), 17.

2. Tocqueville, *The Old Regime,* 156–57.

3. Lynn Hunt, *Politics, Culture, and Class in the French Revolution* (Los Angeles: University of California Press, 1984), 27.

4. Robert Darnton, "The French Revolution: Intellectual and Literature" (lecture at the University of Montana, Missoula, 1 June 1989).

5. Walzer quoted in David L. Kertzer, *Ritual, Politics, and Power* (New Haven, Conn.: Yale University Press, 1988), 6.

6. Edmund Burke, "Letters on a Regicide Peace," in *The Works of Edmund Burke,* 8 vols. (London: George Bell and Sons, 1893), 5:215.

7. Hunt, *Politics, Culture, and Class,* 75.

8. Frédéric Masson, *Le Département des Affaires Etrangères pendant la Révolution* (Paris: E. Plon, 1877), 379.

9. Darnton, "The French Revolution."

10. Quoted in Patrice Higonnet, *Goodness beyond Virtue: Jacobins during the French Revolution* (Cambridge, Mass.: Harvard University Press, 1998), 80.

11. Burke, "Letters on a Regicide Peace," 5:208.

12. Quoted in Albin Mazon, *Histoire de Soulavie* (Paris: Fischbacher, 1893), 164.

13. *Archives parlementaires de 1787 à 1860* (Paris: Librarie administratif de P. Dupont, 1878), 52:314.

14. Quoted in Hunt, *Politics, Culture and Class,* 29.

15. Jennifer Harris, "The Red Cap of Liberty," *Eighteenth-Century Studies* 14 (Spring 1981): 306.

16. Masson, *Le Département des Affaires Etrangères,* 388.

17. Blanning, *The French Revolutionary Wars,* 199.

18. Kelly, *Victims, Authority, and Terror,* 208.

19. Emmet Kennedy, *A Cultural History of the French Revolution* (New Haven, Conn.: Yale University Press, 1989), 215.

20. Ibid., 197.

21. Kennedy, *A Cultural History of the French Revolution,* 78.

22. Ibid., 79.

La France Figurée sous un Globe est soutenu du Peuple
La Noblesse et le Clergé aide au premier
La Ruche represente les trois Ordres reunies

Depiction of the three estates. Reproduced from the Collections of The Library of Congress.

PRISE DE LA BASTILLE

Par les Citoyens de Paris ayant à leurs têtes Mrs les Gardes Françoises, le 14 Juillet 1789

Cette Forteresse fut commencée en 1369 sous le règne de Charles V. Hugues Aubriot Prevot de Paris en posa la 1re Pierre elle ne fut entierement achevée qu'en 1382. Il etoit natif de Dijon. Il y fut un des premiers renfermés sous pretexte d'hérésie Il fut délivré par les Parisiens pendant les troubles qui agitoit la Capitale, et se sauva dans sa patrie.

C'est ainsi que l'on Punit les Traitres.

Seizure of the Bastille and heads of "traitors" on pikes. Reproduced from the Collections of The Library of Congress.

First and Second Estates dancing to the tune of the Third Estate. Demolition of the Bastille in the background. Reproduced from the Collections of The Library of Congress.

Allegory showing three soldiers saving France. Monument to the taking of the Bastille in the background. Reproduced from the Collections of The Library of Congress.

Louis XVI, drinking a toast to the nation, wearing the red cap of liberty. Reproduced from the Collections of The Library of Congress.

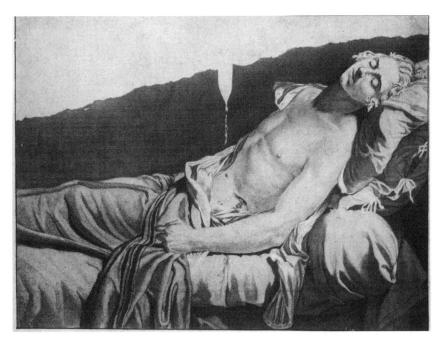

The first martyr of the Revolution, Lepelletier de Saint-Fargeau after his assassination by a royalist. He was a noble who voted for the execution of the king. Reproduced from the Collections of The Library of Congress.

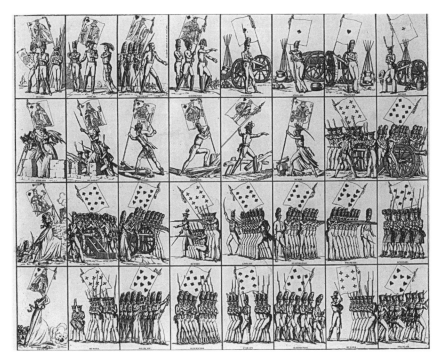

A revolutionary card game. Reproduced from the Collections of The Library of Congress.

Un Sans-culotte instrument de crimes dansant au milieu des horreurs, Vient outrager l'humanité pleurante auprès d'un cenotaphe. Il croit voir l'ombre de l'une des victimes de la revolution qui le saisit à la gorge. Cette effrayante apparition le suffoque et le renverse

A *sans-culotte*, dancing in the midst of horrors. The banner says, "The festival of 21 January, the day the king was guillotined." Reproduced from the Collections of The Library of Congress.

French atrocities in Germany during the Napoleonic Wars. Reproduced from the Collections of The Library of Congress.

The great republican monster having traversed Europe confronts the British lion. Reproduced from the Collections of The Library of Congress.

CHAPTER 5

DIPLOMACY AND REVOLUTION

The reign of the charlatans is over.
Louis-François-Alexandre Goupil de Prefeln,
in *Histoire parlementaire* by Buchez and Roux

The revolutionaries not only wanted to establish a new revolutionary order at home, but also to found a new one abroad; they aimed to jettison the old order and everything associated with it. They rejected the norms and practices of classical diplomacy because they believed that under the Bourbon kings, especially Louis XV and Louis XVI, foreign policy had been immoral, greedy, and aggressive. Moreover, the system was corrupt. For proof, they had to look only to the recent partition of Poland (1772) by Austria, Prussia, and Russia. Even worse, in the eighteenth century, French rulers had been outmaneuvered and outsmarted. Louis XV and Louis XVI had concluded dishonorable treaties that had made France the dupe of Austria. In addition under the old regime, France had betrayed her loyal allies: the Poles and the Turks. The costly wars of the Austrian Succession (1740–48) and the Seven Years' War (1756–63) had ended without advantage for France. France had been defeated on land, at sea, in the colonies, and in Europe.

Concomitant with this attack on the diplomatic system and diplomatic practice was an attack on diplomats. In this new revolutionary world, the French thought that diplomats would no longer be necessary. Diplomats were no more than spies, intriguers who reveled in outward luxury. "The reign of the charlatans is over," one revolutionary joyously proclaimed.[1] The diplomatic system and the diplomats who served in it whom Napoleon derisively dubbed "the brilliant butterflies of the panniers age"[2] were particularly vulnerable because the diplomatic system was so tainted by its association with the aristocracy and the old regime. Throughout the Revolution, those in power periodically purged the diplomatic corps using ideology as their criteria. They attacked not only the nobles but also anyone who had worked under or sympathized with the old regime or who had allied with a certain political faction.

The revolutionaries wanted to employ "simple citizens" with "clear judgments and just hearts" to carry the new ideology abroad.[3] One revolutionary, Jacques Pierre Brissot de Warville, asked: "Is there a greater folly than leaving in the foreign courts those most closely associated with the old regime?"[4] In many instances that was not a problem because beginning in 1790 many of the representatives appointed by the king refused to serve a revolutionary regime and resigned or left their posts: the representatives at Geneva, Venice, Rome, Stockholm, The Hague, the Swiss Diet, Mainz, Darmstadt, St. Petersburg, Naples, Hamburg, Württemberg, Constantinople, Copenhagen, and the Grisons. For many, the king's loss of power, his imprisonment, and his subsequent execution had created a crisis of conscience and made it impossible for them to serve or to take the required oath to the new revolutionary government. One foreign minister condemned such men for "betraying insolently their duties and the interests of their country."[5] Of the few supporters of the king still abroad, many were recalled. Even those who were not nobles lost their positions and pensions and often were imprisoned solely because they had served during the old regime. The revolutionaries purged the diplomatic corps just as they had the army and the administration (see document 13, "Memoirs of Miot de Mélito"). In essence a diplomatic vacuum was created. The consequences abroad were serious: 24 years of warfare ensued. From April 1792, as France found herself at war with more and more of Europe, she needed fewer representatives.

But by September 1793, the French needed few representatives because they concluded they could negotiate only with other republics; that is, the Swiss and the United States. To others France sent only secret agents, secretaries of legations, or *chargés d'affaires*. By 1794, France had only 10 agents abroad, and only Geneva, Malta, and Denmark had representatives in France. Some trumpeted such changes, contending that France had "regenerated" the system. "We are no longer the ministers of despots, we are the agents of a popular government."[6] The appointment of France's representatives illumines the larger issue of loyalty to the Revolution because only certain individuals could be trusted to represent France abroad. Yet the definition of loyalty constantly shifted as factions vied for control. For example, those who had supported Brissot found themselves in danger when Brissot fell from power and the Mountain took over. Edmond Charles Edouard Gênet, for example, the French representative in the United States, was saved from certain death only by President George Washington's refusal to allow the French to seize him.

The French revolutionaries never did completely resolve the problem of such appointments. Individuals with impeccable revolutionary credentials were often those who had the least experience in or understanding of diplomacy. M. A. B. Mangourit, the French representative to Spain, urged the planting of a liberty tree in the courtyard of the embassy, publicly proclaimed that the reigning king would be the last, vilified the queen, and refused to attend any diplomatic receptions at court, for example. He did not survive at court for long—a mere seven months. Gênet, the French representative at Moscow (and later to the U.S.) who tactlessly advocated revolution, was forbidden to appear at court and ultimately was expelled from Russia. Jean-Baptiste-Jules Bernadotte, the French representative at Vienna, ordered his staff to don liberty caps and encouraged dissident Poles to revolt against Austria. These examples were not atypical. French envoys draped their embassies with tricolor flags, painted escutcheons with the image of liberty on embassies and consulates, and commissioned culinary masterpieces with avowedly revolutionary messages. At the congress of Rastatt, for example, the French appalled the Austrian minister Klemens Wenzel Nepomuk Lothar, Fürst von Metternich when they created a tricolor flag in sugar. "I swear to you," Metternich confided to his wife, "that I entirely lost my appetite at the sight of those execrable colors."[7]

These men were determined to refashion diplomacy in the revolutionary image. Instead of the old and elaborate aristocratic dress, they used a simple republican uniform often topped with a red revolutionary plume. Instead of the old deferential, often circuitous language, the revolutionaries relied on a simple, forceful, egalitarian style. Throughout the Revolution, the French envoys abroad either deliberately ignored or

blatantly violated the norms and practices of old-regime diplomacy.
Even on the most trivial of issues French envoys often were confronta-
tional. At Rastatt, when Metternich hung a portrait of Francis I and so
arranged the furniture that a visitor could not turn his back on the
emperor, the French envoy Jean Debry displayed a portrait of
Napoleon. He opposed an idol with another idol. The French envoy
Jean-Baptiste Treilhard, noted for his charm and courtesy, deliberately
ignored the restraint endemic in the old diplomacy. He stupefied the
Austrians when he strode quickly into the room and shouted loudly at
meetings. Such conduct prompted the hardly impartial Metternich to
conclude that he had never seen "such ill conditioned animals. They
see no one, are sealed up in their apartments, and are more savage than
white bears. Good God! How this nation is changed! To extreme neat-
ness, and that elegance which one could hardly imitate, has succeeded
the greatest slovenliness; the most perfect amiability is replaced by a
dull sinister air, which I can only fully describe by calling it Revolutionary! . . . You can form no idea what a pack of wretches they are here. All
these fellows have coarse muddy shoes, great blue pantaloons, a vest of
blue or of all colors, peasants' handkerchiefs, either silk or cotton,
round the neck, the hair, long, black and dirty, and the hideous head
crowned by an enormous hat with a great red feather."[8] Little wonder
these envoys were not welcomed at foreign courts.

Edmund Burke and others realized that these men carried what
William Pitt, the British prime minister, termed "opinions in arms."[9]
They proselytized for the revolutionary creed as much as revolutionary
soldiers. Many outside observers realized the revolutionaries' intent.
George Canning, undersecretary of state for foreign affairs in Great
Britain, saw this French crusade as a crusade "for universal oppression."[10] Burke did as well. In his view the French revolutionaries caused
"a violent breach of the community of Europe," a commonwealth bound
by "laws, customs, manners and habits of life. . . . The changes made by
that Revolution were not the better to accommodate her to the old and
usual relations, but to produce new ones."[11] Burke and others realized
the French intended nothing less than the subversion of the old order
(see document 32, "Edmund Burke's Condemnation"). And they did.
Burke, for one, noted that in violating established patterns of behavior
these men had "made a schism with the whole universe."[12] For Burke,
manners were more important than laws because "manners are what vex

or soothe, corrupt or purify, exalt or debase, barbarize or refine us, by a constant steady, uniform insensible operation, like that of the air we breathe in. They give their whole form and colour to our lives."[13]

As France increasingly realized the necessity of negotiating with other powers, more pragmatic individuals such as Charles-Maurice de Talleyrand-Périgord were appointed to the post of foreign minister. In June 1798, Talleyrand candidly complained that the French employed only "fools" abroad. The Directory had preferred to appoint men who had served in the Convention or—even worse—regicides, those who had voted for the death of the king.[14] The predictable result was that the Europeans abhorred the French republic and its representatives. To compound the problem some countries such as Great Britain, Savoy, Florence, the Holy See, and the bishopric of Liège refused to receive the representatives appointed by the revolutionaries. Charles-Jean-Marie Alquier, the French representative at Munich, complained, "A plague-stricken person whom the police have sequestered . . . is not more watched and dreaded than I am."[15] In 1787, when the foreign minister Charles Gravier, Comte de Vergennes, left the ministry, it was one of the best in Europe. It did not take the revolutionaries long to destroy it. The individual who held the post of foreign minister also was suspect as can be seen in the fate of those who held it from 1789 to 1794: Armand Marc Montmorin de Saint Herem was killed in prison, as was Jean Marie Antoine Claude de Valdec de Lessart. Dumouriez; Victor Scipion Louis Josephe de la Garde, Marquis Chambonas; and Louis Claude Bigot de Sainte-Croix fled. Pierre Henri Hélène Marie Tondu Lebrun was executed; and François Louis Michel Chemin Deforgues was imprisoned but ultimately released.

Concomitant with the attack on the diplomatic system and on diplomats was the revolutionaries' desire to establish a new order based on the brotherhood of man. Many revolutionaries wanted to establish a "fraternity of mankind" or a "fraternity of nations."[16] Some even argued that the progress of equality in France would have as it logical counterpart "the destruction of inequality between nations."[17] They envisioned the creation of a new community based on a rejection of the old regime and its traditions. As one revolutionary idealistically noted: "It is not for ourselves alone, it is not for that part of the globe that one calls France that we have conquered liberty."[18] They wanted to plant the "tree of liberty in a foreign soil."[19]

Ultimately, the revolutionaries thought that foreign policy and diplomacy would be unnecessary. Just as the Revolution had eliminated inequality between men, so, too, it would eliminate the inequality among nations. Universal brotherhood would replace treaties and alliances. This universal brotherhood was to be achieved by following the dictates of natural law. Gênet, the French representative to the United States, stressed this very point when he told then Secretary of State Thomas Jefferson that he would "throw Vattel and Grotius into the sea whenever their principles interfere with my notion of the rights of nations."[20] What these ideas meant in practice was open defiance of past international practices and international law. The French, for example, unilaterally renounced the Family Compact, an offensive and defensive alliance signed with Spain (1761), because such treaties violated the principles of universal fraternity. France, they thought, should conclude only treaties of friendship. In yet another case French revolutionaries insisted on the opening of the Scheldt waterway to international trade. The French forced the Dutch to jettison an old treaty right in favor of the Low Countries' natural right to have access to the sea. The British were not the only ones to realize that the French were attempting to "arrogate the power of annulling at her pleasure . . . the political system of Europe, established by solemn treaties and guaranteed by the consent of all the powers."[21] One revolutionary argued: "It is not the treaties of princes which govern the rights of nations."[22] Implicit in this concept of fraternity, however, was an attack on the old order. When contemporaries referred to the spread of revolutionary ideals, they often compared it to an uncontrollable force of nature: an epidemic, a pestilence, a contagion, a hurricane.

The "propaganda decrees" of November 19 and December 15, 1792, encapsulated the revolutionary challenge to the old order (see document 26, "The First Propaganda Decree, November 20, 1792," and document 27, "The Second Propaganda Decree, December 15, 1792"). In the first, the French promised "fraternity and help to all peoples who wish to recover their liberty" and, in the second, decreed the abolition not only of all established authorities in the occupied lands but also the suppression "of all established authorities, taxes or existing contributions . . . seigneurial rights." The French promised that they would bring not only liberty and equality but also peace and fraternity. That peace came with a price. Article 7 authorized the commissioners in the "liberated" lands to levy contributions to pay for the expenses the republic incurred in providing such fraternity. Article 11 made clear the French intent to "treat as an enemy of the people" those who refused liberty and equality. In addition the occupied had to establish "a free and popular government." A supplemental decree of December 22 stipulated that no citizen could vote or hold office unless that person swore an oath to "liberty and equality" and renounced "all feudal rights and privileges."[23] In effect the French were forcing others to be free. But what if others did not want to be free? Should the French force them? The French agent in Belgium, Pierre Chépy, confronted this very dilemma. But he quickly and chillingly concluded that "it is said that one cannot force a people to be free, I say that one can and that one should."[24]

The French harbored the dangerous illusion that others would quickly and willingly embrace revolutionary ideals. If war had to be waged, it would be short and victory assured. If 1789 marked the first year of French liberty, 1792 (the year that war broke out) would mark that of "universal liberty."[25] World revolution, they thought, was imminent. This extraordinarily optimistic assessment rested on an inflated and unrealistic appraisal of French military capabilities and an unwarranted contempt for their foes coupled with an ingenuous conviction that others would embrace their ideals.

But the old system proved more durable and resilient than many had expected. As the French encountered resistance, their views and policies changed as is best seen in the reports to and from the army. In January 1794, one revolutionary urged the French generals to realize that the Germans "prefer their chains, their apathy to their liberty, the torpor of servitude to the storms of freedom" and to adopt what he termed a "Prussian" attitude; that is, to seize anything that might prove useful to the enemy.[26] In that same year in July, Carnot, the "organizer of Victory," ordered the representative of the army of Sambre-et-Meuse to follow one rule only: "We wish neither to excite the country nor to fraternize with it; it is a conquered country that has large restitutions to make to us; and it is necessary to immediately extract all the resources that might favor a new invasion on the part of the enemy. You should not ignore the fact that the Brabant in general is greatly devoted to the Emperor. . . . It is not therefore a country to spare."[27] As late as January 1795, the French did invoke fraternity, but by that time only as a cynical ploy in a war of propaganda. As Wordsworth observed about the French at the time:

> And now, become oppressors in their turn,
> Frenchmen had changed a war of self-defense
> For one of conquest, losing sight of all
> Which they had struggled for.[28]

The Revolution had by then come full circle. It had changed and so had the revolutionaries. The Comte de Mirabeau's prophecy that in time France would have "only friends and no more allies" had not been borne out.[29] The revolutionary wars had made a mockery of revolutionary ideals. *Freedom* for liberated peoples meant in reality the maintenance of a foreign army, onerous contributions, and oftentimes forcible annexation. The revolutionary slogan "war to the châteaux, peace to the cottages" had been just that—a slogan because both the chateaux and the cottages faced the full brunt of the revolutionary onslaught. As the Revolution had changed so, too, had policy. The idealists had been replaced by the pragmatists. The leaders turned back to the old and well-trodden paths of traditional diplomacy and power politics. In 1797, Napoleon incarnated that view: "The Republic of France is not bound by any treaty to sacrifice its interests and advantages . . . to any other class of individuals. France does not make war on behalf and for the benefit of others. I know it costs nothing for a few chattering declaimers, whom I might better describe as madmen, to talk of a universal republic—I wish they would try a winter campaign."[30]

Notes

1. Goupil de Prefeln, May 27, 1790, in *Histoire parlementaire,* edited by Philippe Joseph Benjamin Buchez and Prosper Charles Roux (Paris: Paulin, 1834), 6:65.

2. Charles De La Roncière, ed., *Napoleon's Letters to Marie Louise* (New York: Hutchinson, 1935), 169.

3. *Réimpression de l'ancien Moniteur seule histoire authentique et inalterée de la Révolution française* (Paris: Plon Frères, 1850), 4 (1790): 411.

4. Quoted in Masson, *Le Département des Affaires Etrangères,* 85–86.

5. A.N., F série administration générale de la France, F/7 Police Générale, comité de sûreté générale, comité diplomatique 4397, 26 August 1792.

6. Ibid., 300.

7. Klemens Wenzel Nepomuk Lothar, Fürst von Metternich, *Memoirs,* edited by Richard Metternich (New York: Charles Scribner's Sons, 1880), 1:368.

8. Ibid., 1:350.

9. Tocqueville, *The Old Regime,* 3.

10. Harold William Vazeille Temperley, *Life of Canning* (London: Finch and Co., 1905), 41.

11. Edmund Burke, *Burke's Politics: Selected Writings and Speeches,* edited by Ross J. S. Hoffman and Paul Levack (New York: Knopf, 1970), 465–66.

12. Burke, "Letters on a Regicide Peace," 5:215.

13. Ibid., 5:208.

14. Paul Bailleu, ed., *Preussen und Frankreich von 1795–1807* (Osnabruck: Otto Zeller, 1965), 211.

15. Quoted in Leonce Pingaud, *Jean de Bry* (Paris: Librairie Plon, 1909), 87.

16. Marie-Jean-Antoine-Nicolas de Caritat, Marquis de Condorcet, *Oeuvres* (Paris: Firmin Didot Freres, 1847), 16:190.

17. Ibid., 16:237.

18. Quoted in Roger Brubaker, *Citizenship and Nationhood in France and Germany* (Cambridge, Mass.: Harvard University Press, 1992), 44.

19. J. P. Brissot, *J. P. Brissot, Deputy of Eure and Loire to His Constituents* (London: Stockdale, 1794), 74.

20. Quoted in William Cobbett, *The Parliamentary History of England* (London: T. S. Hansard, 1817), 30:1251.

21. Harold Temperley and Lillian M. Penson, eds., *Foundations of British Foreign Policy from Pitt (1792) to Salisbury (1902)* (London: Frank Cass, 1966), 4–5.

22. Blanning, *The French Revolutionary Wars,* 50.

23. J. B. Duvergier, ed., *Collection complète des lois, décrets, ordonnances, règlemens* (Paris: Guyot, 1834), 5:93.

24. A.N., F, Belgique, carton 11, Chépy, 18 novembre 1792.

25. Steven Walt, *Revolution and War* (Ithaca, N.Y.: Cornell University Press, 1996), 67 n.

26. T. C. W. Blanning, *Reform and Revolution in Mainz, 1743–1803* (New York: Cambridge University Press, 1974), 326.

27. Quoted in Huntley Dupré, *Lazare Carnot: Republican Patriot* (Philadelphia: Porcupine Press, 1975), 143.

28. Wordsworth, "The Prelude," lines 206–9.

29. Buchez and Roux, *Histoire parlementaire,* 6:77.

30. Quoted in Walter Scott, *Life of Napoleon Bonaparte, Emperor of the French* (Philadelphia: Carey, Lea and Carey, 1827), 1:390–91.

CHAPTER 6

WAR AND REVOLUTION

War to the *châteaux,* peace to the cottages.
French revolutionary slogan

The army in particular and war in general played important roles in the causes, course, and consequences of the French Revolution. As historian Tim Blanning has argued, they were "at the heart of the failure of the old regime."[1] Military collapse was not the only cause of the French Revolution, for it coincided with, for example, an expanding population, a fiscal crisis and economic recession, and an indecisive king and a detested queen, but it was a "necessary" one.[2] The failures of French foreign policy and the collapse of French power abroad bred disaffection and disenchantment at home. The eighteenth-century wars, including the War of the Austrian Succession (1740–48) and the Seven Years' War (1756–63), helped to fuel the crisis of the ancien régime. The costly War of the Austrian Succession ended without advantage to France. When the French saw the conquests in the Netherlands, won at such costs, returned to the Habsburgs in the peace of 1748, a common expression circulated: "stupid as the peace."[3] The war achieved nothing but the aggrandizement of Prussia. And then? In the words of one historian, "France, having played the game of Prussia in the War of the Austrian Succession, was to play that of Austria in the Seven Years' War. . . . She changed partners but remained the dupe."[4]

In the diplomatic revolution of 1756, France had allied with her former enemy Austria. This, "squally marriage of convenience," brought defeat in its wake.[5] In the Seven Years' War with Austria by her side, France was defeated at sea and on land, in the colonies, and—worse of all—on the Continent. In one battle, Rossbach, where 41,000 French and Austrian troops faced 22,000 Prussians, the French panicked and fled. In little more than an hour the Prussians, who suffered less than 500 casualties, would "kill, wound, or capture more than 10,000 French and German troops."[6] Voltaire, for one, thought the French rout a greater humiliation for his country than Crécy (1346), Poitiers (1356), or Agincourt (1415), the catastrophic French defeats in the Hundred Years' War.[7] The description of Rossbach as a "rout and humiliation" seemed to contemporaries an equally apt portrayal of the war as a whole.[8] Militarily, the Seven Years' War was a disaster for France. "France entered the conflict without enthusiasm, fought without distinction and emerged from it without victory."[9]

France had fared no better on the diplomatic front. In the Treaty of Paris of 1763, France lost her territories on the North American continent and witnessed a triumphant Britain gain maritime and colonial supremacy. The king's ministers seemingly sacrificed France's prosperity and glory to Austrian interests. For more than two centuries, the traditional hostility toward Austria had brought France prestige; its reversal brought disaster—military defeat and loss of empire. It was a simple equation. The French ministers had not only sinned; they had failed. They had been outsmarted, outmaneuvered, outnegotiated. Intervention in the American Revolutionary War did not restore morale because at the peace of 1783 the French were exhausted and came away virtually empty-handed, although France did obtain Tobago, Senegal, and some concessions in the Newfoundland fisheries. Only her ally, the United States, profited from the peace; to gain more territory, the Americans concluded a separate peace with Britain and abandoned France.

France's abandonment of her allies only underscored her impotence. Allied with an age-old enemy, France had betrayed the "most loyal of allies," the Turks, to join Austria. Just as shocking were treaties that committed France to pay an annual tribute to the corsairs, who lived only by murder and pillage. Can one believe, one critic asked, that any power would have squandered "its blood and its treasure in order to subscribe to humiliating treaties? Contemplate all these treaties . . . and you will see each page dyed with the blood that the people have shed."[10] French impotence was underscored by events in central and eastern Europe: France was excluded from the partition of Poland in 1772 and was not consulted on the loss of the Crimea by the Turks in 1783, to name but the most obvious instances.

The crisis of confidence worsened in 1787 when the king's principal minister Loménie de Brienne, faced with a budget shortfall, vetoed any intervention to defend the Dutch republic. Prussia then successfully invaded Dutch territory, and the Dutch, abandoned by France, allied with Great Britain and Prussia. France's inability to project its power even into the Netherlands emphasized its impotence. Such failures helped to delegitimatize the ancien régime—and the king because Louis XVI as head of the state was ultimately responsible for war and diplomacy. His personal stature was associated with the prestige of the state. Louis XIV's aphorism "*l'état, c'est moi*" (I am the state) came back to haunt his descendants, Louis XV and Louis XVI. Even more destructive of French influence in Europe was the inability of France to help Sweden, a French ally, in 1788 when she waged war with Russia and Denmark. France's final military and diplomatic retreat was dictated by the growing financial crisis and by Louis XVI's perception that France could be regenerated only in a time of peace. Nonetheless, the response to such debacles "was humiliation, anger, and disaffection."[11] As Tocqueville emphasized, "The political ferment was canalized into literature, the result being that our writers became the leaders of public opinion."[12] And public perception subsequently played a key role in the last crisis of the ancien régime.

To military defeats and diplomatic debacles could be added the demoralization of the army. Reforms put in place after the Seven Years' War only exacerbated the divisions in the army and deepened the discontent. The reforms, designed to increase government control over the army and to maximize efficiency, only fueled the hostility of the officers. After long service, many officers were forced to retire on meager pensions. Direct commissions were reserved for those who could document four generations of nobility, and regimental commands for the nobles who had been presented at court. Furthermore, the government cut the number of officers. Expectations were dashed for many as the lesser officers saw their chances of promotion decrease and those within regiments saw themselves passed over and "outsiders" promoted. The decision to eliminate a number of ceremonial units angered the court nobility in particular. Attempts to close the officer corps to all but those of both noble and military backgrounds embittered the lower and middle ranks and all who had seen the army as an avenue of social promotion. In addition to the reforms, the nearly complete separation of officers and troops and the differences in social status and conditions of service widened the gulf between officers and the enlisted. Soldiers were alienated by the low pay, harsh discipline, exclusion from honors and promotion, peculation by the officers, and similar issues.

The disaffection of the officers and the rifts between the officers and the enlisted also helped to bring down the ancien régime because the army would play a crucial role in the unrest of the summer of 1789. The government had mustered more than 20,000 men in the Paris area by July 1789, but it did not dare use them. The government's perception that the army could not be trusted ensured that the government could not enforce its will. When the crisis came, the king's ministers assumed that the army could not be counted upon to enforce order. The commander's advice not to employ the troops only reinforced the king's indecision. Whether discipline would have held is open to question, because some units remained loyal; but the officers did not believe that the men would obey and were unwilling to test soldiers' loyalty. The government's lack of faith in its own troops most likely quickened the desertion rate because most of the desertions occurred after the fall of the Bastille as the traditional lines of authority collapsed. The perception that the men were unreliable became a self-fulfilling prophecy. The breakdown of discipline within the ranks, the mingling of the soldiers with and their sympathy for the people of Paris, and their disaffection from their officers led the government to withdraw the regular troops from Paris.

The collapse of the army enabled the regime the army was sworn to defend to collapse and forced the king to accept the revolutionaries' demands. Just as the absence or defection of the military had weakened the king's hand, the army also played an active role in various revolutionary crises. Individual soldiers who had left their units helped to precipitate the fall of the Bastille on July 14, 1789. The governor surrendered only after two detachments of 60 French guards aligned with the crowd and aimed four cannons at the main gate. The complicity of the army was also pivotal during the October Days of 1789 when the Parisian crowd marched to Versailles, invaded the palace, murdered two of the queen's bodyguard, and "escorted" the royal family to Paris (see document 6, "Memoirs of the Duchess of Tourzel on the October Days"). In that instance the soldiers of the line could not be depended upon to defend the king. They had done nothing to hinder the movement of the crowd and some had even turned over their cartridges to the National Guard. Others had deserted and joined the National Guard. Again, these actions indicate that the soldiers were too close to the urban populace and too alienated from their officers.

If defeat, humiliation, and a demoralized army played a key role in the collapse of the ancien régime, the revolutionary wars, a medley of ignominious defeats and dazzling victories, played an equally important role. The progress, nature, and duration of the wars that erupted in April 1792 and that did not end until 1815 altered the course of the Revolution and changed its character. The war radicalized the Revolution, ended pluralism, and criminalized dissent. The historian François Furet has even argued that "the war conducted the Revolution far more than the Revolution conducted the war."[13] The war caused or influenced various revolutionary crises: August 10, 1792 (the overthrow of the king), the September Massacres, the fall of the Girondins, the uprising in the Vendée, 9 Thermidor (the fall of Robespierre), and 6 Brumaire (Bonaparte's coup). Tragic fiascoes punctuated the early hostilities: in 1792, French troops panicked, fled, and in one case murdered their general. What saved the French was the inertia of their enemies (Prussia and Austria)—their traditional enmity and distrust of each other, their preoccupation with the impending second partition of Poland, and the dissensions endemic in coalitions. Still, by July, the allies were advancing into France, and on the fifth a declaration was passed that the "country was in danger." Charles William Ferdinand, the Duke of Brunswick and the allied commander in chief, issued a manifesto on July 25 threatening to raze the city of Paris if the royal family was harmed. News of that manifesto reached Paris on July 28. Suspicion of the king's treason combined with fears of allied vengeance triggered the "second revolution" of August 10, 1792, when the crowds besieged the palace, overthrew the king, and massacred the Swiss Guard. The Legislative Assembly recognized the fait accompli and suspended the king.

Shortly thereafter, the September Massacres (September 2–7) occurred. The capitulation of Longwy (August 23), the impending fall of Verdun (September 2) that secured the road to Paris, and rumors that the inmates of the prisons would break out to murder the inhabitants of Paris as the allies approached the capital triggered the mutilation, torture, and massacre of more than 1,400 inmates, including women and children. (See document 12, "Journal of Jourgniac de Saint-Meard.")

The massacres occurred at the instigation of some radicals, with the complicity of the committee of surveillance of the Commune and partially because of the inertia of the authorities. Nine days later, on September 16, the troops of the French commander General Dumouriez fled; as they fled, they spread panic in the lines. The spectacle of 10,000 Frenchmen fleeing before 1,500 Prussians cannot have instilled confidence in the nation. Although Dumouriez rallied his men, the lax discipline boded ill. Still, at Valmy on September 20, 1792, an artillery duel in which the infantry was not engaged signaled a French victory and ended the threat to the capital. After Valmy, the Prussians withdrew, and French troops occupied the Austrian Netherlands, Savoy, and a number of cities on the Left Bank of the Rhine.

The recovery at Valmy and the French surge across the frontiers were followed, however, by another collapse at the front and the threat of another invasion. The so-called third revolution of May 31–June 2,1793, when 20,000 men surrounded the Convention and demanded the arrest of 29 Girondins, occurred amid a backdrop of escalating war and defeat. By the spring of 1793, France was also at war with Sardinia (September 1792), Great Britain (February 1793), the United Provinces (February 1793), and Spain (March 1793). The Austrians defeated Dumouriez at Neerwinden (March 18) and at Louvain (March 21). Dumouriez then launched a preemptive strike and imprisoned the newly appointed French revolutionary minister of war and four commissioners sent to arrest him and turned them over to the Austrians. Four days later on April 5, Dumouriez and his principal staff defected to the Austrians. Dumouriez's defection was important not only because it implicated the Girondins and not only because he turned over key border fortresses to the enemy but also because he, like Lafayette (who had fled in August 1792), had attempted to lead the army on Paris. On another front, Adam Philippe, Comte de Custine, abandoned the Rhineland as the Prussians advanced. The disastrous war also helped to precipitate the Vendée, an insurrection in western France. That rebellion flared up after the local authorities attempted to enforce the military levy of 300,000 men voted by the Convention on February 24. By March, the rebels had seized a number of towns. Despite the ruthless onslaught conducted by the revolutionary authorities, resistance continued until 1799 and stirred again in 1813, 1814, and 1815.

The Terror was above all a wartime emergency measure. The first Committee of Public Safety was created in response to the military crisis of April 1793. Military disasters and defections threatened France and led the beleaguered revolutionaries to declare on September 5, 1793, that "terror is the order of the day" and on October 10, 1793 (19 Vendémiaire, year II), that France was "revolutionary until the peace." The latter declaration created an emergency wartime government. Although military crises helped trigger the onset of the Terror, as Furet points out, the Terror in the spring of 1794 arose when the French were victorious.[14] The stabilization of the military situation and the perception that the Terror was no longer necessary expedited the overthrow of Robespierre in Thermidor. To take but another example, the defeats of 1799 played a role in the Brumaire coup when Napoleon seized power. The war then had momentous consequences: the destruction of the monarchy, the radicalization and ultimately the destruction of the Revolution, the imposition of a political culture that doomed moderation and bred violence, and finally the imposition of a new absolute power.

The demands of the war not only changed the nature of the Revolution and the revolutionary state but also militarized the society. Militarization was reflected, for example, in iconography, in rituals, and in song, such as the *Marseillaise,* which was initially titled "the war song of the Rhine army" and later became the French national anthem (1879). War meant greater centralization and far greater intrusion of the central state into local affairs. It meant more constraint and more compulsion. It meant the imposition of economic regimentation: the wage and price ceilings of the Maximum; control of exports; requisitioning of grain; confiscation of supplies for the armies, and so on. The revolutionaries sustained the war through exploitation of their own people and those they conquered. The *levée en masse* of August 1793 (see document 25, "Decree of August 23, 1793, the *Levée en masse*") called the entire nation, men, women, and children, to contribute to the struggle. It raised over 300,000 new recruits so that by 1794 France had over 750,000 men at arms. France established a mass national army and a conscript army, a new army forged in the ferment of revolution and war. Many of the noble officers had resigned or abandoned their commands in the midst of the revolutionary fervor. From mid-September to the beginning of December 1791, 2,160 officers emigrated.[15] By the end of 1791, over 60 percent, as many as 6,000 officers, had abandoned their commands. After the declaration of war, 600 more followed.[16] Samuel Scott has calculated that "of more than 200 marshals and lieutenant-generals in the French army in mid-1789, only five remained in February 1793. Of the more than 900 brigadier and major-generals before the Revolution, only forty-six remained three years and eight months later."[17] The officers who remained faced the implacable demands of a revolutionary state. Théobald Dillon was lynched by his own men. Augustin-Joseph Isambert was shot in front of his troops for surrendering his post. Jean Nicolas Houchard, a commoner, was guillotined for not pressing his advantage after a victory. Adam Philippe, Comte de Custine met the same fate after the fall of the fortress of Condé and the leveling of false charges. In 1793, the revolutionary government guillotined 17 generals; in 1794, 67. As the eminent historian Blanning notes, "Nothing illustrated better the violence of the French Revolution than the fact that its generals were more likely to die at the hands of their own government than as a result of enemy action."[18]

This new army was also one shorn of the mercenary German and Swiss regiments and militia of the ancien régime. Fewer foreigners staffed the new army. The army was also more representative of France as a whole because it included more peasants and fewer artisans, although it was still disproportionately urban. As many of the noble officers resigned, abandoned their commands, or emigrated, the enlisted soldiers and some provincial nobles, who had little chance of promotion under the ancien régime, moved up to fill the vacated places. Conscription and promotion based on talent also created a new military force that was "clearly recognizable as a modern army."[19]

The coming of war had forged a new spirit in the revolutionary armies, but 23 years of war from 1792 to 1814 distanced the army from the revolutionary government and weakened its commitment to a republican agenda. The army was increasingly a career force loyal to and dependent on its commanders and increasingly disdainful of revolutionary governments. The army was brought more forcibly into politics when it was used to quell the uprising of Vendémiaire (1795), the right-wing revolt launched against the Convention; to implement the coup of Fructidor (1797), when elections were annulled in 49 departments, 65 individuals were deported, and 177 deputies were removed; and to support Napoleon in the coup of Brumaire (1799), the advent of the Consulate. On each occasion the revolutionary government's policy of relying on the military for armed intervention meant that power had ineluctably shifted to the military and away from the civilian authorities. Without clearly defined goals, the war, as Furet points out, could only end in "total victory or total defeat."[20] And it ended in total defeat with France alone losing 1.4 million men in the revolutionary and Napoleonic Wars.[21] As Karl Marx argued, Bonaparte "carried the Terror to its conclusion by replacing the permanent revolution with permanent war."[22] This general at least had learned the lessons of the Revolution.

France waged virtually perpetual war for almost a quarter of a century. The war had engulfed not just France but Europe as whole as the French surged across the frontiers. The Girondins preached universal revolution and contended that France could not be "tranquil until Europe and all of Europe is in flames."[23] Europe witnessed a war in which ideology was mixed with nationalism. It was a heady but deadly brew. Marshal Ferdinand Foch was surely right when he observed, "The wars of kings were at an end; the wars of peoples were beginning."[24] In referring to that war, the contemporary Prussian theorist Karl von Clausewitz notes, "The colossal weight of the whole French people, unhinged by political fanaticism, came crashing down on us. . . . The governments involved had no idea of the fury of the oncoming torrent."[25] The French revolutionary armies found support among some local groups in conquered lands who welcomed the Revolution with its universal claims and its proclamation of human rights. Others, such as Edmund Burke, saw in its abstract principles a danger to the European order and advocated war against revolutionary France. (See document 32, "Edmund Burke's Condemnation.") The unilateral actions of the French (for example, the annexation of the papal territory of Avignon and the opening of Scheldt in contravention of the Peace of Westphalia of 1648) disturbed many.

As the war continued, cosmopolitanism became transformed into a crusade, the crusade into a conquest. This evolution was hardly surprising given that the universalism had been leavened with a strong dose of xenophobia. In the decree of May 1790, subsequently incorporated into the constitution of 1791, title VI, the French renounced "the undertaking of any war with a view to making conquests" and swore never to "employ its forces against the liberty of any people."[26] Less than two years later, they were at war. In the midst of that war, they issued two decrees, one on November 20, 1792 (see document 26, "The First Propaganda Decree, November 20, 1792"), offering to "grant fraternity and aid to all who wish to regain their liberty," and one on December 15, 1792 (see document 27, "The Second Propaganda Decree, December 15, 1792"), providing that the old governments be dissolved, revolutionary provisional administrations be put in their place, and that seigneurial dues, tithes, and the like be abolished. But the mentality changed as the war dragged on. In September 1793, the Convention decreed that generals, "renouncing from henceforth every philanthropic idea previously adopted by the French people with the intention of making foreign nations appreciate the value and benefit of liberty, will behave toward the enemies of France in just the same way that the powers of the coalition have behaved toward them; and they will exercise with regard to the countries and individuals conquered the customary rights of war."[27] But the crusading armies had spread revolution in their wake and set up sister republics, such as the Batavian republic in the former United Provinces (1795); the Cisalpine republic in northern Italy (1797); the Ligurian republic, formerly the Republic of Genoa (1797); and the Roman republic (1798).

The ever-escalating needs of the French military also entailed more demands on the conquered and allied alike. The heavy burden of taxes and the weight of requisitions did nothing to endear the French to the local inhabitants. Nor did the systematic looting and the cultural piracy engaged in by the revolutionaries. The initial illusion that there would be "war to the *châteaux*, peace to the cottages" was soon shattered as the weight of the war fell heavily on the conquered, poor and rich alike (see documents 26–31). The rhetoric of liberation did not hide the reality of expropriation. The horrors of war were magnified by larger armies that were worse supplied and worse disciplined than in the past. The Prussian observer Clausewitz noted that the French "revolutionary leaders cared little for depots. . . . They sent their soldiers into the field and drove their generals into battle—feeding, reinforcing, and stimulating their armies by having them procure, steal, and loot everything they needed."[28] The French general Nicolas Jean de Dieu Soult noted, "We had to live as best we could. . . . One can imagine the distress of the army; it could exist only by plundering. The result was that all the local people rose against us and often we found ourselves having to deal with gangs of armed peasants, who ambushed individual soldiers or small isolated detachments. . . . Another consequence was the destruction of all bonds of discipline throughout the ranks of the army."[29]

The demands of the revolutionary state too often conflicted with humanitarianism. In September 1795, an artillery captain wrote his commander: "I acknowledge with you that the measures we take are cruel, and that they are repugnant to humanity, but I hardly know how to balance the interests of my country with a conquered land."[30] Too few grappled with such scruples. Looting, levies, requisitioning, as well as rape and pillage, brought the brutality of the French Revolution into the lives of many who could not afford to flee as the armies approached. The town council of Speyer reported on the arrival of the French troops and the depredations of the revolutionary commissars in the winter of 1793–1794. The "pitiless commissars" seized "all the public and private property in town. . . . arranged for the emptying of all cellars, all granaries, and the seizing of all basic foodstuffs. . . . They took by force horses, livestock in general, goods lodged at the customs house, and from the shops: cloth, linen, groceries, leather, bedsteads, tin, copper, brass, tools of every kind, furniture, clothing. The windows of all the churches were broken on the orders of the commissars; the interiors were vandalized; the organs dismantled, the lead from the steeples, the slates from the roofs, the wrought-iron work from the windows, doors, and staircases—it was all torn out and taken away."[31]

Even an allied people, such as the Swiss, felt the weight of the French demands (see document 30, "Swiss Protests"). Talleyrand, hardly a starry-eyed idealist, wrote to the minister of war that it was "unjust and dangerous to treat an independent and allied country as a conquered and enemy country."[32] While some Swiss were fighting alongside the French, they witnessed their "homes pillaged, their fellow citizens assassinated, their wives and daughters violated."[33] French exactions were heavy. Still others complained that some villages "are in the most frightful distress, nothing [is] left to them, absolutely nothing but despair. . . . [They have been] pushed to the end."[34] One Swiss patriot lamented that the Swiss had been pushed "to despair . . . one calls us free but one treats us like a conquered country. We are no longer Swiss, we are not French, we are French subjects." He threatened that a Swiss Vendée could erupt as the Swiss were driven by both despair and vengeance. In that letter one of the French Directors noted in the margins that a Swiss "Vendée would be a misfortune to France but a greater misfortune for the Swiss who . . . would be effaced from the list of nations."[35] Not surprisingly, revolts broke out in the Tyrol, in Swabia, in Franconia, in Luxembourg, in the Swiss territory, in the Venetian lands, to name just a few. As Europe was plunged into the maelstrom created by the lethal mix of revolution and war, no state escaped unscathed. Born in military defeat as well as in fiscal crisis and political enervation, the convulsive politics of the Revolution found its outlet in further warfare. A French state that had failed in warfare was succeeded by one that was warfare personified.

Notes

1. Blanning, *The French Revolutionary Wars,* 31.

2. Ibid.

3. Ibid., 21.

4. Albert Sorel, *Europe and the French Revolution* (New York: Doubleday, 1971), 286–87.

5. T. C. W. Blanning, *The Origins of the French Revolutionary Wars* (New York: Longman, 1986), 41.

6. Robert Doughty et al., *Warfare in the Western World,* vol. 1, *Military Operations from 1600 to 1871* (Lexington, Mass.: D. C. Heath, 1996), 93.

7. Quoted in Blanning, *The French Revolutionary Wars,* 5.

8. Claude Louis, Comte de Saint-Germain quoted in Blanning, *The Origins of the French Revolutionary Wars,* 41.

9. V. Dupuis quoted in Steven T. Ross, *From Flintlock to Rifle: Infantry Tactics, 1740–1866* (London: Frank Cass, 1979), 34.

10. *Moniteur* 4 (1790): 389–91.

11. Murphy, *The Diplomatic Retreat of France,* 4.

12. Tocqueville, *The Old Regime,* 142.

13. François Furet, *Interpreting the French Revolution,* translated by Elborg Forster (Cambridge: Cambridge University Press, 1981), 127.

14. Ibid., 128.

15. Alan Forrest, *The Soldiers of the French Revolution* (Durham, N.C.: Duke University Press, 1989), 23.

16. Scott, *The Response of the Royal Army,* 106, 114.

17. Ibid., 204.

18. Blanning, *The French Revolutionary Wars,* 126.

19. Scott, *The Response of the Royal Army,* 208.

20. Furet, *Interpreting the French Revolution,* 127.

21. Yves Blayo, "La Population de la France de 1740 à 1860," *Population* 30, numéro spécial on "Démographie historique" (novembre 1975): 107.

22. Karl Marx quoted in Furet, *Interpreting the French Revolution,* 129.

23. Brissot quoted in Linda Frey and Marsha Frey, " 'The Reign of the Charlatans is Over': The French Revolutionary Attack on Diplomatic Practice," *Journal of Modern History* 65 (December 1993): 712.

24. Marshal Foch quoted in Blanning, *The French Revolutionary Wars,* 82.

25. Karl von Clausewitz, *On War,* edited and translated by Michael Howard and Peter Paret (Princeton, N.J.: Princeton University Press, 1989), 518.

26. Stewart, *A Documentary Survey,* 260.

27. Quoted in Blanning, *The French Revolutionary Wars,* 15.

28. Clausewitz, *On War,* 332.

29. Quoted in T. C. W. Blanning, *The French Revolution in Germany: Occupation and Resistance in the Rhineland, 1792–1802* (Oxford: Clarendon Press, 1983), 87–88.

30. Peter Wetzler, *War and Subsistence: The Sambre and Meuse Army in 1794* (New York: Peter Lang, 1985), xxi.

31. Blanning, *The French Revolution in Germany,* 117.

32. Talleyrand, letter of 18 Brumaire, year VII, in Emile Dunant, ed., *Les Relations diplomatiques de la France et de la République Helvetique 1798–1803: Recueil des documents tirés des archives de Paris* (Basel: Verlag der Basler Buch- und Antiquariatshandlung, 1901), 129.

33. *Résumé* of deeds related by the minister plenipotentiary of the Helvetic republic to the Directory, 7 prairial, year VI, in ibid., 31.

34. Mengaud to Directory, Berne, germinal, year VI, in ibid., 39.

35. Perdonnet, letter of 21 prairial, year VI, and notes of Reubell in ibid., 81.

CHAPTER 7

AN AMBIGUOUS LEGACY

A nursery of future revolutions.
Edmund Burke, *Reflections on the Revolution in France*

The French Revolution broke out at a time of unprecedented change: demographic growth, economic recession, defeat abroad, deficit at home. It also occurred at a time of reform. In the words of the twentieth-century humanitarian Albert Schweitzer, the Revolution was "a fall of snow on blossoming trees."[1] Whether the early Revolution skidded off course or whether it was fatally flawed from the beginning, it nonetheless betrayed most of the ideals it had initially espoused. The costs of that betrayal were enormous. Still, the France of 1815 was considerably different than the France of 1789.

One of the unintended but most important consequences of the Revolution was the growth of the centralizing state. The revolutionaries had intended to decentralize power and to dismantle that apparatus. They overhauled the administration; the former crazy quilt of overlapping fiscal, judicial, legal, religious, and military districts was eliminated as were the provincial structures. In their stead, the revolutionaries in 1789 and 1790 divided the country into equal units based on area and created the 83 departments (today, 96) undergirded with 44,000 communes. Brittany was divided into 5 departments, Provence into 3, and so on. "It was the first time," Burke noted, "that men had ever carved up their own country in so barbarous a fashion," but Tocqueville thought that "they were only cutting up the dead."[2] The newly created departments were to be named after geographical features: mountains, rivers, and so forth. The policy of administrative decentralization, grounded in distrust of royal authority and faith in rational administration, was soon overturned as the departments lost the responsibility to execute revolutionary decisions. Although the intendants were abolished, the revolutionary government brought in *commissaires,* men with a different name but the same function. Under Napoleon, the agents of the central government reappeared as prefects and remained so up to the present (except for a brief period during the 1848 revolution when that government used *commissaires de la république*). Paris and centralism triumphed. The apparatus of the state also expanded. The central administration employed 700 men in the 1780s and 6,000 in 1794.[3] The total number of government officials expanded to 250,000, perhaps 10 percent of the entire bourgeoisie.[4] The bureaucracy was not only larger, it was also different. This new bureaucracy, in which no one owned his office and careers were open to the talented, was also a far more powerful one.

On the social side of the ledger, the Revolution destroyed the corporate society and the society of legal privilege. The antiquated social structure and the medley of seigneurial rights and privileges and prerogatives on which the old regime was based were gone forever. For the nobility, the trauma of the Revolution and the harrowing experience of having their privileges stripped bred a hostility to the Revolution. Every noble family was affected in some way: emigration, imprisonment, execution. After the Revolution, nobles were still prominent, but deference to them came from the respect of the local community or the strength of their economic power, not hereditary status. The nobles became part of a broader elite of the wealthy, that formed regardless of social background, the notables, which included army contractors and land speculators.

Those notables included some of the bourgeoisie. The Revolution enhanced the position of the bourgeoisie, but not the entrepreneurs within it. Their gains as property owners were matched by easier access to the state bureaucracy, which drew in many of the most talented, and to the professions. The standards for admittance to the professions, associated in the revolutionaries' minds with the world of corporatism and privilege, were suspended, and professions, such as, medicine and law, were opened to the public. The Revolution, witnessed a marked increase in charlatans and quacks until Napoleon reimposed admittance qualifications. The bourgeoisie and lower aristocracy also profited from the destruction of the aristocratic monopoly of the army. As in other spheres, careers were open to talent and 70 percent of officers rose from the ranks.[5] Those who remained in the army and did not emigrate had a greater chance of being promoted in a vastly expanded army. Looting and plunder also enriched those who survived the wars.

Within France, the Catholic Church had suffered from such looting. The church was also devastated by the confiscation of its property, the passage of the Civil Constitution of the Clergy, and the imposition of the oath to that constitution. The latter two events tore the church apart and forced many clergymen into counterrevolution. The Catholic Church was decimated in France: between 30,000 and 40,000 clergy emigrated (25 percent of the total).[6] Another 3,000 paid with their lives for allegiance to their faith. The church no longer dominated either education or social services, but the state was unable to fill the vacuum in those areas and literacy rates fell as did relief for the poor and care of the sick. The Concordat of Napoleon provided for free worship and a salaried clergy, but that agreement soon became a *discordat* that haunted church-state relations until the formal separation of church and state in 1905. State oversight of religion increased, but so did the pope's spiritual authority. The Revolution emancipated Protestants and Jews, granting them civil equality and freedom of worship. Protestants had suffered as had Catholics under the dechristianization campaign. The Revolution secularized society; it provided for state registration of births, marriages, and deaths and for civil marriage and, temporarily, for divorce.

The enactment of divorce legislation benefited some women. Regardless of or perhaps because of women's prominent role in the Revolution, the new policies tended to undermine rather than strengthen women's position. During the Revolution, women enjoyed no political rights and only limited legal ones. Only isolated feminists drafted a Declaration of the Rights of Woman and the Citizeness and forged a hope for the future. The liberal divorce laws of the Revolution were curtailed by Napoleon in 1804 and abolished in 1816. Although the Revolution in 1793 had stipulated that all children, including those born out of wedlock, were to inherit equally, Napoleon reinstituted the provision that a portion of the estate could be disposed of as the owner wished and ended the claims of those born outside marriage. Under the Napoleonic Code, women retained the right to inherit equally with their brothers, but married women could not make legal contracts and were under the authority of their fathers and then their husbands. Adulterous women could be imprisoned for up to two years.[7] The code buttressed patriarchal authority and limited the rights of women, children, and bastards. The Revolution did abolish slavery but not until 1794, and Bonaparte reestablished it in 1802. It would last another 46 years in the French colonies. The only exception was Haiti, where the slaves proclaimed a republic and were never reconquered despite repeated attempts. Ironically, Haiti was the only independent state to come into existence as a result of the French Revolution.[8]

The dislocation of war and the uncertainties of revolution also brought economic disaster to France and made the lives of the majority more precarious. But it did not change the production and distribution patterns of the society. The hierarchy of hereditary privilege was destroyed, but a new hierarchy of wealth was created. The nobles lost the income from *banalités* (monopolies of wine presses, mills, etc.) and seigneurial dues and relied more on rents, which increased. The attack on the king, the émigrés, and the church meant a massive transfer of property, but that transfer reinforced preexisting ownership patterns. In the nineteenth century, the nobles still dominated and the overall share of the small peasants was about the same. The Revolution did not expropriate the property of the nobility as a whole but of individuals condemned for some offense. Some noble families lost everything, but others kept their properties intact. After the Revolution, unsold property was returned to the owners, and the indemnity of 1825 enabled others to buy back their estates or other lands. In 1830, two-thirds of the 387 richest men in France were nobles.[9] The economic dislocation of war and revolution reinforced the tendency to shelter money in land. The rampant inflation from 1795 to 1797 encouraged those who could to buy land or buy out leases. Those who gained the most were the urban and rural bourgeoisie who invested in land and who tended to buy land to add to preexisting tracts. The civil code consolidated the landowners' property rights. The peasants who owned their own land benefited from the abolition of tithes and feudal dues. The consolidation of small-scale peasant property underscores the fundamentally conservative nature of the Revolution. The lot of the majority of the peasantry, tenants, and sharecroppers worsened because, although seigneurial dues were eliminated, rents and taxes were higher. The Revolution increased the number of the poorest, those who barely survived in the rural economy, and the tendency of the poorest to cling to collective rights. The Revolution may have accelerated the trend to partible inheritance (that is, the division of the estate among all the heirs) instead of primogeniture (a system in which the eldest son inherits). Those inheritance patterns meant smaller holdings. There were no major innovations in agricultural practices except for increased cultivation of potatoes. As late as the 1840s, agricultural productivity was basically what it had been a century earlier, backward and inefficient.[10] Massive land clearance, in some areas as much as 20 percent, during the Revolution, often interpreted as a disaster for the natural environment, prompted Napoleon to establish a centralized forest policy that attempted to end just such collective use of forests.[11]

The Revolution delayed not only the agrarian revolution, but also the industrial revolution. Inflation disrupted economic relations and consumed capital. And the effects of the Revolution were not temporary: it bred a distrust of paper money and halted public works such as the building of roads and canals. The inflation of the assignats not only channeled more money into land, it also undercut wages, which did not catch up with the cost of living. Wage earners and creditors suffered, but debtors prospered. By 1798, one-tenth of the population of the city of Paris was out of work.[12] The economic policies of the Revolution did not serve the interests of the *sans-culottes*. The biggest economic loss was the destruction of overseas trade, which ruined many traders in the coastal towns. The trade with the colonies was destroyed, although piracy flourished. The colonial trade did not reach pre-1789 levels until 1830. Foreign trade, which had equaled that of Britain in 1789, did not catch up until 1980.[13] The war industries did well, but that was a temporary phenomenon and did not offset the other losses. During the continental system, certain captive markets such as iron, coal, and cotton did flourish. But even this, a kind of barometer of industrial development which often is touted as a success, grew less rapidly than in Great Britain. In 1815, France had 1 million mechanized spindles and Great Britain had 5 million.[14] On the whole, the French protectionist legislation enacted during the revolutionary and Napoleanic era, and the blockade erected during the wars slowed innovation and the transfer of technology. The Revolution throttled France's long-term industrial development: industrial production declined and fell further and further behind that of Great Britain, and that, in turn, reinforced the agrarian nature of French society. On the positive side, some have argued that delayed modernization and delayed urbanization of France created more balanced growth.

In the economic dislocation triggered by the Revolution, the poor, the workers, and the peasants suffered the most. Sixty percent of the official victims of the Terror came from those groups, and almost one-third from the émigrés. The attack on the nobility and church impoverished those who had served them. The crime wave in the cities paralleled that in the country. The lives of the destitute became more precarious. Not surprisingly, there was a marked increase in both crime and urban suicides. The Revolution dealt a major blow to both poorhouses and hospitals that had been staffed and funded by the church. Although the revolutionary governments made gestures toward relief of the poor, they were only that—gestures. By 1847, the number of hospitals was still 42 percent less than in 1789.[15] The Revolution eliminated the multiplicity of taxes, ecclesiastical fees, and feudal dues, but in their stead it created a uniform taxation system. Levies on property and income were assessed on all, but evaded by many. Indirect taxes, however, still weighed most heavily on the poor.

The Revolution removed certain barriers to economic development and growth of a national market such as the restrictive practice of guilds, privileges, monopolies, local tolls, regional tariffs, and internal customs. The government also implemented a uniform system of weights and measures, the metric system, based on the meter, a unit of length, and on the gram, a unit of mass. In one department alone there had been 65 ways of calculating length and 26 for weight. The revolutionaries also adopted a standard currency. Along with standardization went state regulation of the economy for both good and ill. The hands of employers were strengthened. The revolutionary state outlawed labor organizations, collective bargaining, and strikes (not legal until 1864), and Napoleon reintroduced the *livret,* a working-class identity card which detailed a worker's history. Urban workers may have sacrificed the most and gained the least. On the whole, the Revolution and the wars that ensued halted the modernization of France. In the economic maelstrom some benefited: landowners, bureaucrats, soldiers, military contractors, and speculators. Who lost? Some noble families, many of the clergy, creditors, those on fixed incomes, the destitute, the workers, and tenant farmers.

Civilians also suffered. In the wars that raged from 1792 to 1815, civilians were no longer insulated from the effects. When the French called for a *levée en masse,* they initiated a new type of war, a war of peoples. The Prussian theorist Clausewitz argued, "Henceforth, the means available—the efforts which might be called forth—had no longer any definite limits.... The element of War, freed from all conventional restrictions, broke loose, with all its natural force. The cause was the participation of the people in this great affair of State."[16] In response to the demands of war, conscription was implemented not only in France, but also among the allies, such as Austria and Prussia. All European states felt the burden of taxes to fund the war. Others were looted and pillaged by the invading armies. Launched in the name of universal rights of mankind and the fraternity of peoples, the wars, again by the law of unintended consequences, hardened national antagonisms. The French evocation of the sovereignty of the nation was turned against them—and with a vengeance as the reaction to French rapacity provoked a reaction in the occupied areas.

The revolutionary and Napoleonic Wars also triggered major changes in the international arena. A number of Latin America states, triggered by the Napoleonic invasion of the Iberian peninsula, proclaimed their independence from Spain. French revolutionary armies destroyed the city republics of Geneva, Genoa, and Venice. After the defeat of Napoleon in 1815, France lost most of its territorial gains. The Austrian Netherlands was united with the Dutch republic, albeit only temporarily until 1831 when it gained its independence. Luxembourg was made a grand duchy. The Holy Roman Empire was first changed by the provisions of Campo Formio of 1797, which ceded the Left bank of the Rhine to the French, and then was obliterated in 1806 by Napoleonic mandate. In its stead was created a German confederation of consolidated German states. Russia and Prussia pushed farther west. Prussia acquired what would become the German industrial heartland in the Rhineland, and Austria emerged with more territory. Savoy was restored to the kingdom of Sardinia. The British were able to strengthen and extend their trading links in part because during the wars they had destroyed or confiscated the assets of their rivals, such as the Dutch. The real winners were France's enemies. Historian Jeremy Black points out that the revolutionary and Napoleonic Wars created "not only a weaker France in Europe, and a European international system that left few options for France, but also a European overseas world dominated by Britain."[17] The Vienna settlement of 1814–15 left Russia dominant in eastern Europe, Austria in central Europe, and Britain on the seas. The

Revolution and the wars left an impact on Europe, but perhaps not the one the revolutionaries had envisioned.

What of its legacy to the future? Perhaps the best hope of the Revolution lay in its proclamation of liberty, equality, and fraternity. That slogan was officially adopted by the Third Republic (1870–1940) and has continued in France except for the period of Vichy rule during World War II. Liberty at home was defined in the Declaration of the Rights of Man and the Citizen (see document 4, "Declaration of the Rights of Man and of the Citizen") and meant freedom from arbitrary power and from all the old forms of constraint. Equality meant civic equality, equality before the law, and freedom from the old discriminations and from arbitrary and inequitable practices in a society no longer based on privilege, prerogatives, or heredity. Fraternity meant the universality of those rights and the brotherhood of all men. The Revolution did not, however, except for the Conspiracy of Equals, envisage an overturning of property rights or new relationships within families.

Alongside this tradition and inherent in the Revolution from the beginning was a pronounced authoritarian tendency. This should not be surprising because in France there had been no tradition of political dissent. From the beginning, too many ignored conflicting opinions. Libertarian rhetoric masked an intolerance of opposing views. For example, Sieyès could argue that the nobility was outside the nation. The revolutionaries were only too apt to demonize the opposition. The Rousseauist conception of the state, of the general will, of only one single voice invalidated dissent. The supremacy of the general will destroyed the belief that the state power should be checked by ancient fundamental laws or by any intermediary authority. The Jacobin republic was absolute. Tocqueville's contention that the Revolution had brought France democracy and equality but not liberty because of the relentless growth of state power seems even more compelling, given the tendency of the national state to try to obliterate regional identities, distinct languages, and local traditions. This annihilation of intermediary powers pointed the way to totalitarianism. The dispersal of power among corporate bodies was destroyed forever and authority was concentrated in the state. Divine right theory, which vested power in the king, was jettisoned; sovereignty was located then not in the king but in the nation. The legitimacy of political authority no longer rested on hereditary right or prescription. Subjects became citizens; the kingdom, a nation. "The *nation*, not the *people*, as in the United States was to be sovereign," historian J. F. Bosher points out. "The nation and the State played (and play) a characteristically greater part in the French constitution than in the American or British constitutions. Voluntary or local power was (and is) restricted."[18] The Revolution then entailed more state interference in the lives of most Frenchman. The Revolution, which had sought to dismantle the absolutist state, created an even more powerful Leviathan with coercive powers.

Most of the revolutionaries did not intend to put in place a democratic system in the sense of universal suffrage (that would not be implemented for men until 1848 and for women until 1944). The Revolution initially distinguished between active citizens, those with certain property qualifications who could vote, and passive citizens, those who contributed to the state in other ways but could not vote. The only constitution with no property qualification, that of 1793, was never implemented. The closest the Revolution came to the goal of universal manhood suffrage was the charade of democracy under Napoleon, which included indirect voting and plebiscites. Neither had the revolutionaries hesitated to quash elections or to violate parliamentary immunity. The Revolution bequeathed to posterity the terms *left* and *right*, which came from the seating plans of the national assembly. In articulating a modern ideology, the Revolution also spawned its counterpoint, a well-articulated defense of monarchy, religion, social order, and tradition as seen in Edmund Burke, Friedrich von Gentz, and Joseph de Maistre. The Revolution also found a new sense of identity and located that in the nation. The combination of ideology and nationalism posed a powerful threat to Europe as then constituted and proved even more powerful in the future.

The revolutionaries emphasized the legitimacy of revolution, the right of violent insurrection to overthrow an arbitrary order, a tradition that persisted in France as demonstrated in the revolutions of 1830, 1848, and 1871. The violence of the revolutionary movement tore the society apart and left a legacy of political instability; the constitution of the Fifth Republic is the sixteenth (counting 1814 and 1940). This instability prompted one historian to observe, "The constitution has become a special branch of French literature not so well used as the novel, the short story, or the poem."[19] The French Revolution became, in Burke's words, "a nursery of future revolutions."[20] The idea of the

Revolution bred hopes for the future and perpetuated the divisions of the past. That struggle was replayed in the nineteenth and twentieth centuries. The communists could be dubbed the Jacobins of twentieth century, although that identification obscured the real differences. The Vichy regime of World War II suppressed a book on the Revolution by Lefebvre, *Quatre-vingt-neuf,* as subversive. The idea of the Revolution, even more than its reality, lived on because it nurtured hopes of change and of a national regeneration, the dream of a more just and more humane system as seen in the Declaration of the Rights of Man and the Citizen. What proved so seductive about the Revolution was what Darnton has called its "sense of boundless possibility,"[21] the belief that the world as then constituted could be remade in time (with the revolutionary calendar), in space (the metric system), in personal relations (adoption of the informal you, *tu*), and so forth. There was in that Revolution a will to create a new and better world by enacting humanitarian and utilitarian reforms. The legend, or perhaps more accurately, the aspirations of the Revolution would endure. What happened or what is thought to have happened influenced future revolutionaries, such as Karl Marx and Vladimir Lenin, and spawned mimetic revolutionary movements.

Often heralded as a harbinger of democratic and social ideas, the revolutionary legacy is, nonetheless, ambiguous. Europe witnessed "events so terrible that they shook mankind to its core."[22] In its systematic execution of its citizens, its violation of due process, its intolerance of dissent, the Terror left a troubling legacy. Historian Simon Schama argues that violence was not incidental to the Revolution but "in some depressingly unavoidable sense, violence *was* the Revolution."[23] The combination of a secular eschatology with modern nationalism proved a potent and deadly force and a force with a future.[24] The French revolutionary wars cost Europe 5 million men.[25] More Frenchmen were killed in those wars, albeit over a longer period of time, than died in World War I. The dream of a new world became a tragedy.

Notes

1. Alfred Cobban, *A History of Modern France* (Baltimore: Penguin, 1961), 112.

2. Mona Ozouf, "Département," in *A Critical Dictionary of the French Revolution,* edited by François Furet and Mona Ozouf, translated by Arthur Goldhammer (Cambridge, Mass.: Belknap Press, 1989), 494.

3. William Doyle, *The Oxford History of the French Revolution* (Oxford: Oxford University Press, 1989), 408.

4. Ibid., 409.

5. Ibid.

6. McPhee, *The French Revolution,* 199.

7. Ibid., 185.

8. Doyle, *The Oxford History of the French Revolution,* 413.

9. McPhee, *The French Revolution,* 184.

10. Doyle, *The Oxford History of the French Revolution,* 405.

11. McPhee, *The French Revolution,* 195.

12. Doyle, *The Oxford History of the French Revolution,* 403.

13. François Crouzet, "Industrial Anticlimax and Economic Watershed," in *The Place of the French Revolution in French History,* edited by Marvin R. Cox (Boston: Houghton Mifflin, 1998), 206.

14. Ibid., 207.

15. Doyle, *The Oxford History of the French Revolution,* 401.

16. Clausewitz quoted in ibid., 416.

17. Jeremy Black, *European International Relations 1648–1815* (London: Palgrave, 2002), 243.

18. J. F. Bosher, *The French Revolution* (New York: W. W. Norton, 1988), 244.

19. Ibid., 271.

20. Edmund Burke, *Reflections on the Revolution in France,* edited by Conor Cruise O'Brien (Harmondsworth, England: Penguin Books, 1968), 112.

21. Robert Darnton, "A Conflict between 'Possibilism' and 'The Givenness of Things,'" in *The Place of the French Revolution in History,* edited by Marvin R. Cox (Boston: Houghton Mifflin, 1998), 17.

22. Ibid., 19.

23. Schama, *Citizens,* xv.

24. Furet, *Interpreting the French Revolution,* 65.

25. Doyle, *The French Revolution: A Very Short Introduction,* 96.

BIOGRAPHIES:
THE PERSONALITIES OF THE FRENCH REVOLUTION

François Nicolas Babeuf (1760–97) Organized an uprising against the Directory. Born in St. Quentin, 1 of 13 children (only 4 survived to adulthood), Babeuf worked as a common laborer and later as an apprentice to a local surveyor. At age 22 he married a chambermaid who bore his children and who remained loyal to him through his six imprisonments and her own. Babeuf never had access to formal schooling, but was an autodidact. When the *cahiers des doléances* were being drawn up across the nation, he assisted the vocal locals, who were demanding the abolition of seigneurial rights. In 1794, he moved to Paris and established a newspaper, *Journal de la liberté de la presse,* later renamed *Le Tribun du peuple.* He used this paper as a vehicle to attack the moderates, Robespierre's government, the Thermidoreans, the Directory, and the economic results of the Revolution and became a champion of the *sans-culottes.* For such opinions he was frequently jailed. He emerged from his incarcerations even more convinced that the Revolution had not gone far enough in alleviating the misery of the people. In spite of all his hardships he never gave up his conviction that he was destined to be the "savior of the human race."[1] For Babeuf, political equality was not enough; he wanted absolute equality (*l'égalité parfaite*).[2] He wanted to eliminate private property and make education and medical treatment available to all. The plummeting value of the assignat won over some to his views. He gathered together a group called the Society of Equals, which included former Jacobins. Although the Directory banned his journal and his group, Babeuf continued placarding the city with slogans, inciting the people to revolt, urging them to sing the Babouvist song, *"Mourant de faim, mourant de froid"*

(Dying of hunger, dying of cold), and pushing his program of economic equality. This plan envisaged the abolition of property and currency and the free distribution of food and clothing. The Directory knew of the plan to launch an armed uprising on May 11, 1796. Although one of his associate's desire to see "heads falling [and] . . . bowels scattered about the pavement"[3] was perhaps more violent than others wished, the conspirators were planning a bloodbath. They planned to kill the Directors, the ministers, the generals, foreigners, and anyone who refused to give up their foodstuffs. The Directory preempted the plotters and arrested Babeuf and a number of his followers on May 10. Babeuf and one of his colleagues, Augustin-Alexandre-Joseph Darthe, were condemned to death and the others, including Filippo Buonarroti (who would later publish his memoirs about the conspiracy), were exiled or acquitted. Upon hearing the sentence, Babeuf and Darthe attempted—unsuccessfully—to kill themselves. They were both executed on 8 prairial; Babeuf was only 37 years old. Although he died, secret revolutionary societies and leftists kept his ideas alive. The French socialists, for example, honored Babeuf as a great precursor, and the Russian Bolsheviks bought many of his personal papers and put them in the Communist party archives. One historian argues, "Babouvism is like a little red flower which thrusts its head above the mass of the French Revolution," but goes on to observe that "the scarlet petals have been scattered all along the route subsequently trodden by the great revolutionaries."[4]

Jacques Pierre Brissot de Warville (1754–93), the son of a pastry cook, was a lawyer in the ancien régime who wrote a number of pamphlets urging, for example, reform of the criminal laws and abolition of slavery. He traveled widely in both Europe and the United States. Often in debt, he was incarcerated for two months in the Bastille. Because of his precarious finances, he often acted as a police spy. During the Revolution, he was elected to the Paris communal assembly. In that position he wrote a constitution for the city that became a model for municipal constitutions. He was subsequently elected a deputy for Paris and served on the diplomatic committee. He also edited a popular journal, the *Patriot français,* which became the voice of the Girondins. Brissot believed that war would end internal disorder and spread revolutionary principles. It would be, in his words, a "crusade for universal liberty."[5] "We will not be tranquil," he stressed, "until Europe, and all of Europe is in flames."[6] He and his supporters advocated a national referendum on the fate of the king and combated the growing dominance of Paris. Because the Jacobins opposed these positions, a power struggle ensued. As the economy deteriorated and the war effort faltered, many blamed the Girondins. At the end of May 1793, Parisian mobs invaded the Convention, demanding the arrest of Brissot and his supporters. Brissot fled but was caught, arrested, and condemned to death. He died on the guillotine on October 31, 1793.

Charles Alexandre de Calonne (1734–1802), an ambitious controller general of finances (1783–87), was appointed by Louis XVI to solve the financial dilemma that France confronted. He had come to the notice of the king when he served as intendant of Metz (1768) and Lille (1774). He established a sinking fund, supported the Eden Treaty (1786), and attempted to restore public trust with an extensive program of public works. When this program failed, he suggested a number of radical reforms, such as the establishment of a direct tax on land and a stamp tax and the abolition of internal custom duties. Because the situation was so dire, he urged the king to call not the Estates General, which he thought would be too unpredictable, but a handpicked Assembly of Notables, which the king did in 1787. But the Assembly, which included many of Calonne's enemies and Necker's supporters, refused to sanction such reforms. Dismissed, Calonne fled to Great Britain—the first of many émigrés—where he remained until 1802 when he finally returned to France.

Marie Jean Antoine Nicolas de Caritat, Marquis de Condorcet (1743–94), a brilliant mathematician, *philosophe,* and moderate politician, was born in Picardy. He was elected a member of the Academy of Sciences (1769) and the French Academy (1782). In 1786, he married the beautiful Sophie de Grouchy (1764–1822), a sister of the future marshal Grouchy, who transformed their home into a famous salon where the leading intellectual and political figures gathered. When the Revolution broke out, he played an important role, presenting a plan for state education that served as the basis for the system later adopted. He opposed the calling of the Estates General because he feared that this assembly would undermine attempts at reform, but was one of the first to advocate the establishment of a republic and the suspension of the king's power. He was a friend of Brissot and as such an opponent of the Mountain and a supporter of the declaration of war. In the trial of the king he voted against the death penalty. After the Jacobins outlawed him, he went into hiding but was discovered and imprisoned. He died in prison of unknown causes, possibly of suicide. After he was proscribed, his wife—with his permission—divorced him and succeeded in regaining the family property. She subsequently helped with the editing of her husband's 21-volume works and translated Adam Smith's *Theory of Moral Sentiments* into French. Her salon in Paris was an important gathering place for those who opposed the Napoleonic regime.

Condorcet is mainly known for his theory of probability, his belief in progress, and his conviction that man could perfect himself through education. For Condorcet, truth was "the enemy of power and of those who exercise it. . . . The more strength it acquires, the less need societies have of government."[7] Condorcet envisaged a time when the human race would march "with a firm and sure tread on the road to truth, virtue, and happiness."[8] Ironically, this tract on progress was written at a time when Condorcet was in hiding because of the growing power of those on the left and their refusal to tolerate an independent voice.

Georges Jacques Danton (1759–94), a charismatic orator and Parisian lawyer, was influential in the early days of the Cordeliers club and represented his district in the municipal government of Paris in 1790. He was instrumental in the revolution of August 1792 that overthrew the king; he ordered the murder of the commander of the king's troops and exalted in the suspension of Louis XVI. In the aftermath he served as minister of justice and dominated the executive council. After the fall of Verdun, he was morally implicated in the September Massacres. Even if he did not order the massacres, he refused to intervene. Elected a deputy to the Convention, he served on the committee on the constitution and on the diplomatic committee. On the latter, he was an imperialist who wanted to extend the republic to the so-called natural frontiers, a considerable expansion of French territories. He dominated the first Committee of Public Safety but retired from public life in the fall of 1793. Upon his return to Paris in November, he advocated relaxation of the Terror. His popularity in Paris gave him the illusion that he could not be attacked. "They would not dare," he often said.[9] But they did. After the Committee of Public Safety attacked the Hébertists, it attacked his group, dubbed the Indulgents, and charged him with conspiring to overthrow the government. At his trial his oratorical talents enabled him to dominate the courtroom and a guilty verdict was reached only when he was silenced. The trial, like many others, was a mockery. At the guillotine he purportedly told the executioner to show the people his head, remarking that "it is well worth the trouble." Demagogue? Patriot? Statesman? Perhaps all three. His hideous face with its reddish-brown hue dominated his athletic frame, conditioned by his love of physical exercise, particularly swimming, fencing, and tennis. His stature and vitality led one of his admirers to dub him the "Hercules of the Revolution."[10] An extremely bright man, he was a talented linguist who spoke English and Italian fluently. He was a massive man who was careless about his personal appearance, but he was a powerful orator with a resonant voice who spoke "with warmth and energy. . . . His elocution was fiery and always accompanied by violent geticulations."[11] Others remarked that he roared like a lion. Danton could appeal to a crowd and would not hesitate to use scatological expressions. Vulgar, sensuous, and venal; a contemporary remarked that he "made no secret of his love of pleasure and of money, and sneered at vain scruples of conscience and delicacy."[12] Danton had a certain infectious zest for life and for living well. No doubt he had profited from the Revolution and taken money from various savory and unsavory characters, but whether that influenced him is another question. His revolutionary career was marked by a certain elasticity of principles. "The word virtue made Danton laugh," Robespierre noted scornfully.[13]

Jacques Louis David (1748–1825), a famous painter, immortalized the events of the Revolution in a neoclassical style. He was a quarrelsome and combative student who got involved in a number of duels, one of which left a prominent scar on his face. After studying at the Academy of Painting and Sculpture in Paris, he moved to Rome. That experience reinforced his tendency to use scenes from antiquity to evoke civic virtue and to underscore the importance of moral duty as seen in the *Oath of the Horatii* (1785) and the *Death of Socrates* (1787). The themes of patriotism, individual sacrifice, and political loyalty would appear in his later paintings. After the Revolution broke out, he commemorated its famous scenes in paintings such as the *Oath of the Tennis Court* and orchestrated a number of revolutionary festivals and ceremonies. His most famous work may have been his portrayal of Marat, a carefully constructed painting that became a revolutionary icon. His commitment to art was matched by an active engagement in the Revolution. He voted for the death of the king, was elected president of the Convention and of the Jacobin club (despite a marked speech impediment), and served on the Committee of Public Instruction and the Committee of General Security. Closely associated with the Terror, he barely escaped the guillotine after Thermidor. David also served Napoleon and painted the majestic Napoleon crossing, the *Saint Bernard Pass,* and the *Coronation of Napoleon and Josephine.* After the Hundred Days, he retired to Brussels. In his life and painting he encapsulated many of the ideals of the Revolution, especially the primacy of moral duty over personal feelings. A superb technician who was solicitous of his students, he influenced the painting of the revolutionary age by his revival of the classical style in painting, fashion, and interior design.

Charles François du Périer Dumouriez (1739–1823), the son of a war commissary, first saw action in 1758 when he volunteered to serve in a cavalry regiment during the Seven Years' War (1756–63). He was wounded twice and promoted to captain (1761) and then made a knight of St. Louis (1763). Discharged from the army, he sought military service, fighting first with the Genoese against the Corsicans, then for the Corsicans against the Genoese. During this time, he also took part in a French expedition against Corsica (1768) and was promoted to *mestre de camp* (1769). Louis XV entrusted him with a number of secret missions. When his patron at court, Choiseul, fell, he was imprisoned in the Bastille and only released on the accession of Louis XVI, who promoted him to the rank of colonel (1775) and commandant at Cherbourg (1778). By 1788, he had attained the rank of *maréchal de camp.*

During the Revolution, he joined the Jacobin club and received command of the 12th military division at Nantes. Appointed minister of foreign affairs on March 15, 1792, he was instrumental in the declaration of war. Realizing probably more than anyone else that France was not prepared for war, given the disorganized and undisciplined state of the army, he, nonetheless, adopted a belligerent attitude toward other powers in an attempt to win popular support. Such a craven desire also dictated his policies at the Ministry of Foreign Affairs,[14] where he was called the *ministre bonnet rouge* because he donned a red hat when he visited the Jacobins. He intended, he told them, to reform the ministry because most of the diplomatic corps were counterrevolutionaries, "courtesans" who were more occupied with intrigues than with the affairs of France.[15] Within the ministry, Dumouriez's appointment of Guillaume Bonne-Carrère, the secretary of the Jacobins, as director general indicated the new thrust as did the hiring of many who had no experience and even less merit and the dismissal of current employees whose only offense was serving the ancien régime. Unable to earn the trust of the king, Dumouriez was forced to resign.

He became minister of war on June 12, 1792, but resigned a few days later on June 15, fearing that the Assembly would blame him for the French military reverses. He next assumed command of the Army of the North (August 16), defeating the Prussians with the help of François Christophe Kellermann at Valmy (September 20) and the Austrians at the battle of Jemappes (November 6). During the French conquest of the Austrian Netherlands, Dumouriez quarreled with the commissioners over their rapacious policies toward the conquered. When he was defeated at Neerwinden (March 18, 1793), he began negotiating with the Austrians. Undoubtedly, he had cause for concern because 17 generals were executed in 1793.[16] In addition troops often lynched generals—even those who won. He arrested the commissioners and the minister of war, turned them over to the Austrians, and fled on April 5, 1793. The French outlawed the general, and his troops in turn deserted him. Dumouriez spent the remainder of his life abroad. He advised the Spanish on guerrilla warfare and proffered advice to Arthur Wellesley, duke of Wellington before his invasion of France. Because Louis XVIII refused to allow his return, Dumouriez remained an exile to the end.

Philippe François Nazaire Fabre d'Eglantine (1755–94), a French dramatist, was born in Carcassonne. Fabre added *d'Eglantine* to his name to commemorate his award of the golden eglantine, a European rose, in the floral games of Toulouse. He served as secretary of the Cordeliers club, was a member of the Jacobins, and a secretary to Danton. He was present at the attack on the Tuileries on August 10, 1792, and subsequently was elected to represent Paris in the National Convention. A satirist and a dramatist, he is most remembered for creating the poetic names of the republican calendar. To court popular favor, he denounced certain individuals for purportedly conspiring against the republic in an illusionary foreign plot and then the Hébertists for their extremism. He became entangled in a scheme to turn a quick profit by falsifying a decree that liquidated the India Company. This sordid rack-eteering led to his expulsion from the Jacobins. He was indicted for embezzlement and for promoting the foreign plot. He was arrested in January 1794 and possessed enough sangfroid to sing a well-known ditty he had written during his trial and to pass out copies of his poems on his way to the guillotine in April 1794.

Olympe de Gouges (1748–93) was born in Montauban, the daughter of a butcher and a trinket peddler. A self-educated novelist and playwright, she was one of a number of women activists in the Revolution. In 1791, she published her Declaration of the Rights of Woman and the Citizeness, which cleverly paralleled the clauses in the Declaration of the Rights of Man. She also attacked both Robespierre ("the egotistical abomination")[17] and Antoine Quintin Fouqier-Tinville, the public prosecutor and offered to defend the king. But she was not alone in advocating more rights for women. Another, Etta Palm, petitioned for educational and legal equality of men and women; Claire Lacombe organized a club of revolutionary republican citizenesses; and Théroigne de Méricourt donned a National Guard uniform and participated in the uprising of August 10. In November 1793, the Convention ordered the trial and later execution of certain activists, including Olympe de Gouges after she demanded government by plebiscite. Ironically, she had argued earlier that if "a woman has the right to mount the scaffold; she must also have the right to mount the tribune."[18] At the same time she was being executed, her son was in the army fighting for France. The Convention also banned all political activity by women and closed down many clubs, including the Society of Revolutionary Republican Women. Even the radical journalist Louis Marie Prudhomme was not sympathetic and urged women: "Be honest and diligent girls, tender and modest wives, wise mothers, and you will be good patriots. True patriotism consists of fulfilling one's duties and valuing only rights appropriate to each according to sex and age, and not wearing the liberty cap and pantaloons and not carrying pike and pistol. Leave those to men who are born to protect you and make you happy."[19] Neither was he alone in this sentiment: Henri Grégoire, another revolutionary, attacked the influence of "crapulous and seditious women."[20] Women were given some control over their property and more liberal divorce laws, but even the latter did not last. The Napoleonic code greatly restricted the grounds for divorce, and when the Bourbons returned to power, divorce was abolished for the next 70 years.

Jacques René Hébert (1757–94) was nicknamed Père Duchesne after the newspaper he edited from September 1790 until February 1794 and the "Homer of filth" by one historian, an insult to the great Greek poet. Born into a middle-class family, his youthful misadventures landed him in prison and forced him to flee his hometown. His next 11 years in Paris were marked by poverty and misery until he became known for his articles, which were filled with expletives and obscenities. He was a prominent member of the Cordeliers club in 1791 and a member of the revolutionary commune of Paris in 1792. His violent and scurrilous attack on the Girondins led to his arrest in May 1793. The sections freed him several days later. He coveted but was denied various offices in the revolutionary government. He championed the worship of reason and dechristianization, revolutionary war, and ultraterrorist measures. During the trial of the queen, he accused her of sexual abuse of her son. His support among the *sans-culottes* and his influence in the Cordeliers club aroused the suspicion of the revolutionary government and the hostility of Robespierre. His attempts to push the Revolution further to the left and his call for an insurrection on March 4, 1794, alienated the revolutionary committees further. He was arrested on March 12, 1794, accused of plotting to overthrow the government, and guillotined 12 days later. The foul-mouthed spokesman of the streets was taunted by the crowd when he quailed before the guillotine.

Marie Joseph Paul Yves Roch Gilbert du Motier, Marquis de Lafayette (1757–1834), born of an illustrious family, lost his father in 1759 at the battle of Minden. At age 16, he married Marie Adrienne Françoise de Noailles (d. 1807). Carrying on a family tradition, Lafayette entered the Guards and rose to the rank of captain. Upon learning of the revolt of the American colonies against Britain, he determined to fight on the side of the Americans even though the king forbade his leaving France. He arrived in the colonies and fought in a number of battles: Brandywine (1777), Barren Hill (1778), Monmouth (1778), and Yorktown (1781). He forged lasting friendships with prominent revolutionaries, such as George Washington and Thomas Jefferson. Upon returning to France, he served in the Assembly of Notables (1787) and the Estates General and was elected vice president of the National Assembly. It was Lafayette who presented a declaration of rights to the king modeled on the American Declaration of Independence. Lafayette also advocated religious toleration, popular representation, and suppression of the privileged orders. Because of his immense popularity and military experience, he was chosen commander of the National Guard. When the crowd marched to Versailles in October 1789 and stormed the palace, Lafayette followed with the National Guard and intervened, restoring some order. Throughout the tumultuous days that followed, Lafayette attempted to keep the peace. When the National Guard refused to obey his orders and prevented the king from leaving Paris to celebrate Easter in the countryside, Lafayette tendered his resignation but was persuaded to withdraw it. He lost a great deal of popularity in Paris when he ordered his guards to fire on a crowd gathered at the Champ de Mars (July 1791) to draft a petition to dethrone the king. Lafayette, however, never enjoyed the confidence of the king nor of those on the left who accused him of aiding in the flight of the royal family. After the proclamation of the constitution, he resigned and retired. When preparations were being made for the war against Austria, Lafayette accepted one of the commands. He, however, publicly protested the invasion of the Tuileries by the Parisian crowds. When the Assembly ordered him back to Paris and stripped him of his command, he prudently fled abroad with 22 members of his general staff. He was imprisoned by the Prussians and later the Austrians until 1797 when Napoleon procured his release.

Upon his return to France, he voted against a life consulate and later against granting Napoleon the imperial title. He lived in political retirement during the empire but returned to politics with the Bourbon restoration. In 1824–25, he briefly returned to America, where he was fêted and given land and money in recognition of his contribution to the success of the American Revolution. In France, he served in the Chamber of Deputies and in 1830 played a prominent role in the July Revolution, again assuming command of the National Guard. He died in Paris in 1834. Lafayette is honored in both France and the United States for his integrity and his courage, especially his willingness to make decisions and take stands, however unpopular. Several cities in the United States are named after him. His sons, George Washington Motier de Lafayette and Oscar Thomas Gilbert Motier de Lafayette, played prominent political and military roles as well. His direct descendants, the Chambrun family, are to this day honorary U.S. citizens—a distinction granted to very few.

Louis XVI (1754–93), the grandson and successor of Louis XV, was the son of the dauphin Louis (1765) and Marie Josephe of Saxony, both of whom died of tuberculosis in 1765 and 1767, respectively. Physically, he was a very strong man, and intellectually, he was gifted. An autodidact who taught himself English, he was also proficient in Latin and Italian and knew a little German. In 1770, he married the Austrian archduchess, Marie Antoinette, and in 1774—at only 20 years of age—he was crowned king. He loved eating, hunting, and fiddling with locks. He was also a faithful husband and a loving father. But the royal couple's failure to have children for four years led to the circulation of unfounded rumors about his sexuality. The king, unfortunately, was not politically adept. He was hardworking and conscientious, but he tended to let events drive him. Because Louis also wanted to be popular and loved by his people, he dismissed the Maupeou *parlements,* the unpopular courts set up by his predecessor to pass royal edicts into law. Many historians contend that the dismissal of these courts made it impossible to avert revolution. Louis XVI appointed a number of ministers, such as Turgot (see document 1, "Letter of Turgot to Louis XVI"), Necker, Calonne, and Brienne, who suggested a number of reforms. These efforts, however, failed. Because of his inability to push through strong measures, the king called first an Assembly of Notables and finally the Estates General, which had last met in 1614. Some historians have concluded from his behavior that during the later years of his life he suffered from clinical depression. If so, it would be understandable. Unsure of the correct action to take, the king ended up vacillating between the opposing sides. Many never trusted Louis XVI and thought that he intended to betray the Revolution. When he was ultimately brought to trial, Louis decided to defend himself as a constitutional monarch who had fulfilled his duty. He knew at the outset that many would condemn him. As he told his lawyer: "I am sure that they will make me perish."[21] And they did. Condemned to death, he died with great courage on January 21, 1793.

Chrétien Guillaume de Lamoignon de Malesherbes (1721–94) was born in Paris of an old and distinguished family. At age 24, he became a counselor in the *parlement* of Paris, and at age 29 (1750), he succeeded his father and became premier president of the *cour des aides,* which heard appeals about administrative decisions and could issue remonstrances to the king about violations of fundamental laws. In that same year, he was appointed director of the book trade and as such was in charge of press censorship in France. He befriended *philosophes,* such as Voltaire, Rousseau, and Diderot and made it possible for works, such as the *Encyclopédie,* to appear. Malesherbes, who believed in the importance of education, stressed that "ignorance is the cause of most of our faults."[22] Only two kinds of books, in his view, should be banned: those that eroded morality or those that undermined royal authority. He held that position until 1768. In 1771, because of his opposition to the abolition of the *parlements,* he was exiled to his estates. After Louis XVI came to power and restored the old *parlements,* Malesherbes again served as president of the *cour des aides* until 1775 when the king appointed him secretary of state for the king's household. In this position he supported prison reform and restricted the abuses of the *lettres de cachet,* secret warrants of arrest signed by the king. When his friend Turgot fell from power, Malesherbes resigned.

During his retirement, he traveled extensively in Europe and tried to improve the status of Protestants. He also engaged in both scientific and literary pursuits. His distinction won him election to the Academy of Sciences (1750), the Academy of Inscriptions (1759), and the French Academy (1775). When the king was put on trial, Malesherbes offered to defend the beleaguered monarch with two others. He was also the one who informed the king of the verdict. Because of his defense of the king, he was condemned by the Revolutionary Tribunal and guillotined along with his son, daughter-in-law, and granddaughter on April 22, 1794. His sister and two secretaries died as well. Malesherbes died bravely, noting just before his execution that he had been proud to "have sacrificed my existence for him. . . . I would do it again if the situation demanded it."[23]

Jean-Paul Marat (1743–93), the radical editor and Montagnard, was born in Switzerland of a Sardinian father named Mara. He subsequently added the *t* to his name. Unable either to obtain Genevan citizenship or to teach, he studied medicine in Paris and in London. His scientific writings made him famous and won him aristocratic clients. Denied admission to the Academy of Sciences, the embittered scientist turned to politics in 1788 and in 1789 published the journal *L'Ami du Peuple.* Outlawed because of his virulent denunciations of politicians and institutions, he fled to Britain and subsequently to the sewers of

Paris. That last escapade worsened an inflammatory skin disease that he already had contracted and forced him to seek a medicinal bath for relief. Elected to the Convention in 1792, he continued to denounce those he thought were betraying France. Such conspiracies could only be thwarted by purges, by terror, by "200,000 heads." The Girondins had him brought before the Revolutionary Tribunal, where he was acquitted. He did not hesitate to take his revenge. He played a key role in the insurrection of May 31—June 2, which witnessed the proscription of the leading Girondins. Marat was already dying when he admitted to his room a supporter of the Girondins, Charlotte Corday, who stabbed him to death as he was soaking in a medicinal bath. He was immortalized by the painter David in the famous painting of the death scene that became the icon of the Revolution and an emblem of revolutionary propaganda. The revolutionary martyr was commemorated not only in painting and in plaster busts, but in songs and even in names of streets and warships. (Montmartre was renamed Mont-Marat.) The Cordeliers club suspended his embalmed heart from its ceiling. His body was temporarily buried in their garden, then subsequently moved to the Pantheon and after the Themidorean reaction, removed. The father of nine children, his gentleness toward his family makes his revolutionary calls for violence all the more chilling. His demand for massacres, the violence of his polemics, his advocacy of radical revolution, and his calls for a dictator made him a symbol of ultraterrorism.

Marie Antoinette (1755–93) was the wife of Louis XVI of France and the ninth child of the Holy Roman Emperor Francis I and Maria Theresa. Her marriage in 1770 to the then dauphin Louis was designed to strengthen the alliance between France and Austria. Her youth combined with the hostility of many at court who hated the Austrian alliance or disliked her led Marie Antoinette to depend heavily on the Austrian ambassador in France, the competent Florimond Claude Charles, Comte de Mercy-Argenteau, and on a small circle of friends, especially Marie-Thérèse Louise de Savore-Carignan, Princesse de Lamballe and Yolande Comtesse de Polignac. Her dislike of the rigid court etiquette, her love of amusement, and her extravagant spending damaged her reputation as did her interference in court politics on behalf of her favorites. Although both her mother and her brother warned her about the possible consequences of her conduct, her behavior did not change until the birth of her four children (Marie Thérèse Charlotte

[1778], Louis Joseph Xavier François [1781], Louis Charles [1785], and Sophie Hélène Béatrix [1786]), which improved her position but not her popularity. Her enemies exaggerated how much she spent and spread libels, often bawdy, about her. Unusual for the time, Marie Antoinette was both wife and mistress to the king. Although the queen had no understanding of the depth of the economic crisis confronting France and the seriousness of the bread shortage, she never made the oft-quoted callous remark in response to widespread starvation "Let them eat cake." The queen disliked many of the ministers, including both Turgot and Necker, but her influence over court politics, especially during the Revolution, has been exaggerated. It is, nonetheless, true that she abhorred the Revolution and urged the king not to make concessions. Her strong stance on many issues prompted Mirabeau to describe her as "the only man in the family."[24]

The later years of her life were tragic ones. The deaths of her mother (1780); her children, Sophie Hélène Béatrix (1787) and Louis Joseph Xavier François (1789); and her brother Joseph II (1790) greatly saddened her. During the Revolution, she, along with the king, was brought from Versailles to Paris in 1789 (see document 6, "Memoirs of the Duchess of Tourzel on the October Days"), seized at Varennes when the royal family attempted to flee France in 1791, and imprisoned after the mob stormed the Tuileries palace in 1792. Her husband was put on trial and executed in January 1793. Her trial and execution followed in October of that year. The crises of the Revolution showed another side of Marie Antoinette: courage, stoicism, and dignity.

Honore Gabriel Riqueti, Comte de Mirabeau (1749–91), a French revolutionary political leader, was noted for his debauched and extravagant lifestyle, which ruined his health and often landed him in jail. He publicly quarreled with his father, a famous physiocrat who stressed the importance of agriculture and advocated reform of taxation. He was educated at a military school in Paris and, following family tradition, received a commission in a cavalry regiment. He betrayed the government, which had sent him on a secret mission to Prussia in 1786, by publishing his unedited dispatches. He also wrote many pamphlets denouncing the abuses of the ancien régime. In 1789, he was elected a representative of the Third Estate. In the National Assembly he quickly rose to prominence as a moderate. He was a skilled and witty speaker who had the ability to express complicated ideas simply and eloquently. He wanted to establish a constitutional monarchy but was never completely trusted by the court nor by those on the left. Mirabeau also wanted to be a minister of the king, but because the Assembly passed a law that made it illegal for any deputy to accept office from the crown, that avenue was closed. He decided instead to become a secret adviser. In return the king would pay all his debts, which were at the time not insignificant, a monthly stipend, and a large settlement after the Assembly was disbanded. He supported and voted for an absolute veto for the king and urged that the king's authority in foreign affairs be recognized. He tried to serve both camps: the king and the Assembly. When he died suddenly in April 1791, he was buried with much pomp in the Panteón because of his popularity with the people. When his correspondence with the court was discovered, his body was unearthed and moved. In describing Mirabeau's character a contemporary said of him: "He was cowardly but headstrong, with all the intrepidity of impudence. He was dissolute to the greatest degree and boasted of being so; from his youth he had been dishonored by the most shameful of vices, but he set no value upon honor."[25] The historian Furet in characterizing Mirabeau notes that he was an individual "who lived several lives, spoke at least two tongues, one to the king and the other to the assembly, and did not say everything that he believed and did not believe everything that he said."[26]

Jacques Necker (1732–1804), financier, was born in Switzerland. After he moved to Paris, he established his own bank and became a director of the East India Company. He criticized the ideas of the physiocrats, opposed the concept of free trade in grain advanced by Turgot, and loaned the government money, while his wife, Suzanne, hosted an influential salon in Paris. In 1777, the king appointed Necker, who was both a foreigner and a Protestant, director general of finances. In this position he sought to restore financial confidence by enacting reforms and by borrowing at high interest rates to finance the American war. At this time he earned a reputation, probably undeserved, of being a financial genius and a great reformer. As historian Gordon Wright notes, he continued to live on "borrowed time and capital."[27] But it was not to last. In 1781, he published the *Compte Rendu,* which, although it misrepresented the financial situation of France, provided Frenchmen with unprecedented access to the mysteries of the public budget. In the *Compte Rendu* he manipulated the figures to show an excess of income over expenditure and hid the desperate financial plight of the country. When he demanded more power and was refused, he was forced to resign. The critical financial situation forced Louis XVI to recall Necker in 1788. Necker tried to leverage his popularity to convince the king to call the Estates General and agree to the doubling of the Third Estate in order to garner support for financial reform. He was dismissed again in 1789. Later recalled to office, he accepted only with great misgivings, feeling that he was "about to plunge into a pit."[28] As he was. He resigned yet again in 1790, but this time his resignation was greeted only with indifference. Necker opposed the reforms of both Turgot and Calonne and earned the enmity of the queen and the distrust of the king. He was the father of the literary figure Germaine de Staël. Throughout the Revolution, he remained a voice of moderation and as such was attacked by both sides. In his memoirs he noted that it "takes courage to remain loyal to moderate opinions."[29] And he had.

Maximilien François Marie Isidore de Robespierre (1758–94), nicknamed "the Incorruptible" because of the rigor of his principles, was a lawyer from Arras, where he earned a reputation for championing the poor. Self-righteous and personally fastidious, he was a man who hated indecency and uncontrolled emotion. Unquestionably honest and committed to the Revolution, he invariably suspected the intentions of others.He was a slight man of medium height and pale countenance with a curt and affected manner. His tone was "dogmatic and imperious," his laugher "forced and sardonic."[30] Chaste by choice, he scorned licentiousness. He disdained the coarseness of Danton and always dressed elegantly and wore his hair carefully curled and powdered. He was selected at the age of 30 as the representative of Artois to the Estates General. Once in Paris, he became a prominent member of the Jacobin club. Mirabeau said of him that "he will go far; he believes everything he says."[31] In 1791, he proposed and carried the self-denying ordinance by which those who had sat in the previous assembly could not sit in the next. He opposed the declaration of war and founded a journal, *The Defender of the Constitution.* After the overthrow of the king, he was elected to represent Paris in the National Convention. He spoke against the trial of the king, arguing in a famous phrase that "Louis must die, that the country may live." He supported the indictment against the Girondins. On July 27, 1793, he was elected to the Committee of Public Safety. He never dominated that committee, but he did align with Couthon and Saint-Just against the more radical Billaud-Varenne and Collot d'Herbois. A popular and persuasive orator, he defended the committee's policies at the Jacobin club and in the Convention. He participated in the attacks on both Hébert and Danton. As president of the Convention, he presided over the celebration of the Feast of the Supreme Being. His prominence at the celebration forged together a circle of enemies, the representatives on mission who feared that he was moving against them, such as Collot d'Herbois, some dechristianizers on the Committee of General Security, and others who wanted to stop the Terror. After a four-week break, he appeared at the Convention on July 26 and delivered a long harangue full of allegations against unspecified individuals. The next day, he was shouted down, and when he hesitated, was interrupted with "it is the blood of Danton that chokes him." His arrest was voted, but the governor of the prison refused to receive him and the Commune released the other four, Augustin Robespierre, Couthon, Josoph Le Bas, and Saint Just. The five gathered at the city hall and attempted to mobilize the sections. As the forces of the Convention broke in, Robespierre shot himself in the jaw. He and 21 of his supporters were executed on 10 Thermidor (July 28, 1794). Subsequently, 86 others who had supported him paid with their lives.

Jean-Marie Roland de la Platière (1734–93) served as inspector general of commerce and wrote a number of tracts on industry and a number of articles for the *Encyclopédie* under the ancien régime. Widely traveled in Europe, he was outspoken, unbending, irascible, puritanical, and hardworking. He was a member of the Girondins, who came to power in 1792. He and his wife, Jeanne-Marie Manon Plipon (1754–93), 21 years younger than he, made their home in Paris a gathering place for the Girondins and their supporters. Madame Roland, like her husband, was a dedicated revolutionary. She detested the monarchy but had little faith in the common man. To Robespierre she wrote: "The majority of men" were "infinitely contemptible."[32] She was well read, particularly in the *philosophes,* and a great admirer of Rousseau. Although she condemned wars as "scourges for the people,"[33] she supported the Girondins when they declared war against most of Europe. During the Revolution, Roland served twice as minister of the interior: first, appointed by the king in 1792, and second, after the overthrow of the monarchy. Roland supported the Girondins in their call for a vote of the entire people on the guilt of the king and increasingly condemned the Mountain. As the Mountain assumed more power, in 1793, Roland resigned and fled Paris. Madame Roland was condemned to death. Before she was guillotined, she theatrically exclaimed, "O Liberty, what crimes are committed in thy name."[34] Her husband committed suicide after penning a note which ended with "I left my refuge as soon as I heard my wife had been murdered. I no longer desire to remain in a world covered with crime."[35]

Emmanuel Joseph Sieyès (1748–1836), a statesman and theorist, was known as Abbé Sieyès because he had served as a clergyman before the Revolution. He was born in a small town, Fréjus, the fifth child of a minor royal official. He served as canon of Trequier and later as chancellor of the diocese of Chartres. He had the distinction of helping to give birth to the republic and later of burying that same republic. In 1788, he published a small little-noticed tract on privileges. His pamphlet, *What Is the Third Estate?* published in January 1789, made him famous and gained him election to the Estates General as representative of the Third Estate in 1789. He was influential in the writing of the Tennis Court Oath, the Declaration of the Rights of Man and the Citizen, and the constitution of 1791. Most famously, he defined the idea of a nation as a body of individuals living under a common law who voice a common will. He drew a distinction between active citizens, those with property who could vote, and passive citizens, the others, and suggested the division of France into departments. He favored a unicameral assembly but opposed the confiscation of church land as a violation of the right of property. A poor orator who disdained factions, he was not influential in the revolutionary assemblies after 1792. He did not align with either the Girondins or the Jacobins but voted for the death of the king. Silent during the Terror, perhaps because of both timidity and revulsion, he reemerged after Thermidor, was elected to the Council of Five Hundred, and became a Director in 1799. In that same year, he conspired with Talleyrand and Napoleon to overthrow the Directory. Napoleon soon shunted him aside but richly rewarded him for his acquiescence in the new regime with the presidency of the Senate and a generous salary. As a senator, he defended the illegal reprisals against the Jacobins. After the second Bourbon restoration, he went into exile. He returned to Paris with the advent of the Orléanist monarchy in 1830. A commoner who shattered the privileges of an aristocratic elite, a clergyman who had entered the church to make a living and abjured his faith during the Festival of Reason, he had survived.

Charles Maurice de Talleyrand-Périgord (1754–1838) was a member of the old nobility and bishop of Autun. A childhood fall left him lame for life. Because of this accident, he could not join the army but was forced to seek a career in the church. He represented the clergy in the Estates General and was one of the few bishops in the Assembly to take the oath to the Civil Constitution of the Clergy. In 1792 he went to Great Britain, where he was expelled after the execution of the king, and then the United States. He did not return to France until 1796. He briefly served as foreign minister under the Directory (1797–98) and, then under the Consulate and Empire (1799–1807). He supported Napoleon's campaign in Egypt and helped to negotiate the Concordat with the pope in 1801 and Napoleon's marriage to the emperor's daughter, Marie Louise. Napoleon appointed Talleyrand to the lucrative position of grand chamberlain (1803–9). Talleyrand, however, was incapable of loyalty and distrusted Napoleon, who reciprocated, describing him as a piece of horse dung encased in a silk stocking. Talleyrand represented France at the Congress of Vienna (1814–15). After the second Bourbon restoration, he resigned and did not serve again until 1830 when Louis Philippe offered him the ambassadorship to London. Talleyrand was notable for his corruption, his opportunism, and the elasticity of his principles, which enabled him to hold power under the ancien régime, the Revolution, the Consulate and Empire, the Restoration, and the July Monarchy. In his memoirs Talleyrand claimed that he had served 15 governments. When he was dying, he received the last sacrament. Extending his hands, he allegedly said, "Do not forget that I am a bishop."[36]

Notes

1. R. B. Rose, *Tribunes and Amazons, Men and Women of Revolutionary France* (Paddington, Australia: Macleay Press, 1998), 226.

2. R. B. Rose, *Gracchus Babeuf: The First Revolutionary Communist* (Stanford, Calif.: Stanford University Press, 1978), 211.

3. Ibid., 239.

4. Quoted in ibid., 1.

5. Frey and Frey, " 'The Reign of the Charlatans Is Over,' " 711.

6. Quoted in ibid., 712.

7. Keith M. Baker, "Condorcet," in *A Critical Dictionary of the French Revolution,* edited by François Furet and Mona Ozouf (Cambridge, Mass.: Harvard University Press, 1989), 207.

8. Ibid., 209.

9. Miot de Mélito, *Memoirs,* 25.

10. Louis Legendre quoted in ibid., 26.

11. Ibid., 24.

12. Ibid.

13. Quoted in Doyle, *The Oxford History of the French Revolution,* 274.

14. J. Fr. Michaud, *Biographie universelle ancienne et moderne* (1854; reprint, Graz: Akademische Druck u. Verlagsanstalt, 1967), 11: 543–61.

15. Charles François Dumouriez, *La Vie et les mémoires du General Dumouriez* (Paris: Baudouin Frères, 1822), 2:140, 153.

16. Blanning, *The French Revolutionary Wars,* 126.

17. S. Conner, "Olympe de Gouges," in *Historical Dictionary of the French Revolution,* edited by Samuel F. Scott and Barry Rothaus, 2 vols. (Westport, Conn.: Greenwood Press, 1985), 440.

18. Ibid.

19. Doyle, *The Oxford History of the French Revolution,* 421.

20. Ibid., 420.

21. David P. Jordan, *The King's Trial: Louis XVI vs. The French Revolution* (Berkeley,: University of California Press, 1979), 127.

22. John M. S. Allison, *Lamoignon de Malesherbes, Defender and Reformer of the French Monarchy, 1721–1794* (New Haven, Conn.: Yale University Press, 1938), 14.

23. Kelly, *Victims, Authority, and Terror,* 276.

24. Blanning, *The French Revolutionary Wars,* 53.

25. Marmontel, *Memoirs,* 2:257.

26. Furet, *Revolutionary France,* 144.

27. Gordon Wright, *France in Modern Times* (New York: W. W. Norton, 1995), 35.

28. Marcel Gauchet, "Necker," in *A Critical Dictionary of the French Revolution,* edited by François Furet and Mona Ozouf (Cambridge, Mass.: Belknap Press, 1989), 288.

29. Gauchet, "Necker," 287.

30. A. C. Thibadeau, *Mémoires sur la Convention et le Directoire* (Paris: Baudouin Frères, 1824), 1: 58.

31. Furet, *Revolutionary France,* 144.

32. Gita May, *Madame Roland and the Age of Revolution* (New York: Columbia University Press, 1970), 196.

33. Ibid., 211.

34. Ibid., 288.

35. Schama, *Citizens*, 803.

36. E. J. Knapton, "Talleyrand," in *Historical Dictionary of the French Revolution*, edited by Samuel F. Scott and Barry Rothaus, 2 vols. (Westport, Conn.: Greenwood Press, 1985), 931.

Primary Documents of the French Revolution

I Causes

Document 1
Letter of Turgot to Louis XVI

Anne Robert Jacques Turgot (1727–81), the son of a rich merchant, had initially planned to enter the church, but decided instead to become a royal administrator. He served as intendant of Limoges (1761–74), when he instituted a number of key reforms, such as the abolition of manual labor (*corvée*) for public works, and when he wrote a number of works advocating free trade and changes in the tax system. These ideas caught the attention of the king, who appointed him minister of the marine and later comptroller general. In the latter position, he instituted a number of reforms, most notably the preparation of a regular budget and reduction of the deficit. But Turgot's plan for more extensive reforms, presented in his Six Edicts, such as the suppression of forced manual labor (*corvée*) and the abolition of guilds, encountered widespread opposition among powerful individuals including the queen and ultimately led to his downfall in May 1776. An honorable man, he created a powerful coalition of enemies by his attack on privilege and tax exemptions. His contention that only radical reform would avert a revolution unfortunately proved right. His letter to Louis XVI outlines his plans to address the desperate financial plight of France.

August 24, 1774
Sire:

Having just come from the private interview with which your Majesty has honored me, still full of the anxiety produced by the immensity of the duties now imposed upon me, agitated by all the feelings excited by the touching kindness with which you have encouraged me, I hasten to convey to you my respectful gratitude and the devotion of my whole life.

Your Majesty has been good enough to permit me to place on record the engagement you have taken upon you to sustain me in the execution of those plans of economy which are at all times, and to-day more than ever, an indispensable necessity. . . . At this moment, sire, I confine myself to recalling to you these three items:

> No bankruptcy.
> No increase of taxes.
> No loans.
> No *bankruptcy,* either avowed, or disguised in the form of illegal reductions.
> No *increase of taxes;* the reason for this lying in the condition of your people, and, still more, in your Majesty's own generous heart.
> No *loans;* because every loan always diminishes the free revenue and necessitates, at the end of a certain time, either bankruptcy or the increase of taxes. In times of peace it is permissible to borrow only in order to liquidate old debts, or in order to redeem other loans contracted on less advantageous terms.

To meet these three points there is but one means. It is to reduce expenditure below the revenue, and sufficiently below it to insure each year a saving of twenty millions, to be applied to redemption of the old debts. Without that, the first gunshot will force the State into bankruptcy.

The question will be asked incredulously, "On what can we retrench?" and each one, speaking for his own department, will maintain that nearly every particular item of expense is indispensable. They will be able to allege very good reason for their claims, but these must all yield to the absolute necessity of economy. . . .

These are the matters which I have been permitted to recall to your Majesty. You will not forget that in accepting the place of comptroller general I have felt the full value of the confidence with which you honor me; I have felt that you intrust to me the happiness of your people, and, if it be permitted to me to say so, the care of promoting among your people the love of your person and of your authority.

At the same time I feel all the danger to which I expose myself. I foresee that I shall be alone in fighting against abuses of every kind, against the power of those who profit by these abuses, against the crowd of prejudiced people who oppose themselves to all reform, and who are such powerful instruments in the hands of interested parties for perpetuating the disorder. I shall have to struggle even against the natural goodness and generosity of your Majesty, and of the persons who are most dear to you. I shall be feared, hated even, by nearly all the court, by all who solicit favors. They will impute to me all the refusals; they will describe me as a hard man because I shall have advised your Majesty that you ought not to enrich at the expense of your people's subsistence even those that you love.

And this people, for whom I shall sacrifice myself, are so easily deceived that perhaps I shall encounter their hatred by the very measures I take to defend them against exactions. I shall be calumniated (having, perhaps, appearances against me) in order to deprive me of your Majesty's confidence. I shall not regret losing a place which I never solicited. I am ready to resign it to your Majesty as soon as I can no longer hope to be useful in it. . . .

Your Majesty will remember that it is upon the faith of your promises made to me that I charge myself with a burden perhaps beyond my strength, and it is to yourself personally, to the upright man, the just and good man, rather than the king, that I give myself. . . .

Source: James Harvey Robinson and Charles A. Beard, eds., *Readings in Modern European History* (Boston: Ginn and Company, 1908), 1:237–39.

Document 2
Mémoires of Weber

All translations by authors unless otherwise indicated.

Joseph Weber (1755–?), the childhood playmate of Marie Antoinette, followed her to Paris in 1782. He was employed at court until 1789 and witnessed many events of the Revolution, including the August Revolution when he courted danger by attempting to defend the royal family. He was arrested and imprisoned, but luckily escaped the September Massacres, fled to England, and only subsequently returned to the Continent. In this selection he disparages French aid to the American colonies.

One of the most notable Frenchmen to support the American cause was Lafayette (1757–1834) who left officially neutral France to serve in the American army in 1777. Lafayette served as a major general at Valley Forge and at Yorktown and soon won the friendship of George Washington. He was elected to the Estates General and later appointed commander of the National Guard. A moderate who attempted to maintain order, he enjoyed the confidence of neither the court nor the Parisian crowds. He commanded an army in 1792, but when relieved of his command, he fled to the frontier and was captured by the Austrians. Napoleon secured his liberation in 1797.

The enthusiasm of his welcome upon his return from the American colonies in 1779 illustrates the popularity of the American cause. A man of undoubted courage, he became a symbol of the bond between the United States and France. When American troops landed in France in World War I in 1917, John Joseph Pershing allegedly cried out, "Lafayette we are here!" in commemoration of his contribution to the American cause.

A desire to avenge the losses Britain inflicted upon them in the Seven Years' War, along with enthusiasm for the American cause helped to persuade the French to aid the American colonies in 1778. Turgot was one of the few who argued against such intervention on the grounds that it would postpone needed financial reforms. Intervention across the Atlantic helped to trigger the fiscal collapse of the French state. In addition to the financial consequences, that involvement, couched as it was in terms of liberty versus a despotic monarchy, would spread the subversive vocabulary of revolution in France.

But these armies of the land and of the sea, in mixing their flags and their tents with those of the Americans, have heard a new language and have learned to speak it themselves. . . . All these warriors in the prime of life who had run to fight in the new world had left as Frenchmen and returned Americans. They had only sought perils and military glory; they brought back systems and patriotic enthusiasm. They returned in the midst of the court displaying on their chest the scars of wounds received in the fight for liberty and on their clothes the external sign of republican decorations. La Fayette, who had been an ally of the Americans before his king, who with the ardor and the prodigality of all strong passions, but with the secrecy and the perseverance incomprehensible at his age, had armed a ship for the cause of the United States, filled it with munitions of all kinds to the value of a million and had secretly left his family to embark without anyone discovering his secret; La Fayette who had commanded an army of insurgents, who had conquered with them, whom the United States had adopted as its citizen, and whom Washington for six years had called his son; La Fayette returned to his native country, full of the burning desire and the vain illusion of an exotic liberty, which transplanted in France would produce there fruits so different from those that he anticipated.

Source: Joseph Weber, *Mémoires de Weber concernant Marie-Antoinette, archduchesse d'Autriche et reine de France et de Navarre,* edited by Messrs De Berville et Barrière (London: Martin Bossange et Compagnie, 1822), 1: 128–29.

II Early Revolution

Document 3
Memoirs of Miot de Mélito

André-François, Comte de Miot de Mélito (1762–1841), began his career in the military administration, rising to become chief of the bureau, and later chief of the division of the ministry of war. In 1793, he served as secretary general of the department of foreign affairs and, after Thermidor, as commissar. In 1795, the French government sent him to Florence as minister plenipotentiary; in 1796, to Rome as minister extraordinary; and subsequently to Turin. His disagreements with the Directory led to his disgrace. Napoleon brought him back to France, where he was appointed secretary general of the minister of war. Under Napoleon, he served as a member of the Tribunat in 1799, as counselor of state in 1800, as administrator general of Corsica, and as minister of the interior at Naples in 1806. He followed Napoleon's brother Joseph to Madrid and then returned to France and was appointed to the Council of State. During the Restoration, he returned to private life. His translations of Herodotus and of Diodorus won him admission to the French Academy in 1835. His diary was published by his son-in-law. Miot was an eyewitness to many events of the Revolution. The following section records his views of the procession to the church of St. Louis. This religious ceremony preceded the opening of the Estates General on May 5, 1789. As the 1,118 deputies gathered, those of the Third Estate were subjected to numerous slights by the court party and by the decision to follow precedent. Their plain black costumes contrasted with the vestments of the clergy and the silk, swords, and plumes of the nobility. As one deputy noted, "A ridiculous and bizarre law has been imposed upon our arrival by the grand-master of court puerilities."*

Such was the aspect of the Court of Versailles when the States-General were convoked. Neither good faith nor sincerity had dictated this act. Far from seeking to smooth the difficulties as to the method of deliberation, which were raised by the excited state of public feeling, and the twofold representation granted to the Third Estate,** those difficulties were increased by the affected silence maintained on so material a point. The courtiers' last hope was that the obstacles would become so entirely insurmountable as to render the meeting of the States impossible, and for that end they all schemed. As a result of this system, the Deputies arriving at Versailles—and particularly those of the Third Estate—far from being made welcome by the Court, were offended by sarcasms and jests from the Queen's circle and that of the Comte d'Artois. The language, the manners, even the names of these new-comers were turned into ridicule, and the very men who were destined to shine soon afterwards by their superior talent and by their impressive speeches, and to dictate to the Throne and this heedless Court, were at first regarded as provincials whom the fine ladies and gentlemen of Paris and Versailles might mystify with impunity. An obsolete ceremonial, forms of etiquette that had fallen into disuse since greater freedom had penetrated into the atmosphere of the Court, were revived, and thus, between the other two orders and the Deputies of the Third Estate, a line of demarcation, as marked as it was humiliating, was drawn.

In proportion, however, as their reception by the Court was insulting, their welcome in the town was warm and affectionate. They were cordially received into the homes of the citizens, where many of them had arranged to board, and there they freely expressed their resentment and found it shared. Thus, notwithstanding the injunctions of the Court, notwithstanding the dependence upon it of nearly the whole population, the people openly declared themselves in favour of the new opinions, and became so strongly attached to them that in the end they were absolutely hostile to the Court. The sequel has shown that the popular tendencies were not to be despised.

It was in the midst of this agitation that the opening of the States-General took place. I was present, as a spectator, at the ceremony which preceded it on the previous day. In the long procession winding through the wide streets of Versailles, the public remarked with dislike those distinctions of rank and of costume which divided into three separate classes the men on whom our fate was about to depend, and who ought to have possessed equal rights. It was mortifying to see the gold-embroidered cloaks of the noble Deputies, the plumes waving on their caps, the episcopal purple proudly displayed by the clergy, while a humble cloak of black woollen stuff and a plain round cap, a strange costume revived from the feudal ages, marked the Deputies of the Third Estate. Nevertheless, their firm demeanor, their steady gait, their expression of mingled dissatisfaction and confidence, drew all eyes upon them, and they were received with hearty salutations not offered to the other orders. There was a crowd of courtiers round the Princes, but they passed on amid silence. The King's countenance expressed neither emotion nor interest. He advanced, as usual, without dignity, and seemed to be merely accomplishing some duty of etiquette. . . . The Queen, with anxious brow and close-shut lips, made vain endeavors to hide her uneasiness and to impart a look of satisfaction to her noble and majestic countenance; but the weight at her heart, full of anxiety and bitter thoughts, made her unable to maintain it.

    *Quoted in McPhee, *The French Revolution*, 51.

    **The Parlement of Paris's decree of September 1788 that the Estates General would be convoked as in 1614 meant that each order would have an equal number of representatives and voting would be by separate orders. An acrimonious debate had ensued. On December 27, 1788, the king's minister Necker announced that the Third Estate would be doubled; that is, the Third Estate would elect twice as many as each of the other estates. The decree did not, however, stipulate whether they would be voting by head or voting by estate.

Source: André-François, Comte de Miot de Mélito, *Memoirs of Count Miot de Mélito*, edited by General Fleischmann (New York: Scribner, 1881), 6–7.

Document 4
Declaration of the Rights of Man and of the Citizen

Although historians debate who actually drafted this document, they agree that it was influenced by the American Declaration of Independence and the ideas of the Enlightenment and that it is regarded as a sacrosanct part of the French Constitution. On August 26, 1789, the National Assembly adopted this declaration and subsequently incorporated it into the constitution of 1791. The famous historian François Victor Alphonse Aulard referred to it as "the death certificate of the old order"* because it addressed some of the abuses of the old regime. It also reflected the principles of the new revolutionary order because it stressed the rights of the individual and underscored that sovereignty resides in the nation. The universality of its principles echo down to the present day.

Approved by the National Assembly of France, August 26, 1789

The representatives of the French people, organized as a National Assembly, believing that the ignorance, neglect, or contempt of the rights of man are the sole cause of public calamities and of the corruption of governments, have determined to set forth in a solemn declaration the natural, unalienable, and sacred rights of man, in order that this declaration, being constantly before all the members of the social body, shall remind them continually of their rights and duties; in order that the acts of the legislative power, as well as those of the executive power, may be compared at any moment with the objects and purposes of all political institutions and may thus be more respected, and, lastly, in order that the grievances of the citizens, based hereafter upon simple and incontestable principles, shall tend to the maintenance of the constitution and redound to the happiness of all. Therefore the National Assembly recognizes and proclaims, in the presence and under the auspices of the Supreme Being, the following rights of man and of the citizen:

Articles
1. Men are born and remain free and equal in rights. Social distinctions may be founded only upon the general good.
2. The aim of all political association is the preservation of the natural and imprescriptible rights of man. These rights are liberty, property, security, and resistance to oppression.
3. The principle of all sovereignty resides essentially in the nation. No body nor individual may exercise any authority which does not proceed directly from the nation.
4. Liberty consists in the freedom to do everything which injures no one else; hence the exercise of the natural rights of each man has no limits except those which assure to the other members of the society the enjoyment of the same rights. These limits can only be determined by law.

5. Law can only prohibit such actions as are hurtful to society. Nothing may be prevented which is not forbidden by law, and no one may be forced to do anything not provided for by law.

6. Law is the expression of the general will. Every citizen has a right to participate personally, or through his representative, in its foundation. It must be the same for all, whether it protects or punishes. All citizens, being equal in the eyes of the law, are equally eligible to all dignities and to all public positions and occupations, according to their abilities, and without distinction except that of their virtues and talents.

7. No person shall be accused, arrested, or imprisoned except in the cases and according to the forms prescribed by law. Any one soliciting, transmitting, executing, or causing to be executed, any arbitrary order, shall be punished. But any citizen summoned or arrested in virtue of the law shall submit without delay, as resistance constitutes an offense.

8. The law shall provide for such punishments only as are strictly and obviously necessary, and no one shall suffer punishment except it be legally inflicted in virtue of a law passed and promulgated before the commission of the offense.

9. As all persons are held innocent until they shall have been declared guilty, if arrest shall be deemed indispensable, all harshness not essential to the securing of the prisoner's person shall be severely repressed by law.

10. No one shall be disquieted on account of his opinions, including his religious views, provided their manifestation does not disturb the public order established by law.

11. The free communication of ideas and opinions is one of the most precious of the rights of man. Every citizen may, accordingly, speak, write, and print with freedom, but shall be responsible for such abuses of this freedom as shall be defined by law.

12. The security of the rights of man and of the citizen requires public military forces. These forces are, therefore, established for the good of all and not for the personal advantage of those to whom they shall be intrusted.

13. A common contribution is essential for the maintenance of the public forces and for the cost of administration. This should be equitably distributed among all the citizens in proportion to their means.

14. All the citizens have a right to decide, either personally or by their representatives, as to the necessity of the public contribution; to grant this freely; to know to what uses it is put; and to fix the proportion, the mode of assessment and of collection and the duration of the taxes.

15. Society has the right to require of every public agent an account of his administration.
16. A society in which the observance of the law is not assured, nor the separation of powers defined, has no constitution at all.
17. Since property is an inviolable and sacred right, no one shall be deprived thereof except where public necessity, legally determined, shall clearly demand it, and then only on condition that the owner shall have been previously and equitably indemnified.

*Quoted in Sydenham, *The French Revolution,* 64.

Source: Declaration des droits de l'homme et du citoyen / par A. F. Pison du Galland, membre de l'Assemble nationale (Versailles: Chez Baudoin, 1789). (New York Public Library Rare Book Room Call Numbers: KVR KVR 3021; KVR 3022 and KVR 11175) Prepared by Gerald Murphy (The Cleveland Free-Net— aa300). Distributed by the Cybercasting Services Division of the National Public Telecomputing Network (NPTN). http://members.aol.com/agentmess/frenchrev/mancitizen.html

Document 5
Letter of William Eden

William Eden (1745–1814), later Baron Auckland, was educated at Eton and Christ Church, Oxford, and admitted to the bar in 1768. He acted as undersecretary for the northern department from 1772 to 1778, commissioner to North America in 1778, and secretary for Ireland in 1780. As British envoy to France (1786–88), he helped to conclude an important commercial treaty. He subsequently represented Britain as ambassador to Spain (1788–89) and to the United Provinces (1790–94). In this letter he depicts the turmoil in France very early in the Revolution.

　　Francis Godolphin (1751–99), fifth duke of Leeds, served as foreign secretary from 1783 to 1791.

Eden to the Duke of Leeds, September 3, 1789

There are in all the Orders some individuals of great integrity, right meaning, and good talents; but in general they are under intimidation from the lower people of Paris and of the chief Provincial Towns; and there is not yet any man who stands forward with talents and weight to guide the others: In effect the Kingdom of France is at this hour governed by some nameless individuals who assemble every morning and evening at the Hotel de Ville de Paris. The court of Versailles is not only in appearance but in fact in a state of imprisonment. The nominal Ministers of the Country avow without reserve that they are merely nominal. The Church is not only without influence but without respect, and is soon likely to be without bread. The Army is without discipline, and almost without soldiers. The treasury is without money, and nearly without credit; tho' M. Necker's last Rapport (which is an excellent composition) will probably effectuate the new loan of forty millions: and lastly the Magistracy is without power or functions. It is certainly possible that from this chaos some creation may result; but I am satisfied that it must be long before France returns to any state of Existence which can make her a subject of uneasiness to other nations.

Source: Oscar Browning, ed., *Despatches from Paris 1784–1790*, Camden Third series, vol. 19 (London: Camden Society, 1910), 259.

Document 6
Memoirs of the Duchess of Tourzel on the October Days

Louise Elizabeth Félicité Armande Anne Marie Jean Josephine de Croy-Havre, Duchess of Tourzel (1749–1832), provides a vivid eyewitness account of some of the most gripping events of the Revolution. One day after the Bastille fell in 1789, she was appointed governess of the children of Louis XVI and Marie Antoinette, only two of whom were still alive. She succeeded Madame Polignac, who, like many others, chose to emigrate. Unlike many nobles who were devoted to the royal family, the duchess managed to survive.

The scene for the October Days was set on October 1, when the officers of the bodyguard hosted a banquet to celebrate the arrival of the Flanders regiment at Versailles. Rumors spread that the white cockade of the Bourbons and the black of the Habsburgs of Austria had been flaunted and the tricolor trampled. On October 5, a mob of approximately 7,000 women gathered in Paris and marched in the rain and mud to Versailles to demand bread of the Assembly. Upon their arrival, the women were received by the king and promised bread. At dusk, the National Guard of Paris, 15,000 strong, and an additional mob had also marched to Versailles with the intention of "inviting" the king to come to Paris. The next day, some of the crowd burst through an unguarded gate, clashed with the queen's bodyguards, and stabbed the bed from which she had barely escaped. That day, the king agreed to move to Paris as did the Assembly. Force had again trumped the king's indecision. In the following passage Madame Tourzel describes the mob breaking into the palace at Versailles on the morning of October 6.

One portion of the horde spread themselves through the town, forced their way into the barracks of the Body Guard, and massacred everybody they found there, except a few whom they took to the castle gates in order to deliberate as to the punishment they should inflict on them. The other portion forced the gates, and rushed through the courtyards and terraces on the side of the garden with the idea of gaining an entrance into the Castle. These ruffians, who encountered no obstacle, killed two of the Body Guard who were on guard over the apartments of the King's aunts, and had their heads cut off. . . . They then went up the staircase direct to the apartments of the King. The Body guard, though few in number, defended the entrance with the greatest bravery; several of them were dangerously wounded, . . . but they had fortunately time enough to shout, "Save the Queen." Madame Thibaut, her first lady-in-waiting, who luckily had not gone to bed, had only time to give her a dress, and make her take refuge with the King. Hardly had her Majesty left the room than these wretches forced their way in, and furious at not finding her there, they stabbed the bed with their pikes, so as to leave no room for doubt as to the crime they intended to commit.

Source: Louise Elizabeth Félicité Armande Anne Marie Jean Josephine de Croy-Havre, Duchess of Tourzel, *Memoirs of the Duchess de Tourzel* (London: Remington, 1886), 1:33–34.

III Church and State

Document 7
Memoirs of the Duchess of Tourzel on the
Oath to the Civil Constitution of the Clergy

For a background on Madame Tourzel, see Document 6, "Memoirs of the Duchess of Tourzel on the October Days."

The appropriation of church property in November 1789 had been followed by a Civil Constitution of the Clergy adopted in July 1790. That constitution eliminated some bishoprics, reallocated others according to departmental lines, provided for the election of bishops and priests, and stipulated that civil authorities were to pay their salaries. Subsequently, the Assembly passed a law requiring all clergy to take an oath to the civil constitution. Refusal meant loss of office. Swearing the oath mean excommunication. As one bishop declared, "I belong to my flock in life and in death. . . . If God wishes to test his own, the eighteenth century, like the first century, will have its martyrs."* In the Assembly in January 1791, two-thirds of the *curés* and every bishop present, except for Talleyrand and Gobel, refused to take the oath.** In the country, as a whole only four bishops and approximately half of the 50,000 *curés* in France took the oath.*** Some who took the oath later retracted it. Despite the hostility of the crowd and a number of procedural maneuvers, the nonjurors (those who did not take the oath) did not waver. Madame Tourzel describes the atmosphere surrounding the clergy who took or refused to take the oath to the Civil Constitution of the Clergy in the National Assembly.

The Assembly . . . on the 4th of January 1791, the day on which the eight days allowed to the clergy expired, exacted the oath from the bishops, priests, and other ecclesiastics who were members of the Assembly, and decreed that they should present themselves in alphabetical order to take it. The crowds which surrounded the hall made the air resound with their shouts and menaces, hoping by means of their horrid din to succeed in frightening the clergy under such critical circumstances. They failed in their attempts, and the day will be for ever memorable in the annals of the Church. The Bishop of Agen,**** who was the first to speak, declared that he had no regret either for his position or his fortune, but that as he was obliged to listen to the voice of his conscience, he could only express to the Assembly his regret at not being able to take the oath. All the bishops, with the exception of those above enumerated, refused each in his turn. . . . "I am seventy years of age," said the Bishop of Poitiers;***** "I have spent thirty-five of them in the episcopate, in which I have done all the good in my power. Overwhelmed with years and infirmities, I will not dishonour my old age by taking an oath against my conscience and I will bear my fate in patience." This touching speech was received with hooting from the galleries and the Left of the Assembly.

*Quoted in Doyle, *Oxford History of the French Revolution*, 143.

**Jean-Baptiste-Joseph Gobel (1727–94) was later elected constitutional bishop of Paris. He would renounce Christianity in 1793 and be executed with the Hébertists in April 1794. John McManners, *The French Revolution and the Church* (New York: Harper and Row, 1969), 47.

***Aston, *The End of an Elite*, 245.

****Jean-Louis d'Usson de Bonnac (1734–1821) had been appointed in 1767. He went to Switzerland and then to Bavaria.

*****Martial-Louis de Beaupoil de Sainte-Aulaire (1719–1798) had been appointed in 1759.

Source: Tourzel, *Memoirs,* 1:238.

Document 8
Letter of the Archbishop of Embrun

Pierre Louis de Leyssin (1724–1801), the archbishop of Embrun in southeast France from 1767 to 1801, had attended the meeting of the estates of Dauphiné from December 1788 to January 1790. When the archbishop refused to take the oath, seals were put on the cathedral. In 1791, the archbishopric, which had been created circa 800, was eliminated and the area put under the jurisdiction of the new diocese of Gap. In May 1791, the election of a constitutional bishop provoked Leyssin's flight, first to Italy and then to Lausanne in 1796.

He wrote the following letter to François-Joachim de Pierre, Cardinal de Bernis (1715–94), who had served as secretary of state for foreign affairs from 1757 to 1758. Bernis had taken the oath but only after adding a qualification about his religious obligations. That qualification cost him both the ambassadorship at Rome, which he had held since 1769, and the archbishopric of Albi, which he had held since 1764. An opponent of the Revolution, he was proscribed as an émigré and his estates in France looted. He remained in Rome and died there at the age of 79. In 1800, his body was taken back to Nîmes.

Archbishop d'Embrun to Cardinal de Bernis, October 30, 1790
Monseigneur, Your eminence knows the deplorable situation of France. The state is ruined, all the orders are destroyed, and religion especially is totally ruined. The new ecclesiastical constitution puts the realm in a state of schism and heresy. That is the unanimous sentiment of the clergy of France. The bishops of the Assembly have protested, those outside have done so with all the energy that the circumstances demand. They have been silent up to now because of their regard for the papacy. They know that his Majesty has consulted the sovereign pontiff and they await his decision with that filial submission which the clergy of France has never lost. If . . . the Holy Father by some softening, lets subsist in all or in part the actual regime, I see no other expedient, religion is exiled forever from the French empire. We will lack subjects, we will be regarded as base mer-

cenaries whom the people will believe beneath them because they pay them; and you know that the good that one can do depends on the consideration one enjoys. If, on the contrary, the Sovereign Pontiff decides with all the magnificence that surrounds Rome, that this deplorable constitution is not admissible in principle, that it is contrary to the order established by Jesus Christ himself and recognized by all the Catholic church, then courage will be reborn. The *curés* who have lost all by ignorance or by self-interest will have no more excuses. They begin to realize that they have been dupes; they only seek a pretext to abandon their apostasy. Then they will instruct the people, they will have as backing the imposing authority of a solemnly pronounced bull; and I believe that I can assure your eminence of the success of their applications. Opinion begins to change, enthusiasm is dissipating; there are no more aristocrats or democrats. The discontented class absorbs all the others. The bull of the sovereign pontiff, the assignats, the taxes and especially the sentiment of misfortune will do the rest; calm will be reestablished.

Source: R. P. Augustin Theiner, ed., *Documents inédits relatifs aux affaires religieuses de la France 1790 à 1800: Extraits des archives secrètes du Vatican* (Paris: Didot Frères, 1857), 1:297–98.

Document 9
Declaration of Guillaume Tollet

> Nevers in central France was the seat of a bishopric from the sixth century. Guillaume Tollet served as the constitutional bishop of the department of Nièvre, but ultimately felt compelled to resign, as he explains in the following document.

Nevers, July 27, 1795

I, the undersigned, declare that having been nominated to the bishopric of the department of Nièvre whose seat was established at Nevers by the Civil Constitution of the Clergy, decreed by the National Assembly and accepted by the king, I believed immediately after my consecration to prove sufficiently my sincere attachment to the Papacy and my ardent desire to live in the communion of the Church, by my letter of 25 March 1791 dated from Paris, in which in informing the Sovereign Pontiff of my nomination and my consecration, I asked his communion and his apostolic blessing.

But considering that this same Civil Constitution of the Clergy even though it was not annulled by the National Convention of France, was not approved by the pope because it contained many heresies, in brief terms, that even more I was instructed in a definitive way that the universal church had agreed to the condemnation pronounced by the Pope against this same Civil Constitution of the Clergy.

I declare that submissive to the spirit and the heart of decisions of our mother the holy Catholic church, apostolic and roman, I adhere to the judgment of the Church regarding the Civil Constitution of the Clergy.

In consequence, in order to eliminate all cause of division among the faithful and by this means to carry out the grand work of God in the reestablishment of our august religion,

I declare finally to the Sovereign Pontiff, to the entire Church, as well as to all the faithful of this diocese, that I give up my nomination to the bishopric of the department of Nièvre, and that I promise to no longer fulfill any of its duties.

Source: Theiner, *Documents,* 1:438–39.

IV The Fate of the King

Document 10
Letter of Louis XVI

When Louis XVI and his family fled Paris on June 20, 1791, he left a note revealing his true feelings about the Revolution. Unfortunately, he also left behind incriminating evidence that was later used to convict him. The realization that he and his family were prisoners, the conviction that he could not as a good Catholic agree to the confiscation of church land and the oath imposed on the clergy, and his increasing impotence helped to persuade the royal family to flee. Apprehended, they were forced to return to Paris where it is said that the queen's hair turned gray.

Louis XVI's letter, June 20, 1791, presented to the National Assembly June 21, 1791

While the king had any hope of seeing order and happiness restored, by the means employed by the national assembly, and by his residence near the assembly, no sacrifice would have appeared to him too great, . . . he would not even have mentioned his own personal deprivation of liberty, from the month of October 1789. But at present, when the result of every transaction is only the destruction of royalty, the violation of property, and the endangering of persons; when there is an entire anarchy through every part of the empire, without the least appearance of any authority sufficient to control it; the king after protesting against all the acts performed by him during his captivity, thinks it his duty to submit to the French nation the following account of his conduct. . . .

The king thus saw himself a prisoner in his own state; for in what other condition could he be, who was forcibly surrounded by persons whom he suspected? . . .

The societies of friends of the constitution are by much the strongest powers and render void the actions of all others. . . .

The king was declared the head of the government of the kingdom, and he has been unable to change any thing without the consent of the assembly. The chiefs of the prevailing party have thrown out such a defiance to the agents of the king, and the punishment inflicted upon disobedience has excited such apprehensions, that these agents have remained without power.

The form of government is especially vicious in two respects. The assembly exceeds the bounds of their power, in taking cognizance of the administration of justice, and of the interior parts of the kingdom; and exercises, by its committee of researches, the most barbarous of all despotisms. Associations are established under the name of friends of the constitution, which are infinitely more dangerous than the ancient corporations. They deliberate upon all the functions of government, and exercise a power of such preponderance, that all other bodies, without excepting the national assembly itself, can do nothing but by their order. . . .

Frenchmen! Was it this you intended in electing representatives? Do you wish that the despotism of clubs should be substituted for the monarchy under which the kingdom has flourished for fourteen centuries? . . .

Thus perceiving the impossibility of averting any public evil by his influence, it is natural that he should seek a place of safety for himself.

Frenchmen! And you the good inhabitants of Paris, distrust the suggestions of the factious; return to your king, who will always be your friend; your holy religion respected; your government placed upon a permanent footing; and liberty established upon a secure basis.

Source: The Annual Register, or a View of the History, Politics, and Literature for the Year 1791 (London: G. Auld, n.d.), 158–62.

Document 11
Speech of Robespierre, Asking the Death Penalty for Louis XVI

One of the most compelling speakers of the Revolution, Maximilien Robespierre (1758–94), a lawyer, later served on the Committee of Public Safety during the Terror.

After the royal family's abortive flight in 1791, the king's decision to sign the constitution won him a brief reprieve. But the war doomed him. After the second revolution of August 10 and the overthrow of the monarchy, the royal family was imprisoned. The discovery on November 20, 1792, of an iron safe that contained incriminating letters from Louis made a trial inevitable. The king was arraigned in November and tried in December 1792. He was ably defended by Malesherbes, who had volunteered for that dangerous assignment and would later pay with his life for that service. The king was condemned to death and then guillotined on January 21, 1793. He met his fate with undaunted courage.

December 3, 1792

Citizens! . . . The point is not merely that of trying the King. Louis is not the accused. You are not the judges! You are—you cannot be other than statesmen, the representatives of the nation. You have not to give a judgment for or against an individual; on the contrary, you must adopt a measure of public welfare, achieve an act of national wisdom. In a republic, a dethroned king is a source of danger; he will either endanger the safety of the state and attempt to destroy liberty, or he will take steps to consolidate both. . . . Our object should be to engrave deep in the hearts of men a contempt for royalty, and to terrify all the King's supporters. . . .

Louis was King and the Republic was founded. The question before you is disposed of by these few words alone. Louis was dethroned by his crimes. Louis denounced the French people as counter-revolutionaries; to conquer them he summoned the armies of the tyrants, his brothers. The victory and the masses have decided that it was he who was the rebel. Louis cannot be judged. He is already condemned, or we have no republic. To propose now that we begin to try Louis XVI would be equivalent to retracing our steps to royal or constitutional despotism. This is a counter-revolutionary idea, for it means nothing more nor less than to indict the Revolution itself. In fact, if it is still possible to make Louis the object of a trial, it is also possible he may be acquitted. He may be not guilty, nay, even more: it may be assumed, before the sentence is pronounced, that he has committed no crime. But if Louis may be declared guiltless, if Louis may go free of punishment, what will then become of the Revolution? If Louis is guiltless, all the defenders of freedom are liars, all those faithful to the King, all the counter-revolutionaries, are friends of truth and the defenders of oppressed innocence, all the manifestoes, pamphlets and intrigues of foreign courts, all these are merely legitimate and proper articles of complaint. In this case, the arrest of Louis was an injustice, an act of oppression, and the people's committees of Paris, all the patriots of France, these are the guilty ones. . . .

All the bloodthirsty hordes of foreign despotism are ready to wage war against us in the name of Louis XVI. From the recesses of his prison Louis fights us, and yet we still ask whether he is guilty, we still ask whether he may be treated as an enemy? . . .

Louis must die in order that the nation may live. In more peaceful times, once we have secured respect and have consolidated ourselves within and without, it might be possible for us to consider generous proposals. But to-day, when we are refused our freedom; to-day, when, after so many bloody struggles, the severity of the law as yet assails only the unhappy; to-day, when it is still possible for the crimes of tyranny to be made a subject of discussion; on such a day there can be no thought of mercy; at such a moment the people cries for vengeance. I request you to come to a decision at once concerning the fate of Louis. . . . Louis XVI must at once be proclaimed by the National Assembly a traitor to the nation, a criminal against mankind, and the judgment must be carried out on the same square on which the great martyrs of freedom died on August 10.

Source: Speeches of Maximilien Robespierre with a Biographical Sketch (New York: International Publishers, 1927), 46–49, 51.

V The September Massacres

Document 12
Journal of Jourgniac de Saint-Meard

The September Massacres (September 2–7, 1792) were a series of
massacres of those in nine prisons mostly in Paris. Ignited by fears
of counterrevolutionaries and the news that Verdun had fallen to
the Prussians, mobs tortured and butchered approximately 1,300
people, including women and children. The commune of Paris
subsequently reimbursed these killers for their loss of wages. Danton, who was minister of justice in name only, allegedly said that
the prisoners had to look after themselves. These massacres reflect
not only the power of mobs but also the weakness of the revolutionary government.

At half-past two o'clock on Sunday, September 2, we prisoners saw three
carriages attended by a crowd of frantic men and women. They went on
to the Abbey cloister, which had been converted into a prison for the
clergy. In a moment after, we heard that the mob had just butchered all
the ecclesiastics, who, they said, had been put into the fold there.—
Near four o'clock. The piercing cries of a man whom they were hacking
into pieces with hangers, drew us to the turret-window of our prison,
whence we saw a mangled corpse on the ground opposite to the door.
Another was butchered in the same manner a moment afterwards.—
Near seven o'clock. We saw two men enter our cell with drawn swords in
their bloody hands. A turnkey showed the way with a flambeau, and
pointed out the bed of the unfortunate Swiss soldier, Reding. At this
frightful moment, I was clasping his hand, and endeavoring to console
him. One of the assassins was going to lift him up, but the poor Swiss
stopped him by saying in a dying tone of voice, "I am not afraid of
death; pray, sir, let me be killed here." He was, however, borne away on
the men's shoulders, carried into the street, and there murdered.—*Ten
o'clock Monday morning.* The most important matter that now employed
our thoughts, was to consider what posture we should put ourselves in,
when dragged to the place of slaughter, in order to receive death with
the least pain. We sent, from time to time, some of our companions to
the turret-window, to inform us of the attitude of the victims. They
brought us back word, that those who stretched out their hands, suffered the longest, because the blows of the cutlasses were thereby weak-

ened before they reached their head; that even some of the victims lost their hands and arms, before their bodies fell; and that such as put their hands behind their backs, must have suffered much less pain. We calculated the advantages of this last posture and advised one another to adopt it, when it should come to our turn to be butchered. *One o'clock Tuesday morning.* After enduring inconceivable tortures of mind, I was brought before my judges, proclaimed innocent, and set free.

Source: Extract from the journal, entitled "My Thirty-Eight Hours Agony," by M. Jourgniac de Saint-Meard, quoted in Adolphe Thiers, *The History of the French Revolution,* translated by Frederick Shoberl (Philadelphia: Carey and Hart, 1848), 1:360.

Document 13
Memoirs of Miot de Mélito

For the background of Miot, see document 3, "Memoirs of Miot de Mélito."

Miot de Mélito found himself in an increasingly dangerous position as the war ministry became more radical after August 10, 1792, the so-called second revolution, when a mob besieged the palace and overthrew the king. His career of more than 25 years made him suspect with the radical *sans-culottes,* who increasingly staffed the ministry. The politicization and radicalization of the war ministry endangered individuals such as Miot, many of whom were purged on August 10.*

I had been settled in Paris since October 1789, and I continued in the service of the Military Administration which I had entered at Versailles. I occupied at first the post of "Chief of the Bureau," and afterwards that of "Chief of Division," under the different Ministers who succeeded each other at the War Department up to August 10, 1792.

I was included at this period in the proscription which fell upon a great number of Government employees, and I was to have been arrested and thrown into prison, where I should probably have been one of the victims of the massacres of the 2d of September. But, fortunately as it turned out, I was anxious about the health of my wife and daughter, then at Versailles, and on the very morning of the 10th of August I had left Paris by the Clichy Gate, and had made my way to Versailles. . . . During my progress, the noise of cannon and musket shots in Paris caused me terrible anguish of mind; but I only hastened the more quickly on my way, and reached Versailles about noon, trembling with apprehension, ignorant of what had taken place in Paris, and unable to reply to any of the questions put to me. In the evening the details of that terrible day became known. I concealed myself carefully on the morrow, fearing to be arrested as non-domiciled, and on the succeeding day (August 12) I took my place in one of the little carriages that for some time had been running between Versailles and Paris. We passed without difficulty through the gates, which were closed against all who wanted to leave the city, but freely open to all in-comers. On reaching my father's house I found that a warrant for my arrest had been issued, and that a search had been made for me, in order that it might be put in force. I also heard that my brother-in-law, M. Arcambal, Commissioner-Director of War and Secretary-General of the Ministry, and my uncle M. Vauchelle, chief Clerk of Artillery, had already been arrested. After acquainting me with this sad news, my father added that he had stated that he did not know where I was, but I might be heard of at the residence of the War Minister.

Thereupon I quickly decided on my course of action, which was to proceed to the War Office. I learnt there from my fellow-clerks that emissaries of the Commune had in fact come on the previous day to arrest me; that, not finding me, they had left one of their number behind to seize me on my return, and enforce the warrant against me, but that the individual, weary of waiting to no purpose, had departed, and had not since reappeared. The Legislative Assembly had appointed M. Lacuée, one of its members, to administer the department until the arrival of the new Minister of War. I thought it right to wait upon him, and found him, wearing a tricolor sash, and installed in the Minister's cabinet. I told him that I presented myself, in order that he might not suspect me of trying to escape the search now being made for me. He received me politely, said he had no orders to take any steps against me, but that, on the contrary, he requested me to return to my work, and to assist him in the difficult position in which he found himself. He complained of the excesses of the Commune in Paris, which had disorganized every official department by its arbitrary arrests; and in fact he was equally indignant at the acts of that seditious authority as he was powerless to repress them.

I therefore resumed my usual occupations, expecting every instant to be arrested at my desk. But I was not arrested; either it was believed that the warrant had already been executed, or I was forgotten; at all events, I remained at liberty. I even had the very great happiness of saving one of our friends, M. Jullien, who took refuge in my house, and of aiding with him in the release of my uncle and my brother-in-law, whom I have mentioned above, and who were, marvelous to relate, set at liberty a few days before the 2d of September. . . .

When a man appointed by the Paris Commune made his appearance at the Ministry of War, I believed myself irrecoverably lost, and I confidently expected the reappearance of all the officials who had been formerly employed. . . . But, to my great surprise, Bouchotte** [Minister of War] did not reinstate them. He even insisted on retaining me, treated me with the fullest confidence in everything regarding the affairs of the Administration, neither inquired into my political opinions, alluded on any occasion to his own, nor solicited me to embrace them, although I worked with him many hours daily. Nevertheless, I felt my position to be one of constant constraint. A reverse to our troops, an act of forgetfulness or of negligence, anything that should give room for the most trivial denunciation, might bring irretrievable ruin upon me, and I ardently longed to escape from so critical a position. I saw that I owed the consideration with which I was treated solely to the necessity that existed for making use of my experience in the Administration, and that so soon as that necessity should subside, I should be left alone and without a protector to repel the attacks upon me that would inevitably be renewed. I was convinced that the Minister would not willingly dismiss, nor would he denounce me, but I was also aware that he had some difficulty in maintaining his own position, and that, as he was obliged to purchase by continual concessions such protection as was afforded him by the party which had placed him in office, he would be unable to defend me, and certainly would not for my sake put his own popularity in peril. While I was in this state of perplexity, an opportunity of leaving my perilous post offered itself, and I eagerly embraced it. . . . [Miot then moved to the Ministry of Foreign Affairs.]

In this way, with less personal danger that I had hitherto incurred in the terrible storm then devastating France, I passed through the six months which elapsed between June 1793 and the end of the year. . . .

*Howard G. Brown, *War, Revolution and the Bureaucratic State: Politics and Army Administration in France 1791–1799* (Oxford: Clarendon Press, 1995), 8.

**Jean-Baptiste Noël Bouchotte, a radical, had been the president of the Jacobin club at Cambrai but unknown on the national scene. He served as minister of war in April 1793 until April 1794. Under pressure from the Parisian radicals, he filled the posts under him for the most part with extremists.

Source: Miot, *Memoirs*, 18–19, 22–23, 24.

VI Terror

Document 14
Report of Robespierre on the
Principles of a Revolutionary Government

For a background on Robespierre, see document 11, "Speech of Robespierre, Asking the Death Penalty for Louis XVI." In this speech delivered on December 25, 1793, Robespierre offered a justification for the Committee of Public Safety's position. Professor Palmer argues that this speech answered the question "What is the purpose of the Terror?" and served as the "first statement in modern times of a philosophy of dictatorship."*

Citizens, members of the Convention! . . .

The defenders of the Republic will be guided by Caesar's maxim, and believe that nothing has been accomplished so long as anything remains to be accomplished.

To judge by the power and the will of our republican soldiers, it will be easy to defeat the English and the traitors. But we have another task of no less importance, but unfortunately of greater difficulty. This task is the task of frustrating, by an uninterrupted excess of energy, the eternal intrigues of all enemies of freedom within the country, and of paving the way for the victory of the principles on which the general weal depends. . . .

The goal of a constitutional government is the protection of the Republic; that of a revolutionary government is the establishment of the Republic.

The Revolution is the war waged by liberty against its foes—but the Constitution is the regime of victorious and peaceful freedom.

The Revolutionary Government will need to put forth extraordinary activity, because it is at war. It is subject to no constant laws, since the circumstances under which it prevails are those of a storm, and change with every moment. This government is obliged unceasingly to disclose new sources of energy to oppose the rapidly changing face of danger.

Under constitutional rule, it is sufficient to protect individuals against the encroachments of the state power. Under a revolutionary regime, the state power itself must protect itself against all that attack it.

The revolutionary government owes a national protection to good citizens; to its foes it owes only death. . . .

Is the revolutionary government, by reason of the greater rapidity of its course and the greater freedom of its movements than are characteristic of an ordinary government, therefore less just and less legitimate? No, it is based on the most sacred of all laws, on the general weal and on the ironclad law of necessity!

The government has nothing in common with anarchy or disorder; on the contrary, its goal requires the destruction of anarchy and disorder in order to realize a dominion of law. It has nothing in common with autocracy, for it is not inspired by personal passions.

The measure of its strength is the stubbornness and perfidy of its enemies; the more cruelly it proceeds against its enemies, the closer is its intimacy with the republicans; the greater the severities required from it by circumstances, the more must it recoil from unnecessary violations of private interests, unless the latter are demanded by the public necessity. . . .

Let us beware of slaying patriotism in the delusion that we are healing and moderating it. . . .

Either we shall rule, or the tyrants will rule us. What are the resources of our enemies in this war of treachery and corruption waged by them against the Republic? All the vices fight for them; the Republic has all the virtues on its sides. . . .

By virtue of five years of treason, by virtue of feeble precautions, and by virtue of our gullibility, Austria, England, Russia and Italy have had time to set up, as it were, a secret government in France, a government that competes with the French government. They have their secret committees, their treasures, their agents, they absorb men from us and appropriate them to themselves, they have the unity that we lack, they have the policy that we have often neglected, they have the consistency which we have so often failed to show.

Foreign courts have for some time been spewing out on French soil their well-paid criminals. Their agents still infect our armies, . . . All the bravery of our soldiers, all the devotion of our generals, and all the heroism of the members of this Assembly had to be put forth to defeat treason. These gentlemen still speak in our administrative bodies, in the various sections; they secure admission to the clubs; they sometimes may be found sitting among us; they lead the counter-revolution; they lurk about us, they eavesdrop on our secrets; they flatter our passions and seek even to influence our opinions and to turn our own decisions against us. When you are weak, they praise our caution. When you are cautious, they accuse us of weakness. Your courage they designate as audacity, your justice as cruelty. If we spare them, they will conspire publicly; if we threaten them, they will conspire secretly or under the mask of patriotism. . . . We are surrounded by their hired assassins and their spies. We know this, we witness it ourselves, and yet they live! . . . Our only possible answer to their pamphlets and lies is to destroy them. And we shall know how to hate the enemies of our country.

It is not in the hearts of the poor and the patriots that the fear of terror must dwell, but there in the midst of the camp of foreign brigands, who would bargain for our skin, who would drink the blood of the French people. . . .

*Palmer, *Twelve Who Ruled,* 265.

Source: Robespierre, *Speeches,* 61–64, 66–69.

Document 15
The Law of Suspects

The Law of Suspects, passed on September 17, 1793, provided the legal basis of the Terror by endowing the Committee of Public Safety and its agents with considerable power to arrest vaguely defined groups of individuals.

1. Immediately after the publication of the present decree, all suspected persons who are within the territory of the Republic and who are still at liberty, are to be arrested.
2. The following are considered suspected persons: 1. those who by their conduct, association, speech or writings have shown themselves partisans of tyranny or federalism and enemies of liberty; 2. those who cannot justify in the manner prescribed by the decree of 21 March last their means of existence and the performance of their civic duties; 3. those who have been refused certificates of civism; 4. public functionaries who have been suspended or dismissed from their positions by the National Convention or by its commissioners, and not reinstated, notably those who have been or are to be dis-

missed by virtue of the decree of 14 August last; 5. those former nobles, including their husbands, wives, fathers, mothers, sons or daughters and agents of the *émigrés* who have not constantly manifested their attachment to the revolution; 6. those who have emigrated in the interval between 1 July 1789 and the publication of the decree of 30 March–8 April 1792 even though they may have returned to France in the period fixed by the decree or prior to it.

3. The committees of surveillance established by the decree of 21 March last or those substituted for them, either by the orders of the representatives of the people sent to the armies or to the departments, or by virtue of the particular decrees of the National Convention are charged with drawing up each in its own *arrondissement* the list of suspected persons, with issuing a writ for their arrest, and having seals placed on their papers. Commanders of the public force to whom such warrants are sent are responsible for implementing them immediately under penalty of dismissal.

4. The members of the committee may order the arrest of any individual only if seven are present and only with an absolute majority of votes.

5. The individuals arrested as suspects are first to be taken to jails in the place of their detention; in default of jails, they are to be kept under surveillance in their respective dwellings.

6. During the following week, they are to be transferred to national buildings which the administrations of the department are responsible to designate and to prepare for this purpose immediately after the receipt of this decree.

7. The detained may have their essential belongings brought to the buildings; they are to remain there under guard until the peace.

8. The costs of custody are to be charged to the detainees and are to be divided among them equally: this custody shall be confided preferably to fathers of a family and to relatives of citizens who are or may go to the frontiers. The salary for this is fixed for each man of the guard at the value of one and one-half days of labor.

9. The committees of surveillance shall send without delay to the committee of general security of the National Convention, the list of persons who have been arrested, with the reasons for their arrest and the papers they have seized.

10. The civil and criminal tribunals if there is occasion may have detained and sent to the jails described above, those accused of crimes concerning which it has been declared that there was no occasion for indictment or who have been acquitted of charges brought against them.

Source: J. B. Duvergier, ed., *Collection complète des lois, décrets, ordonnances, règlemens* (Paris: Guyot, 1834), 6:172–73.

Document 16
Decree on Revolutionary Government 19
Vendémiaire, year II (October 10, 1793)

After the suspension of the constitution of 1793, this decree served as the legal basis of the government and underscored the dominance of the Committee of Public Safety. Note that the government of this decree is an emergency government and a revolutionary government, but not a constitutional government.

The Government

1. The provisional government of France is revolutionary until the peace.
2. The provisional executive council, the ministers, the generals, and the constituted bodies are placed under the surveillance of the committee of public safety, which will render an account thereof weekly to the Convention.
3. Every measure of security is to be taken by the provisional executive council, under the authorization of the committee, which will render an account thereof to the Convention.
4. The revolutionary laws must be executed quickly. The Government shall correspond immediately with the districts on measures of public safety.
5. The generals in chief are to be appointed by the National Convention on the recommendation of the Committee of Public Safety.
6. Because the inertia of the government is the cause of reverses, the time allowed for the execution of decree and of the measure of public safety are set. The violations of these time periods shall be punished as an attack on liberty.

Supplies

7. The table of grain production of each district, compiled by the committee of public safety, will be printed and distributed to all members of the Convention, to be put into effect without delay.
8. The necessities of each department will be approximately evaluated and guaranteed. The superfluous supplies will be subject to requisition.
9. The table of production of the republic will be sent to the representatives of the people, to the ministers of the marine and of the interior, and to the administrators of supplies. They shall requisition in the *arrondissements* assigned to them. Paris will have a special *arrondissement*.
10. Requisitions for the benefit of the unproductive departments are to be authorized and regulated by the provisional executive council.
11. Paris shall be provisioned for one year on March 1.

General Security

12. The direction and employment of the revolutionary army shall be regulated immediately in order to repress counter-revolutionaries. The committee of public safety shall present a plan to accomplish this.

13. The council shall dispatch a garrison into cities where counterrevolutionary movements have arisen. The garrisons are to be paid and maintained by the wealthy of these cities until the peace.

Finances

14. A tribunal and a jury of accounts shall be created. This tribunal and this jury shall be appointed by the National Convention; they shall be responsible for prosecuting all who have managed public funds since the revolution and with demanding of them an account of their assets. The organization of this tribunal is referred to the legislative committee.

Source: Duvergier, *Collection,* 6:219–20.

Document 17
Camille Desmoulins's Plea for Clemency

Camille Desmoulins (1760–94), a member of the Convention, was a noted journalist and pamphleteer who published the journal *Le Vieux Cordelier.* A painful stammer prevented him from being a skilled orator. Politically, he voted for the death of the king and attacked the Girondins. Robespierre, a friend of Desmoulins for more than 20 years, in an attempt to divorce Desmoulins the man from his writings, urged the burning of his works to which Desmoulins retorted, "I reply—with Rousseau—burning is no answer."* Both he and Danton advocated a more moderate approach; they wanted to mitigate the Terror. In the third issue of *Le Vieux Cordelier,* Desmoulins had allegedly provided a translation of the ancient Roman author Cornelius Tacitus. It depicts a society gripped by fear, violence, duplicity, and denunciation. This attack on extremism was very popular and, as it turned out, dangerous for the author. Robespierre and the rest of the Committee of Public Safety (with the exception of Robert Lindet who purportedly said that he was there "to feed patriots, not to kill them"), signed the death warrant for both Danton and Desmoulins.** At his trial, Desmoulins was not allowed to defend himself. Nor was he present when the sentence of death was passed. His beautiful wife Lucille was executed shortly afterward. Following is an excerpt from the fourth issue of *Le Vieux Cordelier,* 30 Frimaire, year II (December 20, 1793), in which Desmoulins urges a policy of clemency. According to Miot, he was "horror-struck at the terri-

ble scenes which passed before his eyes every day, and was endeav-
ouring to arouse a spirit of humanity."***

Some persons have expressed their disapproval of my third issue,
where, as they allege, I have been pleased to suggest certain compar-
isons which tend to cast an unfavorable light on the Revolution and the
patriots—they should say the excess of revolution and the professional
patriots. My critics think the whole number refuted and everybody justified by the single reflection, "We all know that the present situation is
not one of freedom—but patience! you will be free one of these days.

Such people think apparently that liberty, like infancy, must of
necessity pass through a stage of wailing and tears before it reaches
maturity. On the contrary, it is of the nature of liberty that, in order to
enjoy it, we need only desire it. A people is free the moment that it
wishes to be so—you will recollect that this was one of Lafayette's say-
ings—and the people has entered upon its full rights since the 14th of
July. Liberty has neither infancy nor old age, but is always in the prime
of strength and vigor. . . .

Is this liberty that we desire a mere empty name? Is it only an
opera actress carried about with a red cap on, or even that statue, forty-
six feet high, which David proposes to make? If by liberty you do not
understand, as I do, great principles, but only a bit of stone, there never
was idolatry more stupid and expensive than ours. Oh, my dear fellow-
citizens, have we sunk so low as to prostrate ourselves before such
divinities? No, heaven-born liberty is no nymph of the opera, nor a red
liberty cap, nor a dirty shirt and rags. Liberty is happiness, reason,
equality, justice, the Declaration of Rights, your sublime constitution.

Would you have me recognize this liberty, have me fall at her feet,
and shed all my blood for her? Then open the prison doors to the two
hundred thousand citizens whom you call suspects, for in the Declaration of Rights no prisons for suspicion are provided for, only places of
detention. Suspicion has no prison, but only the public accuser; there
are no suspects, but only those accused of offenses established by law.

Do not think that such a measure would be fatal to the republic. It
would, on the contrary, be the most revolutionary that you have
adopted. You would exterminate all your enemies by the guillotine! But
was there ever greater madness? Can you possibly destroy one enemy
on the scaffold without making ten others among his family and
friends? Do you believe that those whom you have imprisoned—these

women and old men, these self-indulgent valetudinarians, these stragglers of the Revolution—are really dangerous? Only those among your enemies have remained among you who are cowardly or sick. The strong and courageous have emigrated. They have perished at Lyons or in the Vendée. The remnant which still lingers does not deserve your anger. . . .

Moreover it has not been love of the republic, but curiosity, which has every day attracted multitudes to the Place de la Révolution; it was the new drama which was to be enacted but once. I am sure that the majority of those who frequented this spectacle felt a deep contempt in their hearts for those who subscribed for the theater or opera, where they could only see pasteboard daggers and comedians who merely pretended to die. According to Tacitus, a similar insensibility prevailed in Rome, a similar feeling of security and indifference to all issues. . . .

I am of a very different opinion from those who claim that it is necessary to leave Terror on the order of the day. I am confident, on the contrary, that liberty will be assured and Europe conquered so soon as you have a Committee of Clemency. This committee will complete the Revolution, for clemency is itself a Revolutionary measure, the most efficient of all when it is wisely dealt out.

*Palmer, *Twelve Who Ruled*, 268.

**Ibid., 297.

***Miot, *Memoirs*, 27.

Source: Robinson and Beard, *Readings in Modern European History*, 1:307–8.

Document 18
Thibaudeau's *Mémoires*

Antoine-Claire Thibaudeau (1765–1854) was elected to the National Convention in 1792. He voted for the death of the king without appeal and without reprieve. He was influential enough to save his father, brother, and other relations from the charge of federalism, but he became even more influential after Thermidor. Only the intervention of his friends saved him in Fructidor 1797. He rallied to Napoleon in Brumaire and served in the Council of State. He also served as prefect of the Gironde and subsequently in the Bouches-du Rhône. At the first restoration of the Bourbons, the regicide Thibadeau prudently resigned and even more prudently fled the Midi in disguise. He served Napoleon during the Hundred Days. At the second Restoration, he was exiled from France, returning to serve Napoleon III as a senator in 1851. An enlight-

ened revolutionary who was committed to the republic, he played
a key role in the events he described.

The terror of 1793 was not a necessary consequence of the revolution,
it was a wretched deviation. It was more fatal then useful to the foundation of the republic, because it went too far, it was atrocious and it sacrificed friends and enemies, no one person could defend it. It triggered
a reaction that was fatal not only to the terrorists but to liberty and its
defenders. The terror was too violent to last; it ended without premedi-
tation just as it had begun.

Men who were blinded by political fanaticism or who did not suffer from the terror did not worry about when or how it would end.
Those who reflected, or those who felt its oppression could not foresee
its end. In most affairs or political crises the end or the remedy comes
most often unexpectedly. The terror did not end because its leaders
were tired of the slaughter but because they were terrified and divided
among themselves. It was a matter of who attacked first, because if one
remained on the defensive, one was lost.

Source: A. C. Thibaudeau, *Mémoires sur la Convention et le Directoire,* 2 vols.
(Paris: Baudouin Frères, 1824), 1:57–58.

VII Rebellion in the West

Document 19
Letter of Carrier

Jean Baptiste Carrier (1756–94), a radical orator and terrorist, voted
for the death of the king and the establishment of the Revolutionary
Tribunal. He is most famous (or infamous) for his mission to the
west where the civil war was raging. In the Vendée he ordered mass
executions of suspects without any pretense of trials. In the *noyades*
(mass drownings) he "vertically deported" those suspect by loading
them into barges and then drowning them. He euphemistically
referred to these murders as "republican baptisms." His name
became synonymous with the worst aspects of the Terror. Some historians allege that he executed as many as 10,000 of his fellow citizens without even the pretense of a trial. What is unquestioned is
the sadistic cruelty of the executioners who often hacked off the
arms or legs of those, including children, who tried to escape the
boats. Ordered to return to Paris, Carrier helped to overthrow Robespierre, but was in turn condemned by the Revolutionary Tribunal.

Unlike many of his victims he had the benefit of a trial at which he was convicted of crimes of terrorism. He died on the guillotine.

The revolt in the Vendée broke out in March 1793 when the revolutionary government instituted conscription and implemented the Civil Constitution of the Clergy. The revolutionary government launched a counterassault on this popular insurrection, but resistance continued. In August 1793, the Convention approved the destruction of the Vendée. The area was to be made into a desert. The rhetoric of extermination and the mercilessness of the republicans are reflected in the mission of Carrier who was sent there in October 1793. The troops that entered the area in February well after the royalist armies had been defeated were even more ruthless. More than 400,000 died on both sides.* One historian argues, "The slaughter of the Vendéans, along with the destruction of the Vendée, was the greatest collective massacre in the revolutionary Terror."** The savagery of that repression only fanned civil war. Because of the prolonged struggle in that area, the word *Vendéan* would be associated with defense of altar and throne.*** After Thermidor, in December 1794, the government adopted a more conciliatory policy and offered the royalists amnesty. In February 1795, the royalist commander François Athanase de Charette de la Contrie (see document 21, "Charette's Declaration, February 17, 1795") agreed to the peace of La Jaunaye, but that agreement was soon broken. The rebellion was suppressed but not eliminated during the Consulate.

Carrier to General Nicolas Haxo, 1794

It is my plan to carry off from that accursed country, La Vendée, all manner of subsistence or provisions for man or beast: all forage—in a word, everything—give all the buildings to the flames, and exterminate the inhabitants. Oppose their being relieved by a single grain of corn for their subsistence. I give you the most positive—the most imperious orders. You are answerable for the execution from this moment. In a word, leave nothing in that proscribed country—let the means of subsistence, provisions, forage, everything positively everything, be removed to Nantes.

*Blanning, *The French Revolutionary Wars*, 98.

**François Furet, "Vendée," in *A Critical Dictionary of the French Revolution*, edited by François Furet and Mona Ozouf (Cambridge, Mass.: Belknap Press, 1989), 174.

***M. G. Hutt, "Vendée," in *Historical Dictionary of the French Revolution*, edited by Samuel F. Scott and Barry Rothaus, 2 vols. (Westport, Conn.: Greenwood Press, 1985), 1001–3.

Source: Quoted in Thiers, *The History of the French Revolution*, 3:127.

Document 20
Proclamation of the Royalists in the West

Jean-Nicolas Stofflet (1751–96), a game warden, was appointed commander in chief of the royalist forces in 1794. Stofflet was the last leader to reach an agreement with the revolutionary authorities in May 1795. The pacification was short lived. Stofflet, who resumed the struggle against revolutionary authorities, was surrounded and shot on February 23, 1796. He died courageously, embracing his comrades and shouting, "Long live the king!" (Spelling in the following passage has been modernized by this book's authors.)

Proclamation of the Royalists of Anjou and Upper Poitou in Answer, to the pacificatory Proclamation of the Representatives of the People. In the Name of the King. The Military Council of Anjou and Upper Poitou to the Republicans

Deluded Frenchmen,

YOU announce to us words of peace—this is the wish of our hearts; but by what right do you offer us a pardon which it is only your lot to beg? Stained with the blood of our kings, stained by the murder of a million of victims, by the conflagration and devastation of our property, what are your titles to inspire us with confidence and security? Is it the punishment of Robespierre and Carrier? But indignant nature was raised against those bloody monsters! The cries of public vengeance devoted them to death—In proscribing you did nothing more than yield to necessity. Amongst you, one faction supersedes another, and soon perhaps, the same fate awaits that which at present reigns. Is it your pretended victories? But we are not ignorant that falsehood was always presiding over your public press, and that, in experiencing the most severe defeats, you arrogantly assumed the haughty language of the conquerors of Europe, to impose on the credulity of your slaves! Is it the release of our brethren who were prisoners? Was not that liberty due to them which tyranny only could have taken from them? And when you detain them amongst you, unarmed and defenseless, have not we cause to fear that this temporary release is an ambush craftily prepared to blend us all in the same misfortunes? Alas! were we to believe them, our murdered relations and friends would rise from their graves to tell us, "Take care of the poison concealed under those appearances: it was in proclaiming to us life and safety, we were immolated—the same fate undoubtedly awaits you—the faction that was then domineering is still reigning; its spirit is the same; it aims at the same end; means and agents only are changed.

If, however, your wishes are sincere—if your hearts, softened and changed, are bent towards peace, we must tell you, Restore the heir of your king his scepter and crown; to religion its worship and ministers; to the nobility its rights and estates; to the whole kingdom its ancient and respectable constitution, free from the abuses introduced in it by unfortunate events—then, forgetting all your wrongs and enormities, we may fly into your arms, and mingle with yours, our hearts, feelings, and wishes. But, without the previous adoption of these measures, we despise an amnesty that crime should never have dared to offer to virtue—we despise your efforts and threats; supported by our brave and generous warriors, we will fight till death, and you shall reign but on the tomb of the last of us.

Resolved unanimously at Maulevrière, the 28th January, the year of grace 1795, and the third of the reign of Louis XVII. (Signed) Stofflet, general in chief, and others . . .
Printed at the royal printing office at Maulevrière . . .

Source: The Annual Register, 1795, 196–97.

Document 21
Charette's Declaration, February 17, 1795

François Athanase de Charette de la Contrie de la Contrie (1763–96) served in the navy until his resignation in 1790. A master of guerilla warfare, he was appointed supreme commander of the royalist forces in western France in 1795. Republicans emphasized his ruthlessness, but royalists lauded his courage. He was legendary for the red scarves he wore to distinguish himself among his men and for sharing their hardships. He accepted the terms of the treaty of La Jaunaye in February 1795, which promised indemnities for war damages, private exercise of Catholicism, and maintenance of some of his forces. The pacification did not last. Offered passage to England, he refused and chose to fight to the end. "I have sworn," he told his men, "to die as a soldier and as a Christian."* He was surrounded and executed on March 29, 1796. (Spelling in the following document has been modernized by the authors.)
(See also document 19, "Letter of Carrier.")

The Declaration of the Chiefs of La Vendée in the Armies of the Centre and Pay Bas.

UNPRECEDENTED attempts against our liberty, the most cruel intolerance, despotism, injustice, and horrid vexations which we have experienced, have assembled us with arms in our hands. We have seen with horror our unfortunate country delivered over to the ambitious, who, under the appearances of the purest patriotism, and the seductive mask of popularity, aspired to a perpetual dictatorship. . . .

Whilst an oppressive government deprived our fellow-citizens of their most precious rights, we have defended ours with constancy and firmness. . . . Despair . . . engraved on our [hearts] the resolution rather to die than to live under such tyranny.

But now the government of blood has disappeared. The leaders of that impious faction which covered France with cypress and mourning, have paid with their heads the forfeit of their criminal designs. . . . That confidence which had been so lowered by the acts of barbarity . . . begins now to revive. . . . We have informed them [the representatives] of our intentions, and our desire of a sincere pacification, guaranteed by honor. . . . United in the same tent with the representatives of the people, we felt more strongly, if possible, that we were still Frenchmen, and should be animated only by the general good of our country.

It is with these sentiments that we declare to the national convention and to France, our submission to the French republic, one and indivisible, and our acknowledgment of its laws; and that we make a formal engagement not to make any attempt against them. We promise to surrender, as soon as possible, all the artillery and houses in our possession, and we make a solemn promise never to bear arms against the republic.

Done under the tent, the 29th pluviôse, the 3rd year of the republic. Signed Charette and others.

*F. Michaud, *Biographie Universelle: Ancienne et Moderne* (Graz: Akadmische Druck-und Verlagsanstalt, 1966), 7:516.

Source: The Annual Register, 1795, 197–98.

VIII Economic

Document 22
Price Chart

Worsening economic conditions, such as a European-wide recession, high prices for necessities, particularly for the basic staple wheat, and growing unemployment helped to cause the Revolution and the overthrow of the Committee of Public Safety and the Directory. As one historian notes so well, "Hunger moved the masses." The attempt to impose a Maximum on certain necessities proved a dismal failure. The following table shows the price of goods in 1790 and 1795.

Prices 1790–1795

Item	Price in 1790	Price in 1795
Bushel of flour	2 livres	225 livres
Bushel of barley	16 sols*	50 livres
Bushel of oats	18 sols	50 livres
Bushel of peas	4 livres	130 livres
Load of driftwood	20 livres	500 livres
Bushel of charcoal	7 sols	10 livres
Pound of olive oil	1 livre 16 sols	62 livres
Pound of sugar	18 sols	62 livres
Pound of coffee	18 sols	54 livres
Pound of Marseilles soap	18 sols	41 livres
Bundle of turnips	2 sols	4 livres
Pair of shoes	5 livres	200 livres
Pair of sabots (wooden shoes)	8 sols	15 livres
Ell** of linen	4 livres	180 livres
Pound of butter	18 sols	30 livres

*20 sols = 1 livre.

**An *ell* is a linear measure derived from the length of the arm; it varied in different areas (approximately 27 to 45 inches).

Source: François-Alphone Aulard, ed., *Paris pendant la réaction thermidorienne et sous le Directoire* (Paris: L Cerf, 1899), 2:271.

IX The Revolution and Society

Document 23
Decree Regulating Divorce, September 20, 1792

The repudiation of the patriarchal authority of the ancien régime led some to examine the position of women and to call for legal reform. The categorization in the constitution of 1791 of divorce as a civil contract opened up the possibility of its dissolution. Under this law, approximately 30,000 divorces were granted. Women applied for 71 percent of the divorces. Most were economically independent working women.* Under Napoleon, the position of women was less advantageous than it had been under the ancien régime, and divorce was very restricted. Divorce was abolished in France in 1816 and not reestablished until 1884. Although some had raised the issue of women's rights, the Revolution saw the deterioration of their position.

Decree which determines the grounds, the manner, and the results of divorce.

The National Assembly, considering the importance of enabling Frenchmen to enjoy the ability to divorce, a consequence of individual liberty which an indissoluble engagement would destroy; considering that already many spouses have not waited to enjoy the advantages of the constitutional provision according to which marriage is a civil contract, until the law regulated the manner and the consequence of divorce, decrees the following:

I Grounds for Divorce

1. Marriage may be dissolved by divorce.
2. Divorce shall take place by mutual consent of the husband and wife.
3. One of the spouses may have a divorce decreed by the simple allegation of incompatibility of disposition or of character.
4. Either spouse may have divorce decreed on certain determined grounds, namely: 1st insanity, madness, or violence of one of the couple; 2nd on the condemnation of one of the spouses to a penalty involving loss of civil rights or corporal punishment; 3rd for crimes, cruelty, or serious injuries of one against another; 4th for notoriously dissolute morals; 5th for desertion of the wife by the husband or the husband by the wife for at least two years; 6th for the absence of one of them without news for at least five years; 7th for emigration in the cases specified by the laws, notably by the decree of 8 April 1792.
5. Married couples now separated by an executed judgement or in the last resort shall have the mutual ability to have divorce decreed.
6. All demands and suits for separation not adjudicated are extinguished and abolished: each party shall pay their own costs. Judgement of separation not executed, or impugned by appeal or by quashing are considered canceled; reserving to the spouses recourse to means of divorce according to the provisions of the present law.
7. In the future no separation can be pronounced; couples may be disunited only by divorce.

II *Divorce Procedures*
Divorce by mutual consent.

1. The husband and the wife who conjointly request the divorce shall be required to convoke an assembly of at least six of the closest relations or friends in default of relatives; three relatives or friends to be chosen by the husband; three others by the wife.
4. The two spouses shall attend the assembly; there they shall state why they are seeking a divorce. The relatives or friends assembled shall make the observations and representations they deem appropriate. If the couple persists in their intention, a municipal official required for this purpose, shall draw up an act simply stating that the relatives and friends have heard the couple in an assembly duly convoked, and that they cannot reconcile them. . . .
5. In one month at least and six months at most after the date of the act described in the previous article, the couple may present themselves before the public official responsible for recording marriages in the municipality where the husband resides; and on their request this public officer shall be responsible to pronounce their divorce, without taking cognizance of the grounds. . . .
6. After the delay of six months mentioned in the preceding articles, the spouses can be admitted to divorce by mutual consent only by observing again the same formalities and the same delays. . . .

III *Effects of Divorce with Regard to Married Parties*

. . .

2. Divorced spouses may remarry each other. They may not contract a new marriage with others until a year has passed after the divorce, when it has been pronounced after mutual consent or for the mere cause of incompatibility of disposition or of character. . . .
8. In all cases of divorce there will also be allocated by the family arbiters maintenance for the divorced husband or wife in need; nonetheless only to the extent the property of the other spouse can support it, a deduction being made for his (or her) own needs. . . .

IV *Effects of Divorce with Regard to Children*
1. In the case of divorce by mutual consent or by the request of one of the couple for simple cause of incompatibility of disposition or of character, without any other indication of motives, the children born of the dissolved marriage are confided accordingly: the girls to the mother, the boys, aged less than seven years also to the mother; after that age they are sent to and entrusted to the father, nonetheless the father and the mother can make on this subject another arrangement that seems proper to them. . . .

4. If the divorced husband or the wife contracts a new marriage, the assembly of the family will also decide if the children entrusted to them are to be taken away and to whom they will be given.

5. Whether the children, boys or girls, are entrusted to the father alone or to the mother alone, or to both, or to third persons, the father and the mother shall be obliged to contribute to the costs of their education and maintenance; they shall contribute in proportion to the real and commercial means and income of each of them. . . .

*McPhee, *The French Revolution*, 140.

Source: Duvergier, *Collection*, 4:477–82.

Document 24
Report of Amar

Jean-Baptiste-André Amar (1755–1816) came from an affluent family and took a degree in law, which he never practiced. A zealous Jacobin and a passionate advocate for the Mountain, after his appointment to the Committee of General Security, he became its spokesman to the National Convention. He accelerated the Terror and expedited the arrests of both *Hébertistes* and *Dantonistes*. He played an important role in the overthrow of Robespierre, whom he viewed as an obstacle to the continuance of the Terror, but was then himself swept from power. Arrested as a terrorist, Amar was freed in the general amnesty of 1795. Although implicated in the Babeuf conspiracy (1796), he was acquitted and retired to his estates. In the following excerpt he reports to the National Convention on October 31, 1793.

Amar's report triggered a decree outlawing women's societies and clubs, in particular the Society of Revolutionary Women. That society, organized in February 1793, played a key role in the arrest of the Girondins, but as those women pressed for economic legislation and moved closer to the *enragés* (the enraged), they lost the support of the Mountain and aroused the hostility of other women. On October 30, after disputes among women broke out in the streets, the market women petitioned the Convention to outlaw the society. The government seized the opportunity.

Citizens, your committee has been occupied without respite with the means to prevent the consequences of troubles which have taken place the day before yesterday in Paris. . . . Several women, self-proclaimed

Jacobines, from a purportedly revolutionary society, were walking in the morning in the market and under the charnel houses of *les Innocents,* in trousers and red bonnets; they required other citizenesses to adopt the same costume; several testified that they were insulted by them. A mob of about 6,000 women gathered. All the women agreed that violence and threats would not force them to dress in a costume that they honored but they believed should be reserved to men; they would obey laws passed by legislators and the acts of the magistrates of the people, but they would not yield to the wishes and caprices of about a hundred idle and suspect women. They cried out together: Long live the republic, one and indivisible.

Municipal officers and members of the revolutionary committee of the *section du Contrat-Social* calmed people down and dispersed the mob.

That evening the same movement broke out with more violence. A scuffle broke out. Several self-proclaimed revolutionary women were beaten up. Some indulged in acts toward them which decency should have proscribed. Several remarks reported to your committee illustrate that this movement can only be attributed to a plot of the enemies of the state; several of these self-proclaimed revolutionary women may have been led astray by an excess of patriotism; but others were undoubtedly motivated only by malevolence.

Some want to incite disturbances in Paris now when Brissot and his accomplices are being judged just as was the case whenever you [the Convention] were about to reach an important decision or when you were adopting some measure useful to the country.

The *Section des Marchés,* informed of these events, voted to inform your committee that it believed that several malevolent persons have assumed the mask of an exaggerated patriotism in order to incite disturbances in the section and a kind of counter-revolution in Paris. This section requests that it should be forbidden to limit any one's liberty of dress and that the popular societies of women be strictly prohibited, at least during the revolution.

The committee thought that it should carry its examination further. It has posed the following questions: 1. Is it permissible for citizens or a particular society to force other citizens to do that which the law does not demand? 2. Should gatherings of women in a popular society in Paris be permitted? Don't the troubles that societies have already occasioned argue against tolerating their existence any longer? Naturally these questions are complicated and their resolution should be preceded by two more general questions, namely: 1. can women exercise political rights and take an active part in the affairs of government? 2. can they deliberate together in political associations or popular societies? On these two questions the committee decided in the negative. Time does not allow the full development which these major questions and the first especially raise. We are going to put forward some ideas which could clarify them. You with your wisdom will know how to examine them.

1. Should women exercise political rights and involve themselves in the affairs of government? To govern is to rule the commonwealth by laws the drawing up of which demands extensive knowledge, application and a devotion without limits, a severe impassivity and self-abnegation; to govern is also to direct and rectify ceaselessly the action of the constituted authorities. Are women capable of these cares and of the qualities that governance demands? In general, we can respond no. Very few examples would contradict this judgement.

The citizen's political rights are to discuss and to take resolutions relative to the interest of the state by comparative deliberations and to resist oppression. Do women have the moral and physical strength that the exercise of the one and the other of these rights demands? Universal opinion rejects this idea.

2. Should women gather together in political associations? The goal of popular association is to unveil the maneuvers of the enemies of the commonwealth; to oversee citizens as individuals and public functionaries, even the legislative corps; to excite the zeal of one and the other by example of republican virtues; to illumine by public and thorough discussion the shortcomings or reforms of political laws. Can women devote themselves to these useful and difficult functions? No, because they would be obliged to sacrifice the more important cares to which nature calls them. The private functions for which women are destined by their very nature supports the general order of society; this social order results from the differences between men and women. Each sex is called to a type of occupation which is fitting; its action is circumscribed within this circle which it cannot break through, because nature which has set the limits for man commands imperiously and does not recognize any law.

Man is strong, robust, born with great energy, audacity, and courage; he braves perils, the intemperance of seasons by his constitution, he resists all the elements, he is suited for the arts, for difficult work and as he is almost exclusively destined for agriculture, for commerce, for navigation for voyages, for war, for all that demands force, intelligence, capability so it seems he alone appears suited for profound and serious meditations which demand great intellectual effort and long studies which is not given to women to pursue.

What character is suitable for women? Morals and nature itself have assigned her functions; to begin the education of men, to prepare children's minds and hearts for public virtues, to direct them early in life to the good, to elevate their souls, and to instruct them in the public cult of liberty: such are their functions, after the care of the household; woman is naturally destined to incite love of virtue. When they have fulfilled all their duties, they will have deserved well of their country. Without doubt it is necessary that they should instruct themselves in the principles of liberty in order to make their children cherish it; they can attend the deliberations of the sections and the discussions of the popular societies; but made as they are to soften the morals of man should they take an active part in discussions the passion of which is incompatible with the gentleness and moderation which make up the charm of their sex?

We must say that this question is related essentially to morals and without morals, no republic. Does the honesty of woman allow her to display herself in public and to struggle with men? To discuss in public questions on which depend the safety of the republic? In general, women are ill suited for elevated conceptions and for serious meditations: and if, among the ancient peoples, their natural timidity and modesty did not permit them to appear outside their family, then in the French republic would you wish for them to be seen coming to the bar, to the tribune, to political assemblies like men, abandoning both reserve, the source of all virtues of their sex, and the care of their family?

. . . We believe then that a woman should not leave her family to meddle in the affairs of government.

There is another respect in which associations of women appear dangerous. If we consider that the political education of men is at its beginning, that all its principles are not developed and that we are still stammering the word liberty, then how much more reasonable is it for women whose moral education is almost nil, to be less enlightened in principles? Their presence in popular societies would give therefore then an active part in government to persons more exposed to error and to seduction. Let us add that women are disposed by their organization to an excess excitement which would be deadly in public affairs and that the interests of the state would soon be sacrificed to all that the intensity of passion can produce in errors and disorder. Delivered to the heat of public debate, they would inculcate in their children, not love of country but hatreds and suspicions.

We believe therefore and without doubt you will think as we do that it is not possible for women to exercise public rights. You will destroy these alleged popular societies of women that the aristocracy wish to establish to put women into conflict with men, to divide the latter by forcing them to participate in these quarrels and to stir up disorder.

Charlier: Notwithstanding the objections just cited, I do not know on what principle one could lean in order to take away from women the right to assembly peacefully. (Murmurs) Unless you are going to argue that women are not part of the human race, can you take away from them this right common to every thinking being? . . .

Bazaire: . . . Here is how the suspension of these societies can be justified: you have declared yourselves a revolutionary government; in this capacity you can take all measures that public safety dictates. For a short while you have thrown a veil over principles out of fear that they could be abused to lead us into counterrevolution. It is therefore only a question whether these societies of women are dangerous. Experience has illustrated these past days how dangerous they are to the public tranquillity; that granted, let no one say any more to me about principles. I ask that in revolutionary spirit and by way of a measure of public security these associations be prohibited, at least during the revolution.

The decree proposed by Amar is adopted in these terms:

The National Convention, after having heard the report of its committee of general security decrees:

Article 1. Clubs and popular societies of women under whatever name they are known are prohibited.
Article 2. All meetings of popular societies must be public.

Source: Le Moniteur, 31 October 1793.

X War and Imperialism

Document 25
Decree of August 23, 1793, the *Levée en masse*

In response to the allied threat, the revolutionaries mobilized the entire population to repel the enemy. The decree "represents the first wartime mobilization of a nation in modern history."* It brought 300,000 men into the army, raising its total strength to 800,000. Conscription so enthusiastically supported by the *sans-culottes* in Paris engendered considerable hostility in the countryside.

Article 1. From this moment, up until the enemies have been chased from the territory of the Republic, all the French are in permanent requisition for the service of the armies.

    The young men are called to combat; the married men shall forge arms and transport provisions; women shall make tents, clothing and serve in the hospitals; children shall make the old linen into lint; the old men should be carried to public places in order to incite the courage of the warriors, preach hatred of kings and the unity of the Republic.

2. National buildings shall be converted into barracks; public places into arms workshops; the soil of cellars shall be scrubbed to extract saltpeter.

3. Arms of caliber are to be turned over only to those who march against the enemy; service in the interior is to be conducted with sporting guns and with side-arms.

4. Saddle horses are requisitioned for the cavalry corps; draught horses other than those employed in agriculture are to carry artillery and provisions.

5. The committee of public safety is charged to take all measures necessary to establish without delay a special manufacture for arms of all kinds which corresponds to the elan and energy of the French people. It is authorized accordingly to form all establishments, manufactures, workshops and factories judged necessary to the execution of these works, as well to call up for this object in the entire extent of the republic the artists and workers who can contribute to its success. It will put for this end a sum of thirty million at the disposition of the ministry of war, to be taken from the 498,200,000 *livres* in assignats which is reserved in the three key fund. The central establishment of this special manufacture will be in Paris.

6. The representatives of the people sent to execute the present law will have the same authority in their respective *arrondissements,* acting in concert with the committee of public safety; they are invested

with the same unlimited powers as the representatives of the people
with the armies.

7. No one may secure a replacement in the service to which they are
called. Public functionaries will remain at their posts.

8. The levy shall be general. Unmarried citizens or widowers without
children, from eighteen to twenty-five years will march first; they
will gather without delay at the chief town of their districts; where
they will practice daily manual exercises while awaiting the hour of
their departure.

9. The representatives of the people shall regulate the muster and the
marches in a manner so that armed citizens will arrive at the assembly point as supplies, munitions, and all that constitutes army
material exists in sufficient proportion.

10. The points of assembly will be determined by the circumstances
and designated by the representatives of the people sent to execute
the present decree on the advice of the generals, in concert with the
committee of public safety and the provisionary executive council.

11. The battalion to be organized in each district will assemble under a
banner bearing the inscription: the French people standing against
tyrants. . . .

13. In order to collect supplies in sufficient quantity, the farmers and
the stewards of the national lands are to deposit the produce of
these lands in the chief town of their respective districts.

14. The proprietors, farmers and owners of grain are required to pay in
kind taxes in arrears. . . .

17. The Minister of war is responsible for taking all the necessary measures for the prompt execution of the present decree; the National
Treasury will put at his disposition a sum of 50,000,000 [*livres*]. . . .

*Stewart, *A Documentary Survey of the French Revolution*, 472.

Source: Duvergier, *Collection*, 6:107–8.

Document 26
The First Propaganda Decree, November 20, 1792

As the French revolutionary armies moved into enemy territory,
the Convention approved this decree. The revolutionaries, who
had only two years earlier passed a decree renouncing conquests,
henceforth appeared as armed crusaders. Within four months, this
offer of aid was withdrawn.

The National Convention declares, in the name of the French nation,
that it will grant fraternity and help to all peoples who wish to regain
their liberty; and it charges the executive power with giving the gener-

als the necessary orders to bring aid to such people and to defend citizens who have been harassed for the cause of liberty.

Source: Le Moniteur, 20 November 1792.

Document 27
The Second Propaganda Decree, December 15, 1792

The revolutionaries adopted this policy after opposition developed in the Austrian Netherlands. The French revolutionary general Dumouriez bitterly complained that individuals there were "subjected to every kind of vexation; what in their view, were sacred rights of liberty were violated; and their religious feeling impudently insulted."* This policy was applied to all the territories occupied by France. Notice the difference from the first decree. Although the French had declared "war to the *chateaux,* peace to the cottages," this decree made it clear that the occupied were to bear the costs. As historian Simon Schama notes, "A policy of liberation was blurring into one of annexation, euphemistically known as *réunion*."** The French armies were increasingly supported by extortion from the conquered.

The National Convention, having heard the report of its committees of finance, of war, and of diplomacy; faithful to the principles of the sovereignty of the people, which do not allow it to recognize any institutions detrimental to liberty, and wishing to regulate the rules to be followed by the generals of the armies of the Republic in the countries where they bear arms, decrees:

Article 1 In the countries occupied or to be occupied by the armies of the Republic, the generals will proclaim immediately in the name of the French nation, the sovereignty of the people, the suppression of all established authorities, taxes or existing contributions, abolition of the *dîme* [tithe], of feudalism, of seigneurial rights, feudal as well as *censuel* [quit-rent, rent paid in lieu of feudal services], fixed or intermittent, of *banalités* [monopolies by which peasants were forced to use, for example, a lord's mill], of real or personal servitude, of privileges of hunting and fishing, of *corvées,* of nobility and generally all privileges.

2. They will announce to the people that they bring peace, aid, fraternity, liberty, and equality and that they will convoke immediately primary or communal assemblies thereafter in order to create and organize a provisional administration and justice; they will guard the security of persons and property; they will print in the language

or idiom of the country, post, and execute without delay the present decree and the attached proclamation in each commune.

3. All agents and civil or military officers of the former government, as well as individuals formerly deemed nobles or members of any corporation formerly privileged, will be for this time only ineligible to vote in the primary or communal assemblies and cannot be elected to positions in the provisional administration or judiciary.

4. The generals will put under the safeguard and protection of the French Republic all goods, movable and immovable, belonging to the treasury, to the prince, to his supporters, adherents, and voluntary satellites, to public establishments, to the lay and ecclesiastical bodies and communities: they are to draw up without delay a detailed list which is to be sent to the executive council and take all measures in their power to ensure that these properties are respected.

5. The provisionary administration, named by the people, will be charged with the surveillance and stewardship of the objects put under the safeguard and protection of the French republic; it will watch over the security of persons and properties; it will execute vigorously the laws relative to civil and criminal trials, to the police, and to public security; it will take charge of regulating and paying the local expenses and those necessary for the common defense; it will establish contributions, ensuring at all times that they are not supported by the indigent and working classes.

6. From the moment the provisionary administration is organized, the National Convention will name commissioners from its own to fraternize with it.

7. The Executive Council will also name national commissioners who will go consecutively to places to concert with the generals and the provisionary administration named by the people on measures to be taken for the common defense and on means to be employed to procure clothing and necessary subsistence to the armies and to pay the expenses they have incurred and will incur during their stay in the territory.

8. The national commissioners named by the executive council will render an account every fifteen days of their operations. The executive council will approve, modify, or reject them and will forward an account thereafter to the Convention.

9. The provisionary administration named by the people and the functions of the national commissioners will cease as soon as the inhabitants, after having declared the sovereignty and independence of the people, liberty and equality, have a organized free and popular form of government.

10. A statement of the expenses that the French republic will have incurred for the common defense and the sums that it will have received, will be issued and the French nation will make with the

government to be established arrangements for what it due; and in case the common interest demands that the troops of the Republic still remain on foreign soil, they will take appropriate measures for their subsistence.

11. The French nation declares that it will treat as an enemy of the people those who, refusing liberty and equality, or renouncing them, wish to conserve, recall, or treat with the prince and the privileged castes; it promises and engages not to sign any treaty, and not to lay down arms in the territory the troops have entered until the consolidation of the sovereignty and the independence of the people who will adopt principles of equality and establish a free and popular government.

12. The executive council will send the present decree by extraordinary couriers and take the necessary measures to assure its execution .

The French people to the _____ people.

Brothers and friends, we have conquered liberty and we will preserve it. We offer to have you enjoy this inestimable good which has always belonged to us, and that our oppressors are not able to deprive us of without a crime.

We have expelled your tyrants: show yourselves free men and we will protect you from their vengeance, from their projects, from their return.

From this moment, the French nation proclaims the sovereignty of the people, the suppression of all civil and military authorities which have governed you up to this day, of all taxes which you paid, in any existing form; the abolition of the *dîme,* of feudalism, of seigneurial rights, feudal as well as *censuel,* fixed or intermittent, of *banalités,* of real and personal servitude, of hunting and fishing privileges, of *corvées,* of the *gabelle* [salt tax], of tolls, of *octrois* [tolls on goods coming into towns], and generally of all kinds of contributions which you have paid to your usurpers; it proclaims also the abolition among you of all corporations, noble, priestly, and other, and of all the prerogatives and privileges contrary to equality. You are from this moment, brothers and friends, all citizens, all equal in rights, and all called equally to govern, to serve and to defend your country.

Immediately form assemblies, primary or communal, hasten to establish your provisional administrations and courts in conformity to the provisions of article three of the above decree. The agents of the French republic will work with you to assure your happiness and the fraternity which ought to exist henceforth between us.

*Quoted in Schama, *Citizens*, 685.
**Ibid., 643.

Source: Duvergier, *Collection*, 5:82–84.

Document 28
Decree of January 31, 1793

As opposition to revolutionary imperialism developed in occupied territories, the Convention responded with this decree.

Decree relative to the conduct of generals in countries where French armies have entered or will enter.

The National Convention, informed that in some countries presently occupied by the armies of the Republic the execution of the decrees [e.g., that of December 15] . . . have been hindered in all or in part by the enemies of the people united against its sovereignty, decrees the following:

. . .

4. The people of cities and territories who have not assembled in fifteen days at the latest after the promulgation of the decrees . . . are declared to not wish to be friends of the French people. The republic will treat them as people who refuse to adopt or give themselves a government founded on liberty and equality.

Source: Duvergier, *Collection*, 5:130–31.

Document 29
Letter of Carnot

Lazare Nicolas Marguerite Carnot (1753–1823) was dubbed the "organizer of victory" because of his role in mobilizing the French nation. Before the Revolution, he had served as a lieutenant and later a captain in the corps of engineers. His middle-class origins, however, made it impossible for him to be promoted or to marry the girl of his choice, the daughter of an aristocrat. Although a poor speaker and an aloof individual, he was elected to the Legislative Assembly and the Convention and became a committed revolutionary. As such, he voted for the death of the king and the expansion of France's borders. He served as a representative on mission to the Pyrenees (September 1792–January 1793) and to the Army of the North (March–

August 1793). He joined the Committee of Public Safety in August 1793, and worked on military affairs; he helped to train and equip an army of about 1 million. When France was threatened by counterrevolutionaries and foreign invasions, Carnot voiced the opinions of many when he said: "We need expect no peace from our enemies and those at home are worse than those abroad. We must smash them or they will crush us."* His successful military policies and his opposition to Robespierre enabled Carnot to survive the purge of Thermidor. In 1795, he became a member of the Directory, and served until the coup of Fructidor (1797) forced him into exile. He returned to France in 1799 and by 1800 was serving as minister of war. A man of principle, he opposed some of Napoleon's policies; he cast the sole vote against the life consulate and later the establishment of the empire. In 1814, when France was threatened with invasion, he returned to active service, and during the Hundred Days, he served as minister of the interior . When the Bourbons returned to power he was again exiled. The man who had saved France on many occasions died in exile in Prussia. His grandson was elected president of France in large part because of the reputation of his famous ancestor. The following document illustrates the revolutionaries' changing attitude toward conquered territories.

Paris, 23 Messidor, an II (July 11, 1794). Carnot for the Committee of Public Safety to the representatives at the army of Sambre-et-Meuse.

It is necessary to seize all that you can, without permitting the pillage and the misconduct that would incite them against us. Here is the only rule to follow; we do not wish either to stir up the country, or to fraternize with it, it is a conquered country which has many restitutions to make to us and from which it is necessary to extract quickly all the resources which would enable the enemy to launch a new invasion. You ought not to ignore that Brabant in general is totally devoted to the emperor and that it has given all imaginable proofs of its hatred against us. It is not a country to spare but there is everywhere a body of good people and it is necessary more and more to win them over by respecting their persons, customs, and usages and by attacking the rich and the enemies of France.

*Sydenham, *The French Revolution*, 151.

Source: Lazare Carnot, *Correspondance générale de Carnot* (Paris: Imprimerie nationale, 1892[?]), 4:476–77.

Document 30
Swiss Protests

Frédéric-César La Harpe (1754–1838) was trained in the law. His philosophical and liberal ideas impelled Catherine II to bring him to Russia as the tutor to her two grandchildren. During the French Revolution, he returned to Switzerland but was forced to flee after his brochures were deemed seditious by the authorities. In Paris, he intrigued with the Directory to invade Switzerland, and published numerous brochures calling for an insurrection in Switzerland. After the revolution in the Vaud he returned to Switzerland and was put at the head of the revolutionary movement by the French army. He became one of the directors of the Helvetic Republic. In December 1799, he attempted a coup in imitation of Napoleon's but failed and lost all power. La Harpe's influence with Czar Alexander may have protected Switzerland after the allies' victory in 1814. He accompanied Alexander to the Congress of Vienna but soon returned to Switzerland, where he died.

France invaded the territory of Switzerland in January 1798 and proclaimed the Helvetic Republic in March. The Swiss, though not conquered like the Dutch, were henceforth subject to French exactions, French pillaging, and French intervention. Popular uprisings against the French broke out in the fall of 1798, but the presence of French troops insured the survival of the Helvetic Republic until 1803.

La Harpe to Jean Debry, 23 Floréal VI (May 12, 1798), forwarded to Talleyrand

It appears that there is a plan to convert Switzerland into a Vendée. . . . The details of all that my unfortunate fellow citizens have suffered or are still suffering, are a horror; and it is the French whom we have loved, for whom we have sworn, whom we have received as liberators, who have made us so completely wretched! . . . Citizen Representative! In the name of liberty, in the name of humanity, in the name of your country, . . . Do not believe that I wish to alarm you by vain jeremiads; the security of the frontier which extends sixty leagues* is at stake. It will no longer exist, if despair and furor arm the Swiss peasants against you. Your enemies will seize the occasion to recommence hostilities. Our minister should take the necessary official steps, but the urgency is such that I cannot be silent. It is time to take energetic measures to prevent an explosion that 70,000 soldiers will not be able to suppress if it breaks out. It can be averted by curbing the violence and punishing those in Switzerland who have tolerated it.

La Harpe to Talleyrand, 23 Floréal VI (May 12, 1798)

Please, citizen minister, believe a man who has always spoken frankly to you. The vexations which the Swiss people are suffering are insupportable, and the impression that they have left is such that a furious hatred follows in their hearts the tendency which drove them toward those who were announced as their liberators. I repeat with sorrow. Things have come to the point that there are only two alternatives: either to punish severely and immediately those who by their injustices, their rapacity and their insults dishonor the French name among us; or destroy our nation to the last man.

 *A *league* is 4 kilometers.

Source: Emile Dunant, ed., *Les Relations diplomatiques de la France et de la République helvétique, 1798–1803* (Basel: Verlag der Basler Buch-und Antiquariatshandlung, 1901), 25.

Document 31
Proclamation, Signed at The Hague, January 27, 1795

The next three documents indicate the costs of French revolutionary imperialism and the policy of extortion that funded the war. France declared war on the Dutch on February 1, 1793. The expectation of some Dutchmen after the French conquest in January 1794 that they would be allowed to pursue their own policies was not met. As one French general pointed out: "Holland has done nothing to avoid being classed among the general order of our conquests. It was the ice, the indefatigable courage of our troops and the talents of the generals which delivered her and not any revolution. It follows from this that there can be no reason to treat her any differently from a conquered country."* The peace treaty signed in May 1795 required the Dutch to pay a huge indemnity and to cede some southern territories. The costs to what became the Batavian republic were enormous.

The States General of the United Provinces, to all who shall see or hear these presents [sic] greeting . . . know, that the representatives of the French nation now in this country have intimated to us, that it is necessary that speedy provision should be made of several articles appertaining to the subsistence and clothing of the French troops, namely, the following:

> 200,000 quintals of corn.
> 5 millions of rations of hay, at 15 lbs each.
> 5 millions measure of oats, at 10 lb each, heavy weight.
> 200,000 rations of straw at 10 lb each.
> 150,000 pairs of shoes.
> 20,000 pairs of boots.
> 20,000 cloth coats and waistcoats.
> 40,000 pairs of stocking breeches.
> 150,000 pairs of trowsers, [sic] of coarse linen.
> 200,000 shirts.
> 50,000 hats.

All of which are to be delivered at Nimeguen, Thiel, and Bois de Duc within the space of a month, in three instalments—and besides,

> 12,000 oxen within two months.

The above mentioned representatives have also added, that instead of following the practice introduced in other countries which their troops have entered, namely, that the requisitions of similar articles have been made, published, and carried into execution by themselves, they have chosen to treat this republic in another manner, and thereby prove the inclination of the French nation, to consider it in the light of an approaching ally. . . .

We doubt not that the inhabitants will be convinced of the absolute necessity of enabling their provincial sovereigns to furnish these necessary funds without the smallest delay; but we think it nonetheless necessary to hold up to all, conjunctly and severally, the distress to which they must expose themselves, if they manifest the least unwillingness or even procrastination; for we are intimately persuaded of the serious intention of the above-mentioned representatives of the French nation, that these requisitions shall be complied with, at the appointed time, and must therefore warn all in the most impressive manner, that they will have themselves to blame if measures of force and violence must be employed to obtain what we wish to see accomplished with the greatest possible order and regularity. . . .

*Doyle, *The Oxford History of the French Revolution,* 209.

Source: *The Annual Register, 1795,* 208–10.

XII A Conservative Critique

Document 32
Edmund Burke's Condemnation

Edmund Burke (1729–97), a British statesman, was one of the most eloquent theorists attacking the French Revolution. He served as a member of Parliament and later as postmaster general. He also advocated repeal of the Stamp Act, a more conciliatory approach to the North American colonies, and reform in the British Empire. He was a close friend of Charles James Fox, a celebrated reformer. A bitter and public disagreement over the Revolution in Parliament destroyed their lifelong friendship. Burke stressed the importance of tradition and continuity and attacked unrestricted rationalism and the revolutionaries' stress on rights rather than duties. His *Reflections on the Revolution in France* is a conservative classic. Later, after Britain had declared war against France and the British government was attempting to conclude a peace treaty with France, Burke wrote *Letters on a Regicide Peace* in which he reiterated his condemnation of the French Revolution.

Deprived of the old government, deprived in a manner of all government, France fallen as a monarchy, to common speculators might have appeared more likely to be an object of pity or insult, according to the disposition of the circumjacent powers, than to be the scourge and terror of them all; but out of the tomb of the murdered monarchy in France has arisen a vast, tremendous, unformed spectre, in a far more terrific guise than any which ever yet have overpowered the imagination, and subdued the fortitude of man. . . .

The republic of regicide with an annihilated revenue, with defaced manufactures, with a ruined commerce, with an uncultivated and half-depopulated country, with a discontented, distressed, enslaved, and famished people, passing with a rapid, eccentric, incalculable course, from the wildest anarchy to the sternest despotism, has actually conquered the finest parts of Europe, has distressed, disunited, deranged and broken to pieces all the rest; and so subdued the minds of the rulers in every nation, that hardly any resource presents itself to them, except that of entitling themselves to a contemptuous mercy by a display of their imbecility and meanness. Even in their greatest military efforts, and the greatest display of their fortitude, they seem not to hope, they do not even appear to wish, the extinction of what subsists to their certain ruin. Their ambition is only to be admitted to a more favoured class in the order of servitude under that domineering power.

This seems the temper of the day. At first the French force was too much despised. Now it is too much dreaded. As inconsiderate courage has given way to irrational fear, so it may be hoped, that, through the medium of deliberate sober apprehension, we may arrive at steady fortitude. . . .

We are in a war of a *peculiar* nature. It is not with an ordinary community, which is hostile or friendly as passion or as interest may veer about: not with a state which makes war through wantonness, and abandons it through lassitude. We are at war with a system, which, by its essence, is inimical to all other governments, and which makes peace or war, as peace and war may best contribute to their subversion. It is with an *armed doctrine* that we are at war. It has, by its essence, a faction of opinion, and of interest, and of enthusiasm in every country. To us it is a Colossus which bestrides our channel. It has one foot on a foreign shore, the other upon the British soil. Thus advantaged, if it can at all exist, it must finally prevail. . . .

A government of the nature of that set up at our very door has never been hitherto seen, or even imagined, in Europe. What our relation to it will be cannot be judged by other relations. It is a serious thing to have connexion with a people, who live only under positive, arbitrary, and changeable institutions; and those not perfected, nor supplied, nor explained by any common acknowledged rule of moral science. . . . France, since her revolution, is under the sway of a sect, whose leaders have deliberately, at one stroke, demolished the whole body of that jurisprudence which France had pretty nearly in common with other civilized countries. In that jurisprudence were contained the elements and principles of the law of nations, the great ligament of mankind.

. . . They have not only annulled all their old treaties, but they have renounced the law of nations, from whence treaties have their force. With a fixed design they have outlawed themselves, and to their power outlawed all other nations [*sic*].

Instead of the religion and the laws by which they were in a great politic communion with the Christian world, they have constructed their republic on three bases, all fundamentally opposite to those on which the communities of Europe are built. Its foundation is laid in regicide, in Jacobinism, and in atheism; and it has joined to those principles a body of systematic manners, which secure their operation. . . .

Constituted as France was ten years ago, it was not in that France to shake, to shatter, and to overwhelm Europe in the manner that we behold. A sure destruction impends over those infatuated princes, who, in the conflict with this new and unheard-of power, proceed as if they were engaged in a war that bore a resemblance to their former contests; or that they can make peace in the spirit of their former arrangements of pacification. Here the beaten path is the very reverse of the safe road.

As to me, I was always steadily of opinion, that this disorder was not in its nature intermittent. I conceived that the contest, once begun, could not be laid down again, to be resumed at our discretion; but that our first struggle with this evil would also be our last. I never thought we could make peace with the system; because it was not for the sake of an object we pursued in rivalry with each other, but with the system itself that we were at war. As I understood the matter, we were at war not with its conduct, but with its existence; convinced that its existence and its hostility were the same. . . .

All this body of old convention, composing the vast and voluminous collection called the *corps diplomatique,* forms the code or statute law, as the methodized reasonings of the great publicists and jurists from the digest and jurisprudence of the Christian world. In these treasures are to be found the *usual* relations of peace and amity in civilized Europe; and there the relations of ancient France were to be found amongst the rest.

The present system in France is not the ancient France. It is not the ancient France with ordinary ambition and ordinary means. It is not a new power of an old kind. It is a new power of a new species. When such a questionable shape is to be admitted for the first time into the brotherhood of Christendom, it is not a mere matter of idle curiosity to consider how far it is in its nature alliable with the rest, or whether "the relations of peace and amity" with this new state are likely to be of the same nature with the *usual* relations of the states of Europe.

The Revolution in France had the relation of France to other nations as one of its principal objects. The changes made by that Revolution were not the better to accommodate her to the old and usual relations, but to produce new ones. The Revolution was made, not to make France free, but to make her formidable; not to make her a neighbor, but a mistress; not make her more observant of laws, but to put her in a condition to impose them. To make France truly formidable it was necessary that France should be new-modelled. . . .

Exploding, therefore, all sorts of balances, they avow their design to erect themselves into a new description of empire, which is not grounded on any balance, but forms a sort of impious hierarchy, of which France is to be head and the guardian. The law of this their empire is anything rather than the public law of Europe, the ancient conventions of its several states, or the ancient opinions which assign to them superiority or pre-eminence of any sort, or any other kind of connexion in virtue of ancient relations.

Source: Burke, *Works,* 5:155–56, 164–65, 206, 231–32, 244–45, 304.

GLOSSARY OF
SELECT TERMS

Ancien régime   a neologism coined in 1789, refers to the former regime; that is, France or Europe before the revolution.

Assignats   were initially bonds assigned or secured by the confiscated church lands. As the national properties were sold, the assignats were to be returned to the treasury and destroyed. After 1790, these notes were legal tender and non–interest bearing. In 1795, the Directory decided to issue no more because inflation had undermined the currency (0.025 percent in 1796). A new paper currency, the *mandat territorial,* was issued. In 1797, the assignats were formally demonetized. The depreciation of the assignat had allowed some speculators to buy land at ludicrously low prices, but the ensuing inflation ruined creditors, devastated those on fixed incomes and wage earners, and undermined confidence in the economy.

Brissotins,   also known as Girondins or Rolandins, were a loosely knit group that included Brissot; Condorcet; three barristers from Bordeaux: Gensonné, Guadet, Vergniaud; friends of the Rolands; and other deputies. About 130 deputies in the Legislative Assembly, these left-wing deputies were outnumbered by the Feuillants, but effectively used the Jacobin club and the considerable oratorical talents of their members. They pushed for the declaration of war. Radicals in the Legislative Assembly, they became conservatives in the Convention. They championed legality and the provinces and opposed a centralized government in Paris and economic regulation. During the trial of the king, the Girondins were divided among themselves on key issues of the referendum and of the penalty to be imposed. Opposition to the extremists cost them; they soon became a victim of Parisian enmity. On June 2, 1793, 80,000 Parisians surrounded the Convention and demanded a purge of the Girondins. Twenty-nine were subsequently expelled from the Convention. This Montagnard coup has sometimes been dubbed the "third revolution." A number subsequently were executed.

Cahiers   short for *cahiers de doléances,* were lists of grievances that were drawn up by the assemblies that elected deputies to the Estates General. Cahiers provide a glimpse into the public opinion of various constituencies on the eve of the Revolution; they contained the concerns of the area, complaints about abuses, descriptions of local problems, and sometimes recommendations for change.

Civil Constitution of the Clergy   was the reorganization of the church passed on July 12, 1790, after the expropriation of church property. The new diocesan boundaries corresponded to the departments, with one bishop for each department, a reduction from 130 to 83. The parishes also were reorganized. Bishops and priests, like other officials, were to be elected, paid by the local authority, and entitled to a pension. The clergy were required to reside in their area and to take an oath of allegiance. (*See* Juring clergy.) Papal opposition, voiced in the spring of 1791, fueled Catholic resistance to the Revolution and meant a divided church and a divided nation.

Cordeliers Club   (originally called the *Société des amis des droits de l'homme et du citoyen*) was so named because its members originally met in a former Franciscan monastery on the *rue des Cordeliers*. Their symbol was the ever-open eye. They demanded the deposition of the king after his flight to Varennes, and, during the Reign of Terror, they symbolically draped the Declaration of the Rights of Man and the Citizen in black.

Estates General   the national assembly of the three estates, clergy, nobility, and commons, first convened in 1303. Its powers were not clearly defined, but it never controlled finances. The Estates General did not evolve into a parliamentary institution, although its power was stronger when the monarchy was weaker. Before the Revolution, the last time it convened was 1614.

Feuillants   a political club known officially as the *Société des amis de la constitution séante aux Feuillants*, met in the house of a religious order bearing that name. It included the so-called triumvirate of Antoine Barnave, Adrien Duport (both lawyers), and Alexandre de Lameth (a noble and colonel in the army), Lameth's brother Charles and their followers, and Lafayette and his. This group stressed the importance of law and order and urged the nation to forgive the king after his flight. The club was suppressed after the August 10, 1792, uprising. Barnave was executed during the Terror. Duport was arrested, but escaped to Switzerland, and Alexandre de Lameth emigrated with Lafayette. His brother Charles fled to Hamburg after the 1792 revolution. *Feuillants* was a name generally applied to constitutional royalists who believed that only property owners should participate in politics.

Girondins   *See* Brissotins

Jacobins   were members of a club called the Society of Friends of the Constitution. They were dubbed Jacobins because they met in the buildings formerly occupied by the Jacobin order. In the fall of 1791, there were over 1,000 such clubs scattered throughout France, but they mushroomed into 2,000 in the radical phase of the Revolution. Robespierre, among others, played a prominent role. This large network of affiliated societies and its active correspondents enabled the Jacobins to wield enormous power. As the membership, initially limited to the upper middle class, was opened to the poorer elements of society, the society became more radical. By 1793, the Jacobins had fallen under the influence of the Mountain. The Paris club was closed down by the government in November 1794, but its spirit animated the uprisings of Germinal and Prairial, year III (spring 1795).

Juring clergy   were those who swore an oath to the Civil Constitution of the Clergy. When the provision that required clergy to take the oath was generally ignored, the assembly mandated that clerics had to take it or forfeit their positions. The refusal to the swear the oath was the first manifestation of popular opposition to the Revolution. Those who refused to swear were dubbed nonjuring or refractory. In the spring of 1791, the pope denounced the Civil Constitution as heretical and schismatic, declared all elections void, and threatened with excommunication all those who did not retract the oath within 40 days. The regions with the higher proportion of refractory clergy tended to be more rural than urban and had more priests who were natives and who were highly integrated into the local community. The schism in the clergy lasted until 1801 when Napoleon signed the Concordat, although a few on either side refused to accept it.

Levée en masse was decreed on August 23, 1793, and changed the nature of war by putting the nation in arms. It commandeered all individuals and materials to serve the army until France was delivered from her enemies. By the fall of 1794, the Republic had mustered an army of 1,169,000.

Maximum first passed on May 4, 1793, set the legal price of grain and flour. The so-called General Maximum, a wage/price control measure designed as a temporary expedient, was passed by the Convention on September 29, 1793. It regulated the price of certain necessities, such as butter and oil, brandy, coal, candles, salt, tobacco, and paper, and set the level of wages. The Jacobins, ideologically opposed to price regulation, adopted this measure in an attempt to mobilize the resources of the nation in the revolutionary cause and to defuse the demands of the *sans-culottes*. Yet another Maximum (third) was passed on February 24, 1794. After Thermidor, the controls were not enforced and the Maximum was finally abolished on December 24, 1794.

The Mountain was a group of left-wing deputies (Montagnards), variously estimated at between 258 and 302 members, that most famously included Robespierre, Danton, and Marat. The group took its name from its members' habit of sitting in the highest seats when the Convention met in 1792. The Mountain can be defined by its opposition to the group led by Brissot and its support of the Terror. During the king's trial, the Montagnards voted against the referendum and for the king's death. As power passed from the Committee of Public Safety to the Thermidoreans, the Mountain disintegrated, although a few hundred Montagnards survived until April–May 1795.

October Days   were the demonstrations on October 5 and 6, 1789, that forced the king and his family to move to Paris. Subsequently, the National Assembly joined them. The Assembly and the king were both then "prisoners" of Paris.

Parlements   the supreme courts of appeal under the ancien régime. Throughout France there were 13, the most important of which met at Paris. These courts registered all royal edicts before they became law and constituted the chief source of resistance to the monarchy early in the Revolution. The appointments were venal; that is, the officeholders bought their offices and enjoyed security of tenure. As bastions of privilege, they were abolished during the Revolution.

Philosophes   were men of the Enlightenment, such as Voltaire and Montesquieu. who advocated the use of reason and criticism to attack abuses in society.

Physiocrats   were a group of intellectuals, founded by François Quesnay, who believed that land was the basis of wealth and argued for tree trade. They greatly influenced Adam Smith.

Regicides   were those who voted for the death of the king.

Reign of Terror   is sometimes defined as the second phase of the Convention, from June 3, 1793 (after the arrest of Brissot and his colleagues) to July 28, 1794 (the execution of Robespierre). More than 17,000 fell victim to revolutionary legislation, approximately 12,000 were killed either by representatives on mission or after surrendering on the battlefield, and another 11,000 died in the prisons awaiting trial for a total of approximately 40,000 victims (excluding those killed in the Vendée).

Sans-culottes   originally a vulgar term of ridicule, referred to those who did not wear the knee breeches of the aristocracy but instead wore trousers. This group included a varied group of craftsmen, small shopkeepers, and workers in Paris and other cities who espoused direct democracy, government regulation, and cheap bread. They often were depicted carrying pikes, the symbol of popular insurrection.

Thermidor   the eleventh revolutionary month, referred to the overthrow of Robespierre and his partisans and the ending of the Terror. The subsequent dismantling of the revolutionary government is often dubbed the Thermidorean reaction. The Thermidoreans governed from 9 Thermidor until the installation of the Directory in October 1795.

Tricolor   the national flag of France, includes the colors of Paris, red and blue, and that of the king, white.

Vendée   is a department in the west of France, but the term usually referred to the popular insurrection of 1793 that broke out in an area south of the Loire. More than 50,000 men were mobilized to fight the revolutionary government, taking as their symbol the Sacred Heart of Jesus with a cross on it. Initially victorious against the armies sent against them, the Vendéans were defeated in the fall of 1793. The government responded ruthlessly. In February and March 1794, the revolutionary government proceeded to take control of the area with inhumanity and savagery; it ordered the villages to be razed, animals slaughtered, and the area made a "desert." Approximately one-third of the population was massacred. Still, the Vendéan resistance continued sporadically in raids and reprisals. After the overthrow of Robespierre in 1794, the government attempted to placate the insurgents by offering an amnesty and freedom of worship, but revolt broke out again in 1796. In 1799, Napoleon set up a military government there, but revolt stirred again in 1813 and yet again during the Hundred Days, when 20,000 government troops had to be stationed there.

SELECT BIBLIOGRAPHY

Dictionaries/Reference Books

Furet, François, and Mona Ozouf, eds. *A Critical Dictionary of the French Revolution*. Translated by Arthur Goldhammer. Cambridge, Mass.: Belknap Press, 1989. Invaluable guide that includes entries under five major headings: events, actors, institutions and creations, ideas, and historians and commentators.

Jones, Colin. *The Longman Companion to the French Revolution*. London: Longman's, 1988. One of the best reference books available. Includes a detailed chronology and helpful charts.

Scott, Samuel F., and Barry Rothaus, eds. *Historical Dictionary of the French Revolution*. 2 vols. Westport, Conn.: Greenwood Press, 1985. An invaluable guide to the principal actors and events.

Documentary Collections

Baker, Keith Michael, ed. *The Old Regime and the French Revolution*. Chicago: University of Chicago Press, 1987. Excellent compilation that covers major issues.

Beik, Paul, ed. *The French Revolution*. New York: Walker, 1971. Useful collection covering the years 1787 to 1799.

Bienvenu, Richard T., ed. *The Ninth of Thermidor: The Fall of Robespierre*. New York: Oxford University Press, 1968. Excellent coverage of crisis.

Blanc, Olivier, ed. *Last Letters: Prisons and Prisoners of the French Revolution, 1793–1794*. Translated by Alan Sheridan. London: A. Deutsch, 1987. Moving excerpts from those condemned.

Hyslop, Beatrice F. *A Guide to the General Cahiers of 1789 with the Texts of Unedited Cahiers*. New York: Octagon Books, 1968. An invaluable introduction.

Kaplow, Jeffrey, ed. *France on the Eve of Revolution*. New York: John Wiley and Sons, 1991. A well-edited collection of primary materials that reflects the problems France confronted before the Revolution.

Levy, Darlene Gay, Harriet Branson Applewhite, and Mary Durham Johnson. *Women in Revolutionary Paris, 1789–1795: Selected Documents Translated with Notes and Commentary*. Urbana: University of Illinois Press, 1979. Documents women's political role.

Mason, Laura, and Tracey Rizzo, eds. *The French Revolution: A Document Collection*. New York: Houghton Mifflin, 1999. Solid coverage of documents from the old regime through the consulate.

Stewart, John Hall, ed. *A Documentary Survey of the French Revolution*. New York: Macmillan, 1951. Pivotal collection. Covers the years 1788–99.

Walzer, Michael, ed. *Regicide and Revolution: Speeches at the Trial of Louis XVI*. Translated by Marian Rothstein. New York: Columbia University Press, 1992. Interesting selections with solid introduction.

Secondary Accounts

Historiographical

Cox, Marvin R. *The Place of the French Revolution in History*. Boston: Houghton Mifflin, 1998. An excellent analysis by some of the most important historians with excerpts from their works.

Surveys

Aulard, F.-A. *The French Revolution: A Political History, 1789–1804*. Translated by Bernard Miall. 4 vols. New York: Scribner, 1910. A standard account with a leftist and anticlerical bias.

Brinton, Crane. *The Anatomy of Revolution*. New York: Random House, 1965. A classic comparison of the revolutions in the United States, England, France, and Russia.

Carlyle, Thomas. *The French Revolution*. London: Chapman and Hall, 1891. A beautifully written nineteenth-century classic.

Censer, Jack, and Lynn Hunt. *Liberty, Equality, Fraternity: Exploring the French Revolution*. University Park, Pa.: Penn State University Press, 2001. A basic textbook with excerpts from primary documents, illustrations, and maps. Also available on CD-ROM.

Cobban, Alfred. *A History of Modern France*. Vol. I, *1715–1799*. Harmondsworth, Eng: Penguin Books, 1961. A solid study, but sometimes challenging.

———. *The Social Interpretation of the French Revolution*. Cambridge: Cambridge University Press, 1964. Attacks the traditional Marxist interpretation and argues that the Revolution meant a triumph of the officials and landowners.

Doyle, William. *Origins of the French Revolution.* New York: Oxford University Press, 1988. Argues that by August 1789 the Revolution became irreversible.

———. *The Oxford History of the French Revolution.* New York: University Press, 1989. A valuable detailed primarily political history.

Godechot, Jacques. *France and the Atlantic Revolution of 1770–1799.* New York: Free Press, 1965. Analyzes France in the context of the larger Atlantic Revolution as part of a vast philosophical and cultural change.

Lefebvre, Georges. *The French Revolution.* Translated by Elizabeth Moss Evanson. 2 vols. New York: Columbia University Press, 1962–64. Marxist interpretation that the Revolution brought the bourgeoisie to power. Argues that the Thermidorians strengthened both the political power and social predominance of the bourgeoisie. The men of Thermidor and of the Directory shared the same goals of outlawing the Jacobins and preventing the outbreak of any popular movement. Their policies ultimately caused high inflation, ruined the currency, and paved the way for Napoleon.

Mathiez, Albert. *The French Revolution.* Translated by Catherine Alison Phillips. New York: Knopf, 1929. Stresses the economic and social causes of and influence on the Revolution. A Marxist view.

Michelet, Jules. *History of the French Revolution.* Chicago: University of Chicago Press, 1967. A still classic nineteenth-century account in the Romantic style that idealizes the common people and the Revolution.

Palmer, R. R. *The Age of the Democratic Revolution.* 2 vols. Princeton, N.J.: Princeton University Press, 1959 and 1964. Argues that the French Revolution was not unique but part of a much larger democratic revolution that broke out in the late eighteenth century in the United States as well as in western and eastern Europe. A classic.

Popkin, Jeremy. *A Short History of the French Revolution.* Englewood Cliffs, N.J.: Prentice Hall, 1995. A very useful and eminently readable account with a useful bibliography.

Roberts, J. M. *The French Revolution.* Oxford: Oxford University Press, 1978. A short overview. Stresses how the Revolution both continued traditional ways and broke with them and analyzes its impact and legacy.

Schama, Simon. *Citizens: A Chronicle of the French Revolution.* New York: Knopf, 1989. A readable chronicle that underscores the violence and destruction.

Soboul, Albert. *The French Revolution, 1787–1799, from the Storming of the Bastille to Napoleon.* Translated by Alan Forrest and Colin Jones. New York: Random House, 1975. A leftist view.

Sutherland, Donald M. G. *France 1789–1815: Revolution and Counter Revolution.* New York: Oxford University Press, 1986. An excellent general survey that stresses social history.

Sydenham, M. J. *The First French Republic, 1792–1804*. Los Angeles: University of California Press, 1973. Covers the years 1792 to 1802. Stresses the significance of political events and attitudes and argues that by 1804 republicans were thoroughly disillusioned.

Taine, Hippolyte. *The French Revolution*. Translated by John Durand. New York: Henry Holt, 1878–85. The French Revolution increased the centralization already present in France; it did not bring about liberty but greater absolutism.

Thompson, J. M. *The French Revolution*. Oxford: Basil Blackwell, 1962. A readable survey with valuable insights and interesting anecdotes.

Tocqueville, Alexis de. *The Old Regime and the French Revolution*. Translated by Stuart Gilbert. Garden City, N.Y.: Doubleday, 1955. A brilliant interpretation of the linkage between the old regime and the Revolution. The revolutionaries, though unaware of it, took over many of the modes and customs of the old regime to build the new one.

Early Revolution

Godechot, Jacques. *The Taking of the Bastille, July 14, 1789*. Translated by Jean Stewart. New York: Scribner, 1970. Stresses the significant early role of the Parisians, the uniqueness of the seizure of the Bastille and at the same time its part in a larger ongoing revolution in the West.

Greer, Donald. *The Incidence of the Emigration during the French Revolution*. Cambridge, Mass.: Harvard University Press, 1951. An invaluable statistical account.

Hampson, Norman. *Prelude to Terror*. Oxford: Basil Blackwell, 1988. Convincingly traces France's path to the Reign of Terror and demonstrates how the members of the National Assembly confused politics with ethics and demonized their opponents.

Hyslop, Beatrice F. *French Nationalism in 1789 According to the General Cahiers*. New York: Columbia University Press, 1934. Traces the general trend of nationalism in France before the Revolution by examining the lists of grievances.

Lefebvre, Georges. *The Coming of the French Revolution*. Translated by R. R. Palmer. Princeton, N.J.: Princeton University Press, 1979. A stimulating account of the origins. The Revolution progressed in four acts: first the aristocracy, then the bourgeois, then popular revolution in the cities, and finally revolution in the countryside.

———. *The Great Fear of 1789: Rural Panic in Revolutionary France*. Translated by Joan White. New York: Pantheon Books, 1973. A vivid account of the movement that swept the countryside, its causes and its repercussions.

Patrick, Alison. *The Men of the First French Republic: Political Alignments in the Convention of 1792*. Baltimore: Johns Hopkins University Press, 1972. An analysis of the deputies of the first convention. Tables provide information such as voting records, political experience, and place of origin.

Reign of Terror

Greer, Donald. *The Incidence of the Terror during the French Revolution: A Statistical Interpretation.* Gloucester, Mass.: Peter Smith, 1935. Invaluable statistical data on the victims.

Lucas, Colin. *The Structure of the Terror: The Example of Javogues and the Loire.* Oxford: Oxford University Press, 1973. Shows how revolutionary government evolved and functioned and analyzes the terrorists both socially and politically.

Lyons, Martyn. *Revolution in Toulouse: An Essay on Provincial Terrorism.* Las Vegas, Nev.: Lang, 1978. Although those in Toulouse adopted the rhetoric of the Revolution, the excesses of the Terror and the counterrevolution did not occur in part because of the strength of Catholicism and royalism.

Palmer, R. R. *Twelve Who Ruled: The Year of the Terror in the French Revolution.* Princeton, N.J.: Princeton University Press, 1973. A riveting account of France during the Reign of Terror as seen through the Committee of Public Safety.

Scott, W. *Terror and Repression in Revolutionary Marseilles.* New York: Barnes and Noble, 1973. Analyzes the origin and course of a revolt against the Jacobin-dominated Convention and the work and impact of the Revolutionary Tribunal.

Thermidor and the Directory

Lewis, Gwynne, and Colin Lucas. *Beyond the Terror: Essays in French Regional and Social History, 1794–1815.* Cambridge, England: Cambridge University Press, 1983. A series of essays that underscores the importance of the Thermidorean and Directorial period and the popular nature of the resistance to the Revolution.

Lyons, Martyn. *France under the Directory.* Cambridge, England: Cambridge University Press, 1975. A useful explanation of how and why the Directory failed.

Mathiez, Albert. *After Robespierre, the Thermidorian Reaction.* Translated by Catherine Alison Phillips. New York: Knopf, 1931. The Thermidorian reaction strove to destroy the institutions and methods of the Terror and persecute those who had held power. Revolutionary idealism died with Robespierre.

Woloch, Isser. *Jacobin Legacy; the Democratic Movement under the Directory.* Princeton, N.J.: Princeton University Press, 1970. Traces the repression of the Jacobins after Robespierre's fall, their regrouping under the Directory, and their eventual suppression.

Woronoff, Denis. *The Thermidorean Regime and the Directory, 1794–1799.* Translated by Julian Jackson. New York: Cambridge University Press, 1984. The Directory survived because of the weakness of its opponents: those on the left, those on the right, and foreign armies. The Directory did reorganize the tax and financial system as well as the administrative infrastructure.

Counterrevolution

Burke, Edmund. *Reflections on the Revolution in France.* Edited by Conor Cruise O'Brien. Harmondsworth, England: Penguin Books, 1969. A classic, conservative condemnation of the French Revolution.

Godechot, Jacques. *The Counter-Revolution: Doctrine and Action, 1789–1804.* New York: Howard Fertig, 1971. Underscores that the counterrevolution began before 1789, lasted beyond 1804, and extended beyond France. Covers topics such as the White Terror and the views of individuals, such as Mallet du Pan.

Sutherland, Donald M. G. *The Chouans.* Oxford: Oxford University Press, 1982. Provides insights into this counterrevolutionary group.

Tilly, C. *The Vendée.* Cambridge, Mass.: Harvard University Press, 1964. A sociological examination of the counterrevolution that concentrates on two particular phenomena, urbanization and community reorganization.

Biography

Brookner, Anita. *Jacques-Louis David.* New York: Harper and Row, 1980. A study of the life and works of this great neoclassical artist.

Conner, Clifford. *Jean Paul Marat.* Atlantic Highlands, N.J.: Humanities Press International, 1997. Marat, a journalist and politician, wanted to eliminate the gulf between the rich and the poor. He was an excellent strategist and tactician but, unlike Robespierre, was not an organizer.

Curtis, Eugene N. *Saint Just, Colleague of Robespierre.* New York: Columbia University Press, 1935. A sympathetic, balanced account that stresses Saint-Just's character and accomplishments.

Dowd, David Lloyd. *Pageant-Master of the Republic: Jacques-Louis David and the French Revolution.* Lincoln: University of Nebraska Press, 1948. Underscores the artist's political activities.

Eisenstein, Elizabeth L. *The First Professional Revolutionist: Filipo Michel Buonarroti, 1761–1837, a Biographical Essay.* Cambridge, Mass.: Harvard University Press, 1959. Stresses Buonarroti's ardent belief in the Revolution and analyzes his political development.

Erickson, Carolly. *To the Scaffold: The Life of Marie Antoinette.* New York: William Morrow, 1991. A popular readable account of the doomed queen.

Gershoy, Leo. *Bertrand Barère, a Reluctant Terrorist.* Princeton, N.J.: Princeton University Press, 1962. Depicts Barère as a weak and mild-mannered man transformed into a terrorist.

Gottschalk, Louis R. *Jean Paul Marat: A Study in Radicalism.* Chicago: University of Chicago Press, 1927. A realistic portrayal of this radical revolutionary. Points out that Marat did not shape events but was shaped by them and that though he loved the common people he did not trust or respect them.

Gottschalk, Louis R., and Margaret Maddox. *Lafayette in the French Revolution.* Chicago: University of Chicago Press, 1969–73. The standard authority, but a bit difficult.

Greenbaum, Louis S. *Talleyrand: Statesman-Priest; The Agent-General of the Clergy and the Church of France at the End of the Old Regime.* Washington, D.C.: Catholic University of America Press, 1970. Analyzes Talleyrand's early career as a priest and his transformation from uncompromising defender of the church to defrocked priest and excommunicated Catholic.

Hampson, Norman. *Danton.* New York: Holmes and Meier, 1978. An attempt to present this key revolutionary figure as a working politician who appreciated the kind of tactics essential for a radical minority to succeed.

Hardman, John. *Louis XVI.* New Haven, Conn.: Yale University Press, 1993. Depicts the king as intelligent and hardworking but uncharismatic and the collapse of the old regime as inevitable.

———. *Robespierre.* Essex, England: Pearson Education, 1999. A fine account of this important figure of the Terror, an individual who never doubted that he was morally superior to others.

Harris, Robert D. *Necker and the Revolution of 1789.* Lanham, Md.: University Press of America, 1986. A sympathetic look at Necker's first ministry.

Jordan, David P. *The King's Trial: Louis XVI vs. The French Revolution.* Berkeley: University of California Press, 1979. A gripping account of the trial and execution.

———. *The Revolutionary Career of Maximilien Robespierre.* New York: Free Press, 1985. Sees his career as a series of clashes with rivals, analyzes his character, especially his reputation as "the Incorruptible," and depicts him as an individual who refused to compromise and who emphasized the value of ideas.

Kelly, George Armstrong. *Victims, Authority, and Terror: The Parallel Deaths of D'Orleans, Custine, Bailly and Malesherbes.* Chapel Hill: University of North Carolina Press, 1982. A group biography of four important victims of the Terror; each represented a significant group in the nobility.

Luttrell, Barbara. *Mirabeau.* Carbondale: Southern Illinois University Press, 1990. Examines his views, the range of his ideas, and his historical importance.

May, Gita. *Madame Roland and the Age of Revolution.* New York: Columbia University Press, 1970. A study of an enthusiastic supporter of the Revolution and the Girondins.

Roberts, Warren. *Jacques Louis David, Revolutionary Artist.* Chapel Hill: University of North Carolina Press, 1989. An examination of the life and work of the great revolutionary artist. Stresses his devotion to the Revolution.

Robison, Georgia. *Révellière-Lepeaux: Citizen Director, 1753–1824*. New York: Octagon Books, 1972. A well-researched account of a little-known member of the Directory who specialized in public instruction, sciences, and the arts.

Rose, R. B. *Gracchus Babeuf: The First Revolutionary Communist*. Stanford, Calif.: Stanford University Press, 1978. The belief that absolute equality could be achieved through the abolition of private property was a central component of Babeuf's ideology.

Thompson, J. M. *Robespierre and the French Revolution*. New York: Macmillan, 1969. For Thompson, Robespierre was a great man who personified both the strength and weakness of the Revolution, particularly its inhumanity. Argues that the Revolution was primarily social and economic.

Political/Social Groups

Brinton, Crane. *The Jacobins: An Essay in the New History*. New York: Macmillan, 1961. Emphasizes provincial networks.

Kennedy, Michael L. *The Jacobin Club of Marseilles, 1790–1794*. Ithaca, N.Y.: Cornell University Press, 1973. Traces the origins, organization, social composition, policies, and eventual fall from power of one Jacobin club.

———. *The Jacobin Clubs in the French Revolution*. 3 vols. Princeton, N.J.: Princeton University Press, 1982, 1988; New York: Berghahn, 2000. Focuses on the Jacobin clubs outside Paris and argues that Jacobins in the capital did not control the regional groups whose membership changed greatly, especially after 1793 when the number of middle-class members declined.

Rose, R. B. *The Making of the Sans-Culottes: Democratic Ideas and Institutions in Paris, 1789–1792*. Manchester, England: Manchester University Press, 1983. Argues that the *sans-culottes* embodied an alternative democratic tradition that died out by the late 1790s.

Slavin, Morris. *The Hébertistes to the Guillotine, Anatomy of a "Conspiracy" in Revolutionary France*. Baton Rouge: Louisiana State University Press, 1994. The struggle between the *Hébertistes* and the *Dantonistes* led to the end of both and ultimately that of the revolutionary government as well.

———. *The Making of an Insurrection, Parisian Sections and Gironde*. Cambridge, Mass.: Harvard University Press, 1986. An insightful analysis of the background and the impact of the insurrection of May 31–June 2, 1793, that forced the Girondins out of power and ultimately cost many their lives.

Soboul, Albert. *The Sans-Culottes: The Popular Movement and Revolutionary Government, 1793–1794*. Translated by Remy Inglis Hall. Garden City, N.Y.: Anchor Books, 1972. Analyzes the rise, fall, and significance of the Parisian popular movement. The Parisian *sans-culottes* often identified their interests with those of the peasants and opposed those of the bourgeoisie.

Sydenham, M. J. *The Girondins*. London: Athlone Press, 1961. Argues that the Girondins were a historical legend and that the only unified party in the Convention was the Mountain.

Administration/Law

Dawson, Philip. *Provincial Magistrates and Revolutionary Politics in France, 1789–1795*. Cambridge, Mass.: Harvard University Press, 1972. Analyzes the motives, conduct, and fate of an important corporate group—2,700 judicial officeholders.

Doyle, William. *The Parlement of Bordeaux at the End of the Old Regime, 1771–1790*. New York: St. Martin's, 1974. An examination of one of the important *parlements* at a critical period.

Stone, Bailey. *The Parlement of Paris, 1774–1789*. Chapel Hill: University of North Carolina Press, 1981. Examines the Parisian *parlement's* resistance to royal authority and the larger phenomenon, the aristocratic resurgence.

Woloch, Isser. *The New Regime: Transformations of the French Civic Order, 1789–1820's*. New York: W. W. Norton, 1994. The Revolution drastically changed civic institutions as did Napoleon. Yet Napoleon's centralization was not comprehensive. His priorities remained legal codification and conscription.

Art/Culture

Baker, Keith Michael, ed. *Inventing the French Revolution: Essays on French Political Culture in the Eighteenth Century*. New York: Cambridge University Press, 1990. An intellectual analysis of language and discourse.

Boime, Albert. *Art in an Age of Revolution, 1750–1800*. Chicago: University of Chicago Press, 1987. The transition to an urban industrial society was reflected in neoclassicism and romanticism. The works of artists, such as David, reflected the progress and concerns of the middle class.

Carlson, Marvin. *The Theater of the French Revolution*. Ithaca, N.Y.: Cornell University Press, 1966. Analyzes the impact of the Revolution on not only the Comédie française but also other theaters and the reasons for the demise of so many.

Darnton, Robert. *The Kiss of Lamourette: Reflections in Cultural History*. New York: W. W. Norton, 1990. Analyzes a series of events to show how the Revolution "redefined the human condition." A very readable account by one of the masters of the new cultural history.

Gutwirth, Madelyn. *The Twilight of the Goddesses: Women and Representation in the French Revolutionary Era*. New Brunswick, N.J.: Rutgers University Press, 1992. An examination of art and gender relations.

Hunt, Lynn. *Politics, Culture, and Class in the French Revolution*. Los Angeles: University of California Press, 1984. A cultural analysis of the Revolution and its impact, especially in rhetoric, symbols, and images.

Kennedy, Emmet. *A Cultural History of the French Revolution.* New Haven, Conn.: Yale University Press, 1989. Argues that the Revolution had a long-term impact.

Leith, James A. *The Idea of Art as Propaganda in France, 1750–1799: A Study in the History of Ideas.* Toronto: Toronto University Press, 1972. The French revolutionaries tried but failed to mobilize the arts successfully to propagate the revolutionary faith.

Ozouf, Mona. *Festivals and the French Revolution.* Translated by Alan Sheridan. Cambridge, Mass.: Harvard University Press, 1988. Shows how the festivals reflected the new revolutionary society.

Parker, Harold. *The Cult of Antiquity and the French Revolutionaries: A Study in the Development of the Revolutionary Spirit.* Chicago: University of Chicago Press, 1937. What the revolutionaries thought about antiquity and how it affected their actions.

Paulson, Ronald. *Representations of Revolution, 1789–1820.* New Haven, Conn.: Yale University Press, 1983. Analyzes how the Revolution was represented by artists in France, Britain, and Spain.

Sewell, William H. *Work and Revolution in France: The Language of Labor from the Old Regime to 1848.* New York: Cambridge University Press, 1980. Stresses the language and rhetoric.

Starobinski, Jean. *1789: The Emblems of Reason.* Charlottesville: University Press of Virginia, 1982. Stresses the Roman and republican characteristics of neoclassicism and its widespread dissemination, especially in public ceremonial.

Diplomacy/Foreign Policy

Blanning, T. C. W. *The French Revolutionary Wars, 1787–1802.* New York: St. Martin's, 1996. A beautifully written classic that focuses on diplomatic and military issues.

————. *The French Revolution in Germany: Occupation and Resistance in the Rhineland, 1792–1802.* Oxford: Clarendon Press, 1983. Analyzes the impact of French occupation in the Rhineland and the progression of French policy from fraternal liberation to exploitation. A classic analysis of the French occupation and ultimate incorporation of the left bank of the Rhine.

————. *The Origins of the French Revolutionary Wars.* New York: Longman, 1986. Brilliant incisive analysis that emphasizes the role of misunderstanding in igniting wars.

Murphy, Orville. *The Diplomatic Retreat of France and Public Opinion on the Eve of the French Revolution, 1783–1789.* Washington, D.C.: Catholic University of America Press, 1998. An excellent analytical study of the diplomatic retreat of France and its effect on public opinion.

Ross, Steven T. *European Diplomatic History 1789–1815: France against Europe.* New York: Doubleday, 1969. The French revolutionaries, like their predecessors, sought to dominate Europe.

Sorel, Albert. *Europe and the French Revolution.* Translated by Alfred Cobban and J. W. Hunt. New York: Doubleday, 1969. An abridged version of Sorel's classic on the French revolutionaries' diplomatic relations with the rest of Europe. Argues that the revolutionaries followed many of the precedents established during the old regime.

Stone, Bailey. *The Genesis of the French Revolution, a Global-Historical Interpretation.* New York: Cambridge University Press, 1994. Emphasizes the "global geopolitical context" of and reasons for the outbreak of the Revolution.

Stone, Bailey. *Reinterpreting the French Revolution, a Global-Historical Perspective.* New York: Cambridge University Press, 2002. Stresses the impact of international events on the origins and evolution of the Revolution.

Whitehead, Jeremy J. *Reform, Revolution and French Global Policy, 1787–1791.* Hampshire, England: Ashgate Publishing, 2003. Analyzes the relationship between the Revolution and the revolutionaries' international ambitions, and the imperatives of French global policy under the old regime.

Economic

Bosher, J. F. *French Finances, 1770–1795: From Business to Bureaucracy.* Cambridge, England: Cambridge University Press, 1970. An administrative analysis of the financial institutions of the old regime and their transformation.

Harris, Seymour Edwin. *The Assignats.* 1930. Reprint, New York: AMS Press, 1969. An analysis of the origins, impact, and significance of the monetary system.

Education

Barnard, Howard Clive. *Education and the French Revolution.* London: Cambridge University Press, 1969. Shows how the Revolution destroyed the institutions of the old regime and failed to set up a new system of education except in technical and higher education.

Palmer, R. R. *The Improvement of Humanity: Education and the French Revolution.* Princeton, N.J.: Princeton University Press, 1985. Analyzes plans for school reform.

Military/Police

Bertaud, Jean-Paul. *The Army of the French Revolution: From Citizen Soldiers to Instrument of Power.* Translated by R. R. Palmer. Princeton, N.J.: Princeton University Press, 1988. The army reflected the new society but constituted a problem from the onset for the new government. A solid work.

Brown, Howard G. *War, Revolution, and the Bureaucratic State: Politics and Army Administration in France, 1791–1799.* Oxford: Clarendon Press, 1995. Analyzes how war and revolutionary politics increased administrative power.

Cobb, Richard. *The People's Armies: The Armees Revolutionnaires, Instrument of the Terror in the Departments, April 1793 to Floréal, Year Two.* Translated by Marianne Elliott. New Haven, Conn.: Yale University Press, 1987. Underscores the ineffectiveness of the revolutionary government and the importance of local officials, especially the mayor. The *armées,* groups of armed civilians who undertook tasks such as requisitioning grain, were a spontaneous institutional creation of the Terror.

Forrest, Alan. *Conscripts and Deserters: The Army and French Society during the Revolution and Empire.* New York: Oxford University Press, 1989. Concentrates on the effects of the unprecedented militarization in France during the Revolution, especially on local communities.

————. *The Soldiers of the French Revolution.* Durham, N.C.: Duke University Press, 1990. Analyzes such issues as the structure, recruitment, and provisioning of the soldiers in the context of the Revolution and shows how the Revolution transformed the army.

Lynn, John. *The Bayonets of the Republic: Motivations and Tactics of the Army of Revolutionary France, 1791–94.* Urbana: University of Illinois Press, 1984. Examines the tactics and motivations of one of the armies guarding a critical frontier.

Ross, Steven T. *Quest for Victory: French Military Strategy 1792–1799.* New York: A. S. Barnes, 1973. French revolutionary armies placed greater emphasis on open-order techniques such as skirmishing and gave more initiative to junior officers, thus giving the army greater tactical flexibility. Argues that the republic built the best army in Europe but could not control its generals, including Napoleon, who ultimately brought catastrophe.

Scott, Samuel F. *The Response of the Royal Army to the French Revolution: The Role and Development of the Line Army, 1787–1793.* Oxford: Clarendon Press, 1978. The revolutionary assemblies both reorganized and restructured the army. The development of a professional officer corps and the conscription of citizens were natural results of the Revolution just as the improvement in army cohesion and discipline was a result of the wars.

Woloch, Isser. *The French Veteran from the Revolution to the Restoration.* Chapel Hill: University of North Carolina Press, 1979. The revolutionaries transformed and standardized the inequitable system they had inherited. All veterans, both officers and soldiers, received compensation based on rank and years of service.

The Press

Censer, Jack. *Prelude to Power, the Parisian Radical Press, 1789–1791.* Baltimore: Johns Hopkins University Press, 1976. Deals with the role of the press and in particular traces the evolution of ideological radicalism.

Popkin, Jeremy. *Revolutionary News: The Press in France, 1789–1799.* Durham, N.C.: Duke University Press, 1990. During the Revolution, the definition of the freedom of the press was a limited one because many equated a free press with social instability. The execution of Robespierre only temporarily halted the movement toward a government-controlled press, which increased during the Directory and under Napoleon.

————. *The Right Wing Press in France, 1792–1800.* Chapel Hill: University of North Carolina Press, 1980. A comprehensive analysis of the counterrevolutionary newspapers, the domestic roots of counterrevolution, and the importance of the Enlightenment tradition.

Roche, Daniel, and Robert Darnton, eds. *Revolution in Print: The Press in France, 1775–1800.* Berkeley: University of California Press, 1989. Studies revolutionary propaganda.

Religion

Garrett, Clarke. *Respectable Folly: Millenarians and the French Revolution in France and England.* Baltimore: Johns Hopkins University Press, 1975. An arresting study of an overlooked movement. Underscores the interaction between religion and politics.

McManners, John. *The French Revolution and the Church.* New York: Harper & Row, 1969. Points out the interdependence of the throne and the altar and their simultaneous collapse and underscores the important role of the church.

Tackett, T. *Religion, Revolution and Regional Culture in Eighteenth-Century France: The Ecclesiastical Oath of 1791.* Princeton, N.J.: Princeton University Press, 1986. Analyzes the oath and the ensuing religious schism.

Social

Cobb, Richard. *Paris and Its Provinces, 1792–1802.* New York: Oxford University Press, 1975. Addresses issues such as crime, the survival of rural Catholicism, the rivalry between the capital and the countryside, and the Great Fear of year II.

————. *The Police and the People: French Popular Protest, 1789–1820.* Oxford: Clarendon Press, 1970. Analyzes the fragility of the *sans-culotte* movement, the popular recourse to violent solutions, and popular attitudes toward food scarcity.

————. *Reactions to the French Revolution.* New York: Oxford University Press, 1972. Views the Revolution through the perspective of several individuals and examines the impact of revolutionary policies that caused, for example, a shortage of wood, soap, and candles.

Darrow, Margaret. *Revolution in the House: Family, Class, and Inheritance in Southern France, 1775–1825.* Princeton, N.J.: Princeton University Press, 1989. An examination of how the Revolution impacted families, especially in matters of inheritance.

Forrest, Alan. *The French Revolution and the Poor.* New York: St. Martin's, 1981. Analyzes the legislative achievements and their impact on the poor.

————. *Society and Politics in Revolutionary Bordeaux*. Oxford: Oxford University Press, 1975. Underscores the importance of regional identity as reflected in the federalist revolt of 1793 and points out the conservative and commercially oriented nature of Bordeaux.

Hampson, Norman. *A Social History of the Revolution*. London: Routledge and K. Paul, 1963. An analysis of the nature of social conflicts that caused and characterized the Revolution and that influence France to this day.

Hanson, Paul. *Provincial Politics in the French Revolution: Caen and Limoges, 1789–1794*. Baton Rouge: Louisiana State University Press, 1989. Contrasts the provinces with Paris.

Higonnet, Patrice. *Class, Ideology, and the Rights of Nobles during the French Revolution*. Oxford: Clarendon Press, 1981. Analyzes social class and ideology, especially "anti-nobilism."

Hufton, Olwyn. *Women and the Limits of Citizenship in the French Revolution*. Toronto: University of Toronto Press, 1992. Short articles on how the Revolution affected women.

Hunt, Lynn. *Revolution and Urban Politics in Provincial France, Troyes and Reims, 1786–1790*. Stanford, Calif.: Stanford University Press, 1978. The impact of the Revolution on two different towns.

Jones, Peter. *The Peasantry in the French Revolution*. New York: Cambridge University Press, 1988. A synthetic, not archival, study. Questions the myth that the Revolution gave land to peasants, but emphasizes that the Revolution granted peasants municipal self-government and an accessible judicial system.

Kelly, Linda. *Women of the French Revolution*. London: Hamish Hamilton, 1987. A short and popular account of women caught up in the Revolution.

Margadant, Ted. *Urban Rivalries in the French Revolution*. Princeton, N.J.: Princeton University Press, 1992. Examines urban institutional hierarchies before and after the Revolution and the long-term impact of territorial reorganization.

Melzer, Sara, and Leslie Rabine, eds. *Rebel Daughters: Women and the French Revolution*. New York: Oxford University Press, 1992. A series of articles examining topics such as women's exclusion from the body politic.

Rudé, George. *The Crowd in the French Revolution*. Oxford: Clarendon Press, 1959. A classic account of the seminal role of the crowd and its composition.

Slavin, Morris. *The French Revolution in Miniature, Section Droits-de-l'Homme, 1789–1795*. Princeton, N.J.: Princeton University Press, 1984. Interesting analysis of the impact of the Revolution on one section in the Marais district.

Weiner, Dora. *The Citizen Patient in Revolutionary and Imperial Paris*. Baltimore: Johns Hopkins University Press, 1993. The revolutionaries' vision was one of "citizen-patients" with access to health care, but paucity of funds limited its execution.

Weiner, Margery. *The French Exiles, 1789–1815.* New York: Morrow, 1961. Analysis of a small group of émigrés in London.

CD-ROMs/Web Sites

Censer, Jack, and Lynn Hunt. *Liberty, Equality, Fraternity: Exploring the French Revolution.* New York: American Social History Productions, 2001. A basic text organized thematically. It also includes 400 documents, 300 images, and 13 songs.

http://chnm.gmu.edu/revolution. A site on the Revolution that includes 338 texts, 245 images, 13 songs, maps, a comprehensive time line, and a glossary.

Movies

Danton, directed by Wajda, 1982.

La Marseillaise, Renoir production, 1937.

The Scarlet Pimpernel with Ronald Coleman. For a more comprehensive listing, see *La Légende de la Révolution.* Paris: Flammarion, 1988.

INDEX

About the Authors

LINDA S. FREY is Professor of History at the University of Montana.

MARSHA L. FREY is Professor of History at Kansas State University. With Linda S. Frey, she is co-author of *A History of Diplomatic Immunity* and also serves as series editor for the Greenwood Guides to Historic Events 1500–1900.